PHAC

D1194020

A Half Baked Idea

A Half Baked Idea

*How grief, love and cake took me from
the courtroom to Le Cordon Bleu*

OLIVIA POTTS

FIG TREE
an imprint of
PENGUIN BOOKS

FIG TREE

UK | USA | Canada | Ireland | Australia
India | New Zealand | South Africa

Fig Tree is part of the Penguin Random House group of companies
whose addresses can be found at global.penguinrandomhouse.com.

First published 2019
003

Copyright © Olivia Potts, 2019

The moral right of the author has been asserted

Grateful acknowledgement is made for permission to quote from the following:
on pp. 5, 19, excerpts from *A Grief Observed* by C. S. Lewis © copyright C. S. Lewis Pte Ltd 1961;
on p. 19, an excerpt from *Death's Door* by Sandra Gilbert published by W. W. Norton and Company,
2006; on p. 21, a quotation from *Love Actually*, screenplay © Richard Curtis (2003), reprinted by
kind permission of Portobello Studios; on p. 96, an excerpt from *From Attachment and
Loss Volume 3: Loss, Sadness and Depression* by John Bowlby published by The Hogarth Press.
Reproduced by kind permission of The Random House Group Ltd. © 1980.

This book is a work of non-fiction based on the life, experiences and recollections
of Olivia Potts. In some cases names of people, places, dates and sequences of
the detail of events have been changed to protect the privacy of others.

Set in 13.5/16 pt Garamond MT Std
Typeset by Jouve (UK), Milton Keynes
Printed and bound in Great Britain by Clays Ltd, Elcograf S.p.A.

A CIP catalogue record for this book is available from the British Library

ISBN: 978–0–241–38045–1

www.greenpenguin.co.uk

For Mummy, but because of Sam

I

When someone close to you dies, an odd thing happens. Whatever is happening at the time takes on a special resonance. Maybe you were watching *Emmerdale*, or on your way to a Pilates class, or buying a particular brand of chocolate biscuit.

There needn't be anything special about the activity; indeed, usually, there isn't. Death has a knack of arriving at the most mundane moments. But it is mundane moments that make up most of our lives. And so, without meaning to, you'll probably find yourself returning to that activity, and reliving the death, over and over. *Emmerdale* becomes harder to watch; Pilates loses its appeal. As time passes, grief slows, it moves from a gasping stab to a dull ache; it moves from standing in front of you, obscuring your vision, to one pace behind you, present, distracting, but unremarkable. But those biscuits? They will always bring you right back to that moment, in a way that will take your breath away, and break your heart in two.

It's sensible, then, to do your best to avoid that activity. To solve the problem by running away from it, as fast as you can. *Coronation Street* scratches a similar itch to *Emmerdale*; no one really likes Pilates anyway. And there are always new biscuits to try. The problem comes when you find out, to your surprise, that the tainted activity is one you want to spend the rest of your life doing.

When my mother died, I was cooking. I was not a cook. I did not cook. I ate high-street-chain sandwiches, supermarket filled pasta, and more takeaway kebabs than I was comfortable admitting. My rare, haphazard forays into the kitchen led to fallen cakes, burnt biscuits, and stringy stews. But I had recently started dating a man – a man who was very keen on cooking, and whom I was keen to impress. One weekend, he suggested we cook together for friends. And I thought, *Oh God, that sounds like a terrible idea.* But I said, 'Sounds great.' And so I found myself standing in a kitchen that was not my own, baking a cake alongside a man I didn't know.

Meanwhile, 275 miles away, my mother was dying.

I'd spoken to my mother earlier that day on the phone. I'd told her about this man, and what I took to be his faults: he wasn't sure he wanted children, and he'd recently returned to vegetarianism, something I had inexplicably taken as an affront. 'Don't worry, darling,' Mum had replied. 'Bring him home to meet your mother: I'll point out your child-bearing hips, and feed him my shepherd's pie. That'll sort him out. When I met your father, he was wearing a blue velvet dinner suit. You can change anything,' she had concluded. I'd laughed, and told her it would be a good story to recount if we ever got married. She'd yawned, and we'd said goodbye to one another.

I didn't know then what I would know sixteen hours later: that that yawn was a death knell, a swan song; a yawn – so commonplace, so trivial – that meant she wasn't getting enough oxygen. A yawn that said she was dying. Later, I would replay that conversation, that yawn, over and over again. Her body was already preparing itself for what would happen over the next few hours. Entirely self-interested, I hadn't even asked her how she was, though I did promise to call her the next day with a full post-mortem on the supper. The irony would only occur to me later.

My mother was 275 miles away, and she was dying. But I didn't know this. So I drank, and I laughed, and I presented the cake I had made for the evening – a clementine and almond cake, the one cake I knew how to bake – proudly. I did the washing up, badly, drunkenly. The man who was not my boyfriend later redid this washing up, not mentioning the shoddiness of the original job, in that quiet way that is peculiar to a couple who have not yet established their status as a couple. I'd half-done the washing up, then I'd slid into a bed that was not my own. And 275 miles away, my mother was dead.

The next afternoon, an impossibly blue February day, as cold as it was bright, my phone rang. My home phone number flashed up on the screen. I didn't get to it in time and the screen darkened. Then a voicemail flashed up. It doesn't matter how many times I ask my father not to leave voicemails, he persists in doing so. I rolled my eyes, irritated. He knows how I feel about voicemails.

Begrudgingly, I called my voicemail, sitting on the loo. All he said was to call him back, but I could immediately tell that something serious had happened. I hung up, and rang home. He answered instantly. And though I may not want to remember what followed, I do.

One of the realities of the death of someone close to you is that you will have to relay that news to other people, over and over again. It's not surprising that this becomes easier, although it never loses its inherent awkwardness, a peculiar embarrassment that manifests itself as an apology: 'I'm so sorry, I have some awful news . . .' The apologetic self-consciousness intensifies at their shock, their sadness. Your grief feels like an inconvenience, sparking a cringing guilt.

You do get better at it. Of course you do. You have variations on the same conversation repeatedly, every day for years. You create a formula of words that makes the whole thing as painless as possible. You find a way of making it as easy for the other person as you can. You make it quick, efficient, like ripping off a plaster. Perhaps you even find a gentle joke that you can tack on to the end of the conversation to break the tension.

But nothing quite compares to the first time you have to articulate the words.

I walked back into the bedroom, where I'd left Sam reading a book. He looked up, clearly surprised to see me standing stock-still, but with the casual calm of a man whose life hasn't just been ripped apart by a single phone call. 'My mum's . . . dead?'

The physical effort of saying those words was like a dam bursting. Grief broke over me like a wave, adrenaline coursing through me, and I realized I was almost certainly going to be sick or pass out. I was literally knocked off my feet, doubled over, on to my knees, a parody of sorrow, like the protagonist in a Greek tragedy.

My mother was dead. My mother was dead. My beautiful, brilliant, infuriating, mad mother, who I'd spoken to less than twenty-four hours ago, who'd joked about shepherd's pie and child-bearing hips, was dead. I had that weightless feeling you have when you lie down after drinking too much, or spending the day at a water park.

In *A Grief Observed*, C. S. Lewis wrote, 'No one ever told me that grief felt so like fear. I am not afraid, but the sensation is like being afraid.' But I knew in that moment that he was wrong. I *was* afraid. I was so terrified it was visceral, physical. I felt like I needed to wee and be sick and be held tight, simultaneously. I felt like I would shatter if I were touched. I was scared of not having a mother. I was scared of losing that person who was contractually, biologically, genetically obligated to love me. I was scared of not having anywhere to put my love for her.

It suddenly occurred to me that I didn't really know this man whose bedroom I was standing in, on whose loo I'd been sitting when I listened to the voicemail, who was now looking at me in horror as I tried to gather my things from around his house. And I felt terribly, terribly alone. 'Do you want me to come . . . up north with you?' he asked.

Christ, no.

But the reality of the task ahead of me suddenly hit. I had to go home. I had to get back up north. Now. I was a criminal barrister, and I was due in Kingston Crown

Court in just over twelve hours. I was in south London, but my papers were in north London. My father was in Sunderland, where I needed to be. It was a Sunday evening, no one would be in chambers, so I rang my supervisor's mobile, interrupting the end of their weekend, to impart the information that I'd received minutes before, strangling the important words, but eventually getting the message across, and hanging up as fast as I could. Sam walked me to the Tube station, where we said an awkward goodbye. I'd worn heels to the dinner party that night and, having no other shoes with me, skittered down the stairs to the platform at Stockwell.

The alienating numbness that goes hand in hand with grief, that makes the bereaved seem distant, dazed, even rude, was still days away. Those clichéd stages of grief that we've all heard about – denial, anger, bargaining, depression – serve a purpose. They protect you; they wrap you up and remove you from reality. Their ferocity provides a buffer against the new world in which you find yourself. But they only kick in after the shock abates. Before that, without those blankets and duvets that shroud you as true grief takes hold, you are undressed before the world. No, more than that, you are raw. A mass of bone and pulsing muscle, unprotected by skin. As I crossed London, there was nothing to shield me from a world that hadn't been heartbroken. The assault of King's Cross station was acute. The bustle and banality of people going about their lives felt like a personal attack.

I went through the motions of organizing a journey I'd done a hundred times, none of the individual actions signalling that this journey was unlike previous ones. I bristled, for just a moment, at the cost of an on-the-day ticket from London to Newcastle, before catching myself with a horror that almost tipped into hysteria. I couldn't believe that those around me couldn't sense my sorrow, notice it dripping off me, marking me out as grief-stricken, as different.

The train to Newcastle was packed, as it tends to be on a Sunday evening, with people going back to their jobs or their families, returning from jaunts and visits. I sat pressed into a window seat. Unable to handle speaking to my dad or to my sister, Madeleine, I texted Maddy's boyfriend, and looked down a moment later to see that I was out of battery. I was sitting on a train with a dead phone, nothing to distract me from my dead mother. *My mum's dead, my mum's dead, my mum's dead.* It repeated in my head with the rhythm of the train.

At some point during the journey, the man sitting next to me asked if I was OK, and I realized I was crying. We can talk about it if you like, he offered. I briefly considered his offer: when I tell the story in the future, years from now, I make it a funny one. 'Imagine,' I say, 'if I'd turned to this well-meaning man and unburdened myself!' *My mum's dead, my mum's dead, my mum's dead!* But of course, it wouldn't have been an unburdening. It would have given the thought shape and form. I couldn't say those words again, not yet.

My mother dying was my greatest fear. I don't mean that in an abstract way. I thought about my greatest fears a lot – which perhaps tells you a bit about my general disposition – and this was at the top of the list. I have always been anxious, a trait I inherited, not unironically, from my mother, though she'd had it worse, at least up to that point. My mother was hobbled by fear of death. Her father had died from cancer when she was thirteen. She dearly loved dogs, but we were never allowed one, or any other pet for that matter, because she knew that, having given our love to this hypothetical dog, it would go and die on us. She loved horses, too. She grew up riding, and went to the stables every day, until her best friend died, age sixteen, when she was thrown from a horse, and that was that: no more horses. Mum was desperately, constantly scared for us, her daughters. Every parent worries, of course, but I guarantee you my mother had it worse. No activity, from cross-stitch to tennis, was truly safe. Panic bubbled under the surface.

Well, I am my mother's daughter. I inherited her dark straight hair, her voice and her laugh, her competitive nature, but it is her anxiety that rose above all the other similarities like a flare. That's how it felt, every time almost anything bad, or potentially bad, or even just new happened: it was like someone had set off a flare within me, which whooshed up through my body until my head was filled with blinding light, and with one overwhelming thought: something terrible had happened. Someone I loved was dead.

This feeling was most associated with phone calls. Mum never left me voicemails, because she knew this feeling, and felt it too. True, she was also a technophobe, who carried an old brick of a mobile phone in her handbag but never turned it on, who didn't even have an email address. I never received a single text message from her. But even if she were Bill Gates, or Mark Zuckerberg, she still never, ever would have left me a voicemail. Because she was me, only twenty-nine years older. Because she knew.

In a way, I hadn't needed to call my dad back. I listened to the voicemail, to my dad's voice breaking as he told me to call him, and I knew. I'd spent my whole life expecting this to happen. Now, here I was, reeling, as the prophecy was fulfilled.

Sam phoned me that first night. I padded downstairs from my childhood bedroom, dressed in the T-shirt I'd been wearing the day before. I sat on the sofa, feet curled underneath me, and I gave him a get-out-of-jail-free card. 'This is not what you signed up for,' I told him. 'You are allowed to back out of this without being the bad guy.' 'I know,' he said. 'But I don't want to.' I sat on the sofa staring at my phone long after we'd said our goodbyes. I didn't believe him.

I was in that peculiar hinterland of adulthood. I was twenty-five; to all intents and purposes, a grown-up. I lived 300 miles from my parents, I paid rent, I earned money, I represented other grown adults (and children!) in court, and argued for their liberty. I had a cat! But I was still a child. And, unlike my sister, I didn't have a partner really, not someone I could lean on, depend on. Just this guy I'd flirted with online and had dinner with a couple of times.

I can't remember the last time I saw my mum. I guess it must have been Christmas. Was she dying even then? Was her body already quietly betraying her? Did she know something was deeply wrong? I don't know, but I think the answer to all of those questions was probably yes. Just as she avoided technology, she avoided doctors, but I suspect she knew something wasn't right. Of course, it doesn't really matter. It doesn't change the outcome. But also, it does matter. It matters. It matters to me. When we were very little, our favourite book was a picture book called *Owl Babies*, by Martin Waddell. It is about three little owlets, who wake one night to find their mother has disappeared. Sarah and Percy, the older owlets, remain fairly stoical. Sarah and Percy try to figure out where their mother might be. Perhaps she's gone hunting! To get food! But Bill is inconsolable. *'I want my mummy,'* he says. We probably read that line together a thousand times. It was so simple, so impossible to imagine. Of course, in *Owl Babies*, the Mummy comes back: *'What's the fuss?'* she asks.

*

Sam never got to eat my mother's shepherd's pie. For a long time, I didn't eat it either. Death makes even the most banal memories painful, tangled in grief – even eating mashed potato. You have to work hard to soften those memories, to allow them to bring comfort in the way they once did. This is one of my favourite memories of my mother: Mum, standing in her kitchen, carefully, systematically dicing vegetables, the smell of leeks frying, gently in butter, and the *schlup* of the mandatory tin of baked beans making their appearance. I use Henderson's Relish here: a vegan version of Worcestershire sauce, and a Yorkshire institution, but Worcestershire will do just fine if you can't find the northern stuff. My mother always claimed her shepherd's pie had magical powers. It turns out she was right.

Shepherd's pie

Makes: Enough for 4 (although make this much for 2, and keep the leftovers: it's even better reheated the next day, and eaten with brown sauce)

Takes: 25 minutes

Bakes: 1½ hours, including unattended time on the hob

For the filling
2 tablespoons olive oil
400g lamb mince
2 medium carrots, diced
2 ribs of celery, diced
2 small onions, diced
1 x 400g tin of baked beans
2 tablespoons tomato purée
½ tablespoon Henderson's Relish
200ml lamb stock
Salt and pepper

For the topping
1kg potatoes, peeled and cut into 5cm cubes
50g butter
50g mature Cheddar cheese, grated
1 leek, finely sliced

1. Place a large casserole dish over a high heat on the hob: add 1 tablespoon of olive oil and the mince, and cook until browned. Set the mince to one side, and pour off any liquid that's been produced.

2. Heat a tablespoon of oil in the casserole dish and turn the heat down to low; add the diced vegetables and cook gently, until soft but not coloured.

3. Return the mince to the pan and add the baked beans, tomato purée, Henderson's Relish, lamb stock, and a generous sprinkling of salt and pepper. Bring to the boil, then cover the pan and cook over a very low heat for an hour. After an hour, check on the mixture: if it is still quite liquid, remove the lid, turn the heat up a little, and cook for another 20 minutes until it is thick and casserole-like.

4. Place the potatoes in boiling water and cook until tender, about 15 minutes, but you can test by spearing a potato with a sharp knife: if it slides off the knife back into the water, it is cooked. Drain and leave to steam for 5 minutes.

Mash the potatoes, or push them through a
ricer, until very smooth; beat the butter into
the mash.

5. Preheat the oven to 200°C fan/220°C/gas 7.
Mix two-thirds of the cheese and all the leeks
into the mash and spoon on top of the meat.
Flatten with the back of a spoon, then drag the
back of a fork in concentric circles. Sprinkle with
the remaining cheese. Cook for 25 minutes,
until the top is golden, and starting to crisp at
the edges.

2

Sam and I met through Twitter. We'd been at university together, in the same year, but even though we had dozens of mutual friends, our lives had never collided. We had first spoken over Twitter in 2009. We met at a Wetherspoon's in 2011, as part of what was then tweely referred to as a 'tweet-up'. He stood outside with me while I smoked a cigarette, and we exchanged the names of familiar acquaintances, and marvelled at how we'd never met before. But that was it. I had a boyfriend and he had a girlfriend. I didn't see him again until much later, after both of us were unceremoniously dumped within weeks of each other.

On our first date, before everything happened – before all of this – he invited me round for supper. It was just before Christmas. We'd already agreed to spend New Year's Eve together, coming up with tenuous reasons why we should forgo parties to hang out with a near stranger, but had both decided we wanted to meet up before then, because who has their first date (if that's what it was) on New Year's Eve? We'd arranged it last minute, and I, for the first time, had enjoyed spending a day in Milton Keynes Magistrates' Court, everything made more palatable by the prospect of romance and excitement. I thought all of this, despite knowing – via

Twitter, of course – that he had a stinking cold. When my train pulled into Euston, I had time to kill, and loaded up with painkillers and packets of tissues and clementines to take with me. I thought I was being charming.

He did indeed look full of cold when he opened the door, and I wondered if perhaps we should have just waited a couple more weeks, and had that first date on New Year's Eve after all. But here we were, so I might as well make the best of it, I thought. 'How does Welsh rarebit sound?' he asked. 'Sure,' I replied, 'whatever's easy for you,' thinking: *yes, even I could do cheese on toast*. Through a haze of stuffy nose and blocked sinuses, he picked his way around his kitchen, using up the end of a loaf of homemade bread, and herbs he'd grown on the window ledge. He melted butter in a pan, then stirred flour into it, until it sizzled. He sloshed milk into the pan, until it was a sauce, thick, and velvety. He grated strong cheese into the mixture, along with mustard and Worcestershire sauce, placed thick slices of bread under the grill and then spooned the cheese sauce on top, before returning them to the grill and leaving them to blister. I followed him around the kitchen, trying to think of interesting things to say, but really, just talking about my job. I was a brand new barrister, and it consumed me. I watched him as he pottered and cooked, thinking: *I am being so boring, what am I doing?* The rarebit came out bubbling, spots of primrose yellow and mahogany brown. This was like no cheese on toast I'd ever had. He'd done the whole thing without reference to recipes, without fuss or head-scratching. We ate it at his small dining table, and then sat on the sofa and talked (both of us) and sniffed (him). He insisted on walking me to the Tube station. He kissed me outside Stockwell Tube and, despite his cold, I let him do it. 'I'd like to see you again,' he said. 'Well, you will!' I said. 'On New Year's Eve!' But what I thought was: *me too*. I sat on the Victoria Line all the way to Finsbury Park and smiled. Because I was twenty-five, and excited by the prospect of romance and, well, my mother was still alive.

The first days of grief are drawn out, stretched like taffy. It's too early to begin sorting through possessions. Moments of frenetic activity and decision-making are interspersed with endless cups of tea, and lots of aimless sitting around. There's no plan. Everyone exists in a state of shock, a state of in-between-y, don't-know-what-to-do-with-yourself-ness. Like Boxing Day, if Boxing Day was awful.

No one around me could sleep. I, on the other hand, was practically narcoleptic. I slept. I slept and I slept and I slept. I needed only to sit down for a moment before my eyes would begin to close. I felt so guilty about it. I was sad about my mum's death, wasn't I? So how come I slept like a baby? I fell asleep on sofas and in chairs, I had afternoon naps and early nights. I longed for days to end so that I could sink into my childhood bed, and fall into oblivion.

Maddy and Dad seemed synced in their grieving: denied sleep, they were quiet, contemplative, whereas I, fully rested, felt manic during my waking hours. I clung to tasks, to-do lists, busywork.

On the other hand, I couldn't eat. Or rather, I wouldn't eat. At breakfast, my father and sister would tuck into bacon sandwiches prepared by aunts and uncles, dark circles under their eyes, while I just sat there and watched. The thought of eating turned my stomach. Eating felt like such an inherently pleasurable activity, especially eating at home, around my mum's table, that to do so in her absence, to take any such pleasure, felt like a kind of betrayal.

Dad is a probate solicitor, which means that death has been part of our lives for as long as I can remember. Each evening he would open the local paper and flick straight to the obituaries, to see if any of his clients had died. He was at a funeral most weeks. And nor were we new to death or bereavement on a more personal level. By the time my mother died, I had, at various stages and through various illnesses, lost all my grandparents. I was also better versed in *ER* and *Grey's Anatomy* than I was in any of the texts I studied for my degree.

So I was well acquainted with death, whether near or remote, sudden or slow. But this was different. Entirely different. You may think – I used to think – that grieving is just a matter of degree, and if you lose someone close to you, if you lose them suddenly, if you lose them too soon, it hurts more. But this wasn't merely a deeper, darker sadness. This was like being hollowed out and filled to the brim with loss. It coursed through me, to the ends of my fingers, the roots of my hair.

Despite our familiarity with death as a concept, our family was not made for grieving. Perhaps we were *too* well acquainted with death; unsure how to react when gallows humour failed. We dealt with most of life's challenges via jokes. Both Maddy and I would rather die than be earnest about anything – and, well, we'd already had quite enough of death. So we made jokes. We joked incessantly about what Mummy would have wanted – about how, for example, she would have scolded us for crying over her. Actually, this bit was only half a joke. Mum had very firm opinions on propriety around death (and weddings, and parties, and correspondence, and any social interaction whatsoever). In retrospect, these opinions were at best esoteric. According to her, crying at funerals was terribly gauche, as was running out of sandwiches or beer.

Grief, or at least expressing grief in public, can be exquisitely socially embarrassing. This isn't a feeling unique to me, or even my bonkers mother: it's a phenomenon that lots of those dealing with new loss find themselves feeling. Sandra Gilbert, the academic and critic, describes the experience of showing her grief outwardly as a 'persistent barely conscious feeling [. . .] a strangely muffled sense of *wrongness*', whereas C. S. Lewis takes it a couple of steps further and suggests colonies for the grieving: 'an odd byproduct of my loss is that I'm aware of being an embarrassment to everyone I meet [. . .] Perhaps the bereaved ought to be isolated in special settlements like lepers.'

I joked about Mum's firmly held beliefs, but I also took them to heart, dealing with Mum's death, however singular it was, in the same way as we dealt with each of my grandparents': by carrying on. For better or worse, I am my mother's daughter. I carried on as if my life could continue to function as before if only I focused hard enough, as if Mum's death was trivial. The least we could do as we mourned her was grieve as she would wish. I made the decision there and then: whatever happened, I would just cope.

I was drowning in paper. No one tells you about the admin of death. Amid the shock and confusion, the sheer quantity of paperwork and logistics is overwhelming. Mum had only been dead two days, and already there were so many decisions to be made over the minutiae of it: coffins, venues, readings, flowers, charities, newspaper announcements. So many opportunities to second-guess those decisions.

I don't remember who decided that we'd have the funeral at the village church, but at some point the decision had been made without debate. I sat in the sitting room, the room that was only used for guests, Christmas, piano practice and, it now transpired, death, staring at the antimacassars, thinking, *This is* not *what Mummy would have wanted.* But dear God, what *would* she have wanted? I realized I knew much more about what she disapproved of than what she actually liked, as though she were a forest clearing or a cave, defined by the negative, by what wasn't there. I knew that my mother had kept a list of hymns she wanted at her funeral in her bureau, but I couldn't find it. I had no idea what readings she'd want, or what kind of service she should have.

I had no idea about anything. My mind was blank, and I was crushed by the weight of it. In the one thing that really mattered, the one thing left, I was failing her.

There's a scene in *Love, Actually* where Daniel, played by Liam Neeson, is giving a eulogy for his wife, who has died of cancer. She wants the Bay City Rollers' 'Bye Bye Baby' played as the casket goes out. Daniel says to the congregation: 'When she first mentioned what was about to happen, I said, "Over my dead body." And she said, "No, Daniel, over mine . . ."' Then the distinctive first notes of the song begin to play. But if that person dies unexpectedly, before their time, whatever that means, how can you know? If the worst happened, do you know now what your middle-aged parents or your brothers and sisters or children would want? The undertaker asked if we wanted a large picture of Mum propped at the front, or a photo on the programme. Relief coursed through me that I knew the right answer for once: 'God, no,' I said.

And then, of course, there was the food. We had a meeting. No, more than that – we had a *tasting*. Dad, Maddy and I sat around a table sampling dishes that could form part of the wake buffet, like you might in the run-up to your wedding, only considerably bleaker. Wake cake. Wake pies. Wake sandwiches. Every choice felt crucial. How many pork pies should there be? There was a frisson of panic that went around the table when it was suggested that perhaps we were lowballing the pork pie consumption of mourners. Yes, we definitely wanted tuna finger sandwiches; she loved tuna sandwiches. Presented with little pots of seafood, we discussed seriously whether they were what Mummy would have wanted at her funeral. Mum was allergic to shellfish. In the context of these cockle pots, of course, she was literally the least important person. There were so many things to care about, to be troubled by: why would we care about what she could or couldn't have eaten at her own wake?

I had always sought Mum's approval above all else, so it made sense, in a perverse, grief-stricken way, that here, in this final game, I would want to impress her. Everything I had done had been success-oriented. Achievement-focused. This was very much my mother's doing. I approached grief similarly. Mourning was something I could be a high-achiever in. I treated every aspect of the funeral planning as an administrative task, to be ticked off a long to-do list that was headed Seeing Mum Off. I needed, very urgently, to be a good funeral hostess.

I found myself volunteering to do the eulogy. This really was what Mum would have wanted. Wasn't it? I didn't really know; as with everything else, I honestly had no idea. But I latched on to the idea that this was one final way in which I could make her proud. As children, Maddy and I had entered drama and public speaking competitions like our lives depended on it. For each one, we would spend hours in the sitting room, being coached by Mum over each pause, each intonation. 'OK, that time was better,' she'd say after the fourteenth recitation, 'but this time, make sure you pay attention to the comma at the end of line five.' This time, I stood in the sitting room alone.

*

The next day, we began making phone calls. Dozens of phone calls. Dad and I divided the address book up and set about our tasks. I sound like my mother, more so on the phone. 'Hello!' I would say, as brightly as I could muster, when one of Mum's friends or colleagues answered.

'Ruth!' they would reply. 'It's so lovely to hear from you!' Frequently, they embarked on full conversations with her before I was able to interject and explain that it was me they were speaking to. As I made phone call after phone call, I apologized over and over. 'I'm sorry, it's not actually Ruth. I'm afraid I have some bad news about her actually. I'm sorry.' I apologized again and again, but I couldn't bring myself to use a euphemism, to sugar-coat the awful information I was about to give them. 'My mother is dead.' Then I would add, for good measure: 'I'm so sorry.'

That night, I spent half an hour on the phone to a friend from chambers, who would be covering one of my cases the following day. He'd rung to get the lowdown on the case. It's not unusual to cover a chamber mate's case at short notice; it's how we keep the criminal bar ticking along with its myriad commitments and changeable nature. Often, you'll call up the person whose case it is to make sure you've got everything you should have, and to ensure there isn't anything you should know which isn't on the papers – a particularly tricksy client, a difficult instructing solicitor, a capricious judge. He'd been told I couldn't do the case, but not why, so we spent a strange half hour, with me pulling what I could from my tired brain and scrambled memory, assuming we were skirting round my unfortunate circumstances. I made a reference to being up in Newcastle, which prompted him to ask if I was on holiday. 'Actually, my Mum died,' I said, wincing as the words came out almost without my bidding. The poor guy. 'Oh my God. The clerks didn't tell me. Why didn't they tell me?' 'I'm so sorry,' I replied. 'I'm so sorry.'

We put a notice in the newspaper announcing Mum's death. It was both accurate and wholly incorrect at the same time:

POTTS. Ruth Anne (née Littlehales) suddenly at home on Sunday February 10th after a long illness aged 54 years.

This was exactly what had happened – but there was so much it didn't say. It didn't really say that she'd been ill for several *years*, nor that it wasn't that illness – or at least, no predictable, expected part of it – that killed her. 'Sudden' didn't seem to capture the debilitating, breath-stealing, ground-tremoring shock of it all. The notice didn't tell you that it was wrong, so wrong; that it never, ever should have happened. That it was so desperately unfair. That if she had to endure ill health for such a long time, the least she and we should have got in return was the opportunity to say goodbye, to know that this was the end. That although she was at home, she was alone. Because we didn't know. She didn't know.

'Adored.' That's how she was described in the rest of the announcement. 'Adored mother of Olivia and Madeleine.' The word catches me physically as I re-read it. It sounds overblown, saccharine, but it was the only word that came close to describing how consumed Maddy and I had felt by her love for us and our love for her, how it blew me up like a balloon, and how, without her, I couldn't make sense of anything.

I overheard Dad on the phone to someone expressing their condolences. 'Yes, Livvy and Maddy are doing well. Too well, really.' I was at once furious and perversely pleased. It felt like a warm swell within me. I felt proud. Anyone else would fall apart, right? I was doing better than every-one else was doing, than anyone could be expected to do. I was sticking to my promise of being the perfect bereaved daughter. I was going to be the best griever ever. You wouldn't even notice I was grieving! I would be so high-functioning, no one would think I was flighty or unreliable or, God forbid, unstable. The one thing I didn't want was for it to be dramatic. I have a tendency towards the dra-matic, but now, everything was quite dramatic enough, thank you very much. And I didn't want to make this about me. So I needed to redress the balance. So the answer was to be quiet, and good, and cope. Don't make a spectacle of yourself. I would show no weakness. Grief was weakness. Grief was failure. Of course, in doing so, I made it entirely about myself. I needed people to attempt to pity me so that I could confound them with my level-headedness.

My job, at this point, was still exceedingly precarious. The previous year, I'd finished law school, passed my Bar exams, and joined a set of criminal law chambers in the heart of Temple in London. Barristers are self-employed, but band together in groups to share premises, clerks, office resources and, often, values. Young barristers spend the early part of their training as 'pupils': these pupils spend the first six months shadowing more senior barristers – their pupilmaster or pupilmistress – getting the lie of the land, learning from them, and doing small pieces of work for them. After the first six months, they are allowed to undertake their own cases, but remain under the technical supervision of their pupilmaster. They check in with them, consult them when they encounter tricky areas of law or ethics, and will likely rely on them for a reference at the end of their pupillage. The end game for pupils is tenancy: this is a permanent position in chambers, one that can last the length of your entire career. The process for getting tenancy differs amongst chambers, but essentially requires your set of chambers formally 'accepting' you. If you are unsuccessful in seeking tenancy – which is not unusual – you must begin again at a different chambers. The stakes are high in what amounts to a year-long job interview. Your heart is weighed against a feather.

I was due for my tenancy decision in just three weeks' time. My senior clerk was kind but firm: I was not to come back to work until I was ready. But I was nervous. I had been out of court four days, and had a big case the following day. The hearing itself wasn't a big one, but it was for one of the few privately paying solicitors I was instructed by, and had been my case since day one. Privately paying cases are few and far between in the world of criminal law, with the majority of cases being funded by legal aid, and I was convinced that if I were replaced for this single, unimportant hearing, my solicitor would realize that not only was I not all he thought I was cracked up to be, but he would cease instructing me entirely, preferring one of my more competent or charismatic colleagues. I had to go back for this case.

Dad drove me down from Newcastle to my flat in London. We were trying to decide on music for the cremation, and I'd hastily grabbed a handful of CDs from home. How do you sum up a life in two pieces of music? Methodically, we worked our way through them, listening to the music that had made up my mum: the Housemartins and Beautiful South, Billy Joel and Trisha Yearwood. We listened to Kirsty MacColl, Mum's favourite singer, in silence. And when 'Days' started playing, we both began to cry. Dad looked sideways at me: 'This is it, this is the one, isn't it?' I nodded silently.

When I got home to my flat, I went upstairs to dump my handbag, and the carrier bag with clothes I'd had to buy at Asda to see me through my short time up north. My bedroom was not as I'd left it. I am not a naturally tidy person. My clothes were never contained by my flatshare wardrobe, shoes and books littered the floor, and papers were scattered everywhere. But now, piles of clean clothes were neatly folded on a made bed boasting clean sheets. Heading down to the kitchen, I found oven pizza and filled pasta stacked in the fridge, alongside big fat bars of Dairy Milk, smoked salmon, bread and butter. All my favourite things – courtesy of my housemates, Suzy and Rachel. I started crying again.

Before Mum's death, Sam and I had decided to skip Valentine's Day; we were still new to each other, we hadn't worked out what or who we were together. Valentine's Day was an unnecessary pressure. We'd hang out that week, just the two of us, in a quasi-romantic fashion – but we'd do it two days before the big V, on Pancake Day. With me stuck in Newcastle, organizing coffins and coroners, Pancake Day came and went, but Valentine's Day still loomed large. In fact, when we looked at my movements, it was the only day we could meet at all.

And so, two days later, I sat in Sam's flat, feeling guilty that I still had any interest in this man at all. I must have something seriously wrong with me if I was able to focus on my love life when we hadn't even had Mum's funeral. The last time I'd been here, I'd found out that my mother was dead. Now, I sat at the small table in his living room, while he moved around the kitchen making pancakes. I read the first draft of my eulogy out to him, the only person I'd properly spoken to over a fortnight who didn't know my mother. I tried out my jokes on him, and practised not crying at the difficult bits. We sat down to eat his pancakes, and I marvelled once again at his ability to pull together a simple meal not only without breaking a sweat, but without reference to a recipe. He tried to introduce me to his family speciality: a pancake spread two-thirds with Marmite and one third with jam. I declined. But around him I felt, for the first time, like I could breathe again.

The next morning, I was in court for the case that had dragged me back down south to Luton Crown Court. I loaded up my suitcase with files for the hearing, my wig, my gown, my books. It often happens that you end up in a groove with a particular court – sometimes because a solicitor decides they like you, and that court is on their beat, sometimes just by coincidence. Luton had become such a court for me. Out of all the courts in the country, the dozens I could be sent to on any given day, I found myself at Luton almost every week. I knew it so intimately, I was able to go about my day on autopilot. Ignoring the usual eye-rolling from fellow commuters as I lugged my enormous suitcase on to the train, I arrived at St Pancras, and waited on the platform for the Thameslink to Luton. I trundled through the shopping mall that smelt of popcorn, the worn-out wheels of my suitcase clattering noisily. I passed through the court's security – two very bored men and a metal detector – and stamped in the code for the robing room, which I knew off by heart. The robing room is the area reserved for barristers to change into their wigs and gowns; it's like a locker room, if footballers dressed like Batman. I took off my jacket, put on my collarette, a white cotton bib that I smoothed down over my black T-shirt, and replaced my jacket, buttoning it up, so only the lace collar and white tapes showed beneath. I slung my gown on my shoulders, put on my wig, and stepped into the heels that lived in my suitcase. I stalked upstairs, and sat outside the courtroom waiting for my solicitor to arrive. I was aware that I looked entirely normal. Or as normal as you can look wearing a cape and horsehair in 2013. It's easier to play a part when you're wearing a costume that, for all its drama, in the right context, allows you to fade into the background.

As my solicitor arrived, I smiled to see him, and the smile was at once both pasted on and genuine; hiding my tiredness and my sadness, but also a real expression of relief at a component of my old life, unchanged. The hearing was over in a matter of minutes, and the solicitor and I stood chatting afterwards at the bottom of the stairs, about the progression of the case, the next steps to be taken, and other upcoming cases that we were working on together.

And then, just before I made my excuses and left to get changed, I told him I was heading back up north for my mother's funeral. My solicitor was horrified. As the words came out of my mouth, *I* was horrified. Why did I tell him? For the second time in forty-eight hours, I'd managed to make a colleague feel horrible. Was I that desperate for him to know that I'd dragged myself from a house of grief in Newcastle to Luton Crown Court for a mention hearing in a benefit fraud case? What was wrong with me? If anything, surely I had just shown myself to be entirely unhinged, rather than robust and professional. Idiot. Idiot.

Two days later, I was getting dressed for the funeral in my childhood bedroom, surrounded by posters from plays I'd been in at university, shelves lined with books not important enough to move into my London home, but which I'd refused to throw away. I carefully applied my makeup, painfully aware that I would be on a perverse kind of display. The whole act felt surreal, like I was dressing up. I suppose I was. I'd decided to wear one of Mum's dresses. I don't know why. I was a barrister: I had black, formal dresses coming out of my ears. But I chose to wear hers. Was I trying to bring myself some kind of comfort? Or was I making a point? If I was, what the hell was it?

We waited nervously for the hearse and funeral cars. We had a slightly curved drive that obscured the view of the road, and I had to fight the urge to repeatedly check to see if they'd arrived, as if they were a taxi that would scarper if we exceeded our five minutes' waiting time.

The funeral was split into a service at the crematorium, followed by one at the local church. After that, the guests were invited back to our house for the wake. We were really only expecting a handful of people at the crematorium, where we'd have a small, private gathering; the church was supposed to be the main event. But as our car pulled up, I saw a huge crowd of people. There were so many more than I'd thought: dozens of people, spilling out from the steps of the crematorium building on to the pavement. I was completely overwhelmed. My whole body flashed cold then hot. At the front, I spotted my best friend, Ruth.

Ruth and I had been friends our whole lives: she was born a month before me, and she – our parents, being best friends – had been my mum's practice baby. Mum had spent the final month of her pregnancy with me learning how to hold baby Ruth and change her nappies. Her name, the same as my mum's, was a coincidence in origin, and of course, not an uncommon name, but had always made her feel even more like family to me. We were at school together, went on family holidays together,

31

and started Brownies and Guides together. We'd had baths together, and visited the set of *Last of the Summer Wine* together (no, really). She credited my mum's tuna sandwiches with bringing her back from vegetarianism. At the same university, she was the one who came to me when I broke up with my teenage boyfriend, bearing cake, and sat on my grubby floor and fed it to me. Ruth was stitched into every bit of my life.

Our eyes locked, and hers filled with tears. I had been trying so hard not to cry, not to let Mum down. It was the first time I had seen Ruth since Mum's death. The distance I had been carefully curating that morning from those around me, from the occasion itself, from anything I was feeling, disappeared. It was our car – our funeral car – approaching the crowd, but when I looked at Ruth, it felt like the crowd was rushing towards me, fast, crashing, unstoppable. My breath caught in my chest.

That morning, Dad had asked me to make sure that the flowers from the crematorium were taken to the church for the service. I was so relieved to have a job to do that I channelled all my energy into it. Moving flowers was my calling. Nothing mattered more. I cornered several undertakers and members of the crematorium staff to make them aware of how critical it was that the flowers be moved with the mourners. I was thorough: there was no way that this could go wrong. Dad had chosen the right person for the job.

Did you know that when the coffin is taken behind the curtains for cremation, there is a moment when the body is removed from it, rather than the whole thing being chucked, wholesale, into the incinerator, like some sort of garbage chute? Reader, I did not know this. This was the first funeral where I'd had any meaningful production assistant role; I was clueless. Taking my flower-protector role seriously, I had harangued no fewer than four separate people about the flowers since arriving at the crematorium: why did none of them mention that contrary to appearance, they weren't going to burn my flowers? I'm not sure. This could hardly have been a situation unique to us. I had spent hours with the undertakers; yet no mention was made of these more useful pragmatics. The moment of panic when the curtains opened, and the coffin, along with my precious flowers, slid into the fiery abyss, was acute. I fought the urge to leap from my seat and cling to the coffin; not in a bereft, grief-stricken way, but simply to save the flower arrangement perched on top.

The music began, Kirsty MacColl, the first few seconds missing, thanks to technical difficulties, and we filed out, on to the church, to the next part of the god-awful process.

I took a deep breath and began.

'Ruth Anne Potts, neé Littlehales – Mummy – was born in 1958 . . .'

My memories of the eulogy are juddering, stilted. I remember walking up to the lectern, touching it, gripping it, holding on to it for dear life. If I held it tightly enough, I could hide the fact my hands were trembling, an old courtroom trick. I remember fighting my voice as it tried to quaver, and the strange surge of pride that accompanied that successful repression. I remember there were jokes, though I don't remember what they were. I remember looking out and seeing my friends from college sitting in a row together, in the pew that my mother sat in every Sunday for the first twelve years of my life, before she lost her faith – the pew in which I would join her after Sunday school.

I'd been christened here, in this village church. I'm not remotely religious, but this church was a huge part of my childhood. I'd read the Bible from this very lectern, gone to confirmation classes here. I'd played Mary in the Nativity, aged five, when my toddler sister, cast as an angel, refused to leave my side, following me round, holding my hand, through the entire performance. I'd carried the big church candle up the aisle one Easter Sunday, before fainting dramatically during the Lord's Prayer – cutting my youthful role as a server short. I had lit more tea lights than I could ever recall in the small side chapel, in remembrance of my maternal grandfather. What was my mother thinking every week as we sat in that deathly quiet chapel? For me, a tiny child, putting the small change into the donation pot, choosing a tea light, lighting it, was a treat. For her, who knows? She was crouching there with her small daughter, who'd never met her grandfather. What did that feel like? Was it as hard as this?

Now, I stood ten feet from where we used to sit, telling all the people who knew Mum what Mum meant to me, or trying to; trying to fit into a five-minute speech a woman's life. I told them about how she grew up, and the course her life took. It was a eulogy full of the things you are supposed to say in a eulogy, and as I gave it, inside, I was disowning it. Because reducing my and Mum's relationship to a few telling anecdotes and vignettes was impossible, and insulting. It could never convey her smell and her laugh, how much she drove me up the bloody wall, and how I felt like there was a physical fire inside of me burning with her love, how I ached to smell her, just once more, and how I knew, deep down, that no one would or could ever love me like she did again. Somehow, I made it through, and bolted back to my seat.

After my eulogy, the vicar said some platitudes about Mum, though she didn't know Mum. The vicar who had been at the church when we attended regularly had left years before. There's something very peculiar about someone who has never met or known the deceased giving an address about them. Speaking passionately, emotively about not only someone they don't know, but someone they won't even remember tomorrow.

I stood at the doors to the church, where I'd collected in the hymnals when I was little, and the three of us gathered in a procession line, ready to greet each of the mourners as they filed past. Each of them introduced themselves to me, assuming I would have forgotten them. I hadn't. But each was a tiny electric shock: dozens and dozens of people, hundreds, all of whom I knew in the context of Mum. To see them here, without her, was to see them displaced, like the first time you see a teacher in the supermarket. There's a standard line when you greet someone who is bereaved: 'I'm so sorry for your loss.' You really don't need to say anything else. But the response?

The response is harder. Actually, in hindsight it's easy: a simple 'Thank you' would have done. 'Thank you for coming' would be better. Instead, I plumped for trying to persuade people to come for a drink at the wake, like some sort of manic club promoter.

At the wake, I was bright-eyed and bushy-tailed; I was in hostess mode, which felt like much firmer ground. I was polite when asked how I was doing, told them I was coping. Really, though, I was emotionally catatonic. I talked about the flowers, which now stood proudly on our dining table and had not, in fact, been incinerated, declaiming their beauty in increasingly overblown terms as the afternoon wore on. There were enough pork pies. No one touched the seafood pots. Piles of banana cake that I don't remember ordering flanked the table.

Halfway through the wake, I ducked out into the garden with Ruth. I sat in Mum's garden, on her bench, and smoked her cigarettes. She hadn't known she was going to die, so there was half a carton of cigarettes in the dresser in the morning room, where she'd always kept them. I say that like, if she'd had some kind of warning, she'd have bought the correct number of cigarettes, rationed them so that she smoked her last before she died. I don't mean that. But it was just one of the many things we found after she'd gone. Hairdresser appointments that needed cancelling. Library books that needed returning. More tiny objects that pointed to a future snatched away. I wasn't sentimental enough to hold on to her cigarettes, though. I smoked them all, one after the other. It's what Mummy would have wanted.

I was heading back to London that night, and as I packed up my stuff in the kitchen, my father stood over the sink, washing brine off dozens of pots of seafood. 'What are you doing?' I asked incredulously. 'I'm rinsing the cockles!' he replied. 'For paella!' We had never as a household eaten paella, and I would be prepared to bet substantial amounts of money that my father, in all his fifty-six years, had never made paella. We'd never even been to Spain together, for God's sake. But it was clearly very, very important to him at this precise moment in time that the seafood be preserved, that ordering it need not have been an error, another waste. The seafood would go on to sit in his freezer for about two years, until he sold the house, at which point it was thankfully all thrown away. The sound of the tap on the polystyrene cups was like heavy rain.

On the other side of the small kitchen, I loaded up slice after slice of leftover banana cake into a rectangular green biscuit tin that, turned over, bore a little white label with the name POTTS written in my mother's clean, clear, distinctive handwriting – block capitals, just like her death announcement. It was a part of the house, a part of her life, and I was taking it back to London with me. This was far from the best banana cake I'd ever eaten. It was slightly insipid, a little rubbery. But it was sweet. And as I ate it on the train, I found my appetite had returned.

*

If you asked me now, with the benefit of hindsight, I think I'd prescribe banana bread for grief. It has everything you need: stodge for heartache, sugar for wobbliness, and potassium for fatigue. I don't say this flippantly. There is a reason we turn to food for comfort. Certain dishes have ways of bringing contentment, or at least a nudge towards equilibrium. I'd never have thought that those fingers of unexceptional banana cake could do that, but I was wrong.

This is a much better banana cake than the one I ate on the train. It's dark and damp, with pockets of caramel and chocolate, and the demerara sprinkled on top gives an addictive crunch. But it provides the same comfort as that first banana cake. It's not a cake I often make for others, but it's the cake I'll invariably make when I want cake for myself.

When I have bananas that are slightly on the turn, I throw them into the freezer, whole and unpeeled. Although they might look unchanged when you remove them from the freezer, as they thaw, they will turn jet black: the freezing and thawing causes them to oxidize and ripen, so the fruit emerges broken down, sweeter, and, well, banana-ier. It's up to you how long you leave them frozen, but I recommend at least a day. Defrost them before baking by plunging them unpeeled into warm water for ten to fifteen minutes until they have completely softened. This process has improved my banana cakes no end, and I commend it to you.

Banana and Rolo cake

Makes: One loaf
Takes: 1 hour
Bakes: 40–50 minutes

125g butter
150g dark brown muscovado sugar
85g light brown muscovado sugar
250g plain flour
2 eggs
3 bananas (must be over-ripe)
2 teaspoons baking powder
1 teaspoon salt
2 packets of Rolos
A handful of demerara sugar

1. Preheat your oven to 180°C fan/200°C/gas 6.
   Line a 900g loaf tin with two strips of paper, one
   running the width of the tin, and one the length,
   both with grabbable overhang.

2. Cream the butter and sugars together using a
   stand mixer, a hand-held mixer, or a spatula and
   determination. When ready, the mixture should
   be light and fluffy, and noticeably paler than
   when you began.

3. Measure out your flour into a separate bowl. Add
   the eggs to the butter and sugar mix one by one,
   fully incorporating each one in turn. If the

mixture looks like it's going to curdle, add
1 tablespoon from your pre-measured flour,
and continue.

4. Add the bananas one by one. Smoosh them into
   the mixture, so that they run all the way
   through, but not so that you lose all the lumps.

5. Fold in the pre-measured flour, the baking
   powder, and the salt. Fold through the Rolos.

6. Spoon into the cake tin and give it a jiggle to
   smooth out the surface. Sprinkle with the
   demerara sugar.

7. Bake for 40–50 minutes, until the cake is set
   when carefully pressed with a fingertip, and
   doesn't wobble when gently shaken. Leave to
   cool, then slice into thick slabs.

3

What people don't tell you about grieving is quite how boring it is. Not straight away, of course. In the immediate aftermath of death, it's anything but. But quickly, surprisingly quickly, it all becomes very boring. Desperate to be useful, to plough my energies into something which would stop me thinking about my new reality, I insisted on shouldering the bulk of the admin, snatching it away from Maddy and Dad. Naturally I viewed this as me swooping in with competence and efficiency, but you know, tactfully, effortlessly, whereas the reality was a clunkier cross between inexplicable hero complex and martyrdom. However it presented, I really did want to help, I wanted to do something to take away the pain from Maddy and Dad, and if that meant making phone calls to banks and sending emails to lawyers, so be it. This admin is boring: there are accounts to close and appointments to cancel, paperwork to file, wills to execute, solicitors to meet, phone calls to make, clothes to take to charity shops. Exhibits of a life interrupted.

But everything else is boring, too. The inside of your head is boring. Grief, after the first few hours of pure, raw shock, is indescribably tedious. As you try to process the loss of this person, the same thoughts spring up again and again. You are surprised again and again by their absence, and each time, you have to remind yourself of the reality. Missing someone and knowing that there is no way of alleviating that loss is exquisitely boring.

When people talk about grief, they often use water metaphors: drowning in grief, waves of grief, being swamped. People say it's like breathing underwater. But this all feels much too dramatic for me. The first day or two aside, I didn't feel like I was drowning. If I had to use a water metaphor, I'd say grieving is sitting in a cooling bath you can't get out of. Your fingers slowly prune. Did you know that this is thought to be an evolutionary trick – that the pads of your fingers develop ridges to give you a better grip underwater? Isn't that amazing? Not in this metaphor. Because in this metaphor, there's nothing to hold on to. Your cooling bath is a giant, smooth semi-circle, and it's now uncomfortably chilly, and you are languishing. There is no one there to tell you to come out. No one there to wrap you in a towel and make you feel better. Sure, there may be people nearby who offer support – who tell you to get out of the damn bath and wrap yourself in a towel. But you can't. I wasn't sinking. I was floating: aimlessly, unwillingly but irresistibly.

The boredom and the floating and everything else is made unbearable by not knowing when it will end, or if it ever will, in the same way that waiting for a bus is far worse if you have no idea when it will arrive. Time stretches ahead of you. You go to work. You pay your bills. You water the plants, and start thinking about whether you should buy some poles for when the beans come through in the spring. You live your life, but every part of it feels a little greyer, a little more pointless. A little colder.

Sadness used to be codified. The Victorians had explicit rules around mourning periods, dress and etiquette. A widow could lift the veil on her bonnet after three months, but the veiled bonnet was to be worn for a full year, and mourning colours for two years. Crêpe tied with ribbon was hung from doors, not to discourage visitors, but to alert them to the death within, and encourage them to enter quietly, without ringing the doorbell. For the young, white crêpe and ribbon were used, and black for the elderly. Close friends could visit the bereaved after ten days, but acquaintances had to wait until the family attended church. The bereaved could invite sympathy on their own schedule, by sending out black-edged mourning cards that told the world they were ready to receive condolences.

These rules loosened at the start of the twentieth century, and particularly during the First World War. In the face of so much death, elaborate mourning rituals became both impractical and absurd, and the 'stiff upper lip' prevailed. A century later, we are in much the same place, even though death is a much smaller part of most of our lives. We go to the funeral. We eat pork pies and banana bread. We go home, and carry on with our lives. For better or worse, most of us are left to grieve in our own private way. For worse, I'm pretty sure it was for worse. Our grief was unstructured.

In other countries and other cultures, they do things differently. In Vietnamese culture, people who are grieving wear a black band, a sort of baby-on-board sticker for bereavement: bereavement on board. I like that. Maybe if I had worn a black armband, or full-on mourning dress, people would have known that I was fragile, and that they should treat me with kid gloves. Maybe I would have felt I had permission to openly grieve.

With the exception of the more pared-down Christian denominations, most religions still provide some kind of structure for grieving, some rituals to go through. In Hinduism, the grieving family's bathing and eating is stipulated: twice daily baths, vegetarian meals. Men do not shave or cut their hair for ten days following the death, nor do women wash their hair; white clothes are worn to indicate mourning during this period. On that tenth day – *Daswan* – hair is washed, beards are shaved. With us, life got in the way: Maddy went back to Sheffield, I went back to London. Rather than the three of us being a physical presence and comfort to one another, we scattered.

The Jewish community view mourning as a process through which the bereaved can come to terms with their grief and, slowly, return to normal life. In the immediate aftermath, they 'sit shiva': a week-long mourning period spent at home. This is followed by sheloshim, a thirty-day period during which the bereaved are encouraged to slowly return to their activities. The idea is that each of the stages of mourning requires incrementally more of the mourner, until they are able to rejoin society. The mourning period for the death of a parent is one year.

Perhaps if I'd been born into one of these cultures or religions that stipulates an engagement with death in a structured way, that invited me to acknowledge my pain, or grapple with the reality of my situation, I would have had the skillset to grieve. But I am an atheist, brought up in the unemotive Church of England. For me, mourning was always going to be as brief and unexpressive as possible. I thought I was avoiding dwelling on death, but really, I was boxing myself in. Inside, my grief was unspooling.

Mum was born in Leeds in 1958. She had an older sister, Jan. Her father died of lung cancer when she was thirteen. Her mother moved the family to Ponteland, near Newcastle, where she got married again, to a solicitor.

From a young age, Mum loved books perhaps more than anything, but was encouraged to read law at university. She loved her three years at Durham, but was never terribly interested in law. She went to Collingwood College, which is high up on the hill, and credited walking up and down that hill four times a day to and from college and lectures for her objectively excellent legs. She thought perhaps she wanted to be a barrister, but her stepfather told her she cried too easily to stand up in court, so she trained to be a solicitor. She moved to Guildford for that, where she felt thoroughly isolated and miserable (although while there she was once mistaken for Prince Charles's new girlfriend by paparazzi waiting outside her best friend's apartment. So there's that). She moved back up north, and joined her stepfather's law firm where she qualified as a full solicitor. She met my father at a Law Society dinner in 1980. He was wearing the aforementioned blue velvet dinner suit, and tried to impress her and her best friend, Mac, by drinking the horrible sweet wine they'd been served. Unbelievably, it worked. He invited her to join him on a jaunt to Llandudno for a hockey game that he was captaining. There, he asked her to marry him. They'd known each other for three weeks. She told him she'd have to think about it.

They were married in Ponteland, in the north-east, with a reception at her mother and stepfather's home. Granny, wanting to get value for money out of her marquee hire, threw a second party the following morning, to which the happy couple were not invited.

Mum and Dad planned to set up a law firm, just the two of them: Potts and Potts. But then Mum became pregnant with me, and Dad was offered a partnership at Mum's firm – that is, his new father-in-law's firm. It was, as they say, a no-brainer.

I was born in 1987. Just before I was born, Mum and Dad moved into the house that would become the only family home I ever knew. It was a Victorian house, the servants' quarters of the rather grander house next door. It had a big garden with an apple tree right at the centre. A swing hung from the apple tree for a short time, until Mum became too worried Maddy or I would die on it.

I used to love the story of my birth. Three weeks premature and jaundiced, I was whisked away and put into an incubator with premature-baby-sized sunglasses to protect my eyes. But as I get older, I'm struck by how absolutely terrifying the whole thing must have been for my parents.

Maddy was born in 1990, three years my junior. I

resented her initially, like all good big sisters do, then grudgingly accepted her as sometime-playmate, sometime-nemesis. Identical to me as a baby, she grew into a smiley squidge of a toddler, grinning in every photo, with wayward auburn curls, where my hair was dark and poker straight.

That's a potted biography of my mother. I could also give you any number of bits of trivia. She was terrified of flying, but loved trains. She was allergic to shellfish and penicillin. She collected blue glass bottles. She could whistle like no one else I've ever met. She loved lemons in every guise. She was heart-stoppingly scary when angry, with a shouting voice that could halt tanks or rhinos in their tracks. *Gone with the Wind* was her desert island book, and I suspect her luxury would have been a pack of 20 Silk Cut and a lighter.

The last few years of Mum's life were dominated by illness. It began in 2007, with a swelling on her abdomen like an enormous baby bump. Her back hurt and she couldn't eat. She came to visit me at university, and I was shocked at how much she'd changed since I'd seen her just a few weeks previously. Many tests later, she was diagnosed with cryptogenic cirrhosis of the liver – liver disease whose origin could not be identified as, for example, alcohol abuse. It made her very poorly for the following four years, but not in a way that was thought to be life-threatening. I knew that one day she would probably need a liver transplant, and that she, like me, was terrified of that.

What neither of us knew was that her cirrhosis would

be complicated by the development of a stomach ulcer that haemorrhaged with fatal consequences. The biography I've just given you, the various events and quirks and twists and turns that make up a life – it was all over. On 10 February 2013, Ruth Anne Potts died. And nothing was ever the same again.

It wasn't just us who were shocked by her death; it was her GP, whom she'd seen not long before she died, and to whom she'd given no inkling of the stomach ulcer. Perhaps Mum didn't mention her symptoms, perhaps she didn't understand what was going on inside her. Either way, a post-mortem was ordered. I suddenly wished that I wasn't a barrister, that I didn't know what happened at post-mortems. That I hadn't seen photos.

My mother was my best friend. Does that sound trite? Rose-tinted? Maybe. But it's true. After she died, I felt so fucking lonely. The only person I wanted to talk to about my grief was her. She'd lost a parent prematurely; she'd understand. Maybe she was the only person who would understand. I couldn't talk to Dad or Madeleine. I couldn't bear to hear the grief in their voices. I feared betraying the grief in mine. When we spoke, I kept it as light as I could. I ignored the Mum-shaped elephant in the room. Sam was wonderful, as were my housemates, but they were always going to be somewhat removed. The only person who could help me was the one who was missing, and however much love and support people gave me, all I could focus on was how alone I felt. She was my person, and she was gone, and she was literally irreplaceable.

*

My mother gave me many things, but an education in cookery was not one of them. She liked eating rather more than she loved cooking. She loved cheese scones, moussaka, and bolognese pizza – which was exactly what it sounds like: meat ragù on top of a pizza crust, and a non-negotiable part of our order when we got takeaway pizza. When she was ill, she became obsessed with clementines, and before then, she was obsessed with tuna pâté – tuna anything, really – and cherry tomatoes and Marks & Spencer BLTs. Also fig rolls, dry white wine, and Marmite. She was incapable of going to a pub for tea and not ordering ham, egg and chips, more so if it came with a ring of pineapple, which in the kind of pubs we went to it always did. Though she was allergic to saltwater prawns, she delighted in the freshwater prawns you'd get in Indian restaurants sometimes, which made going for a curry with her a thrilling game of Russian roulette. She loved baked beans beyond all reason, even cold: 'sneaky beans', she'd call the spoonful straight from the tin, before heating the rest. She was easy to please when it came to birthdays because all she really desired was a box of Thornton's fruit-filled chocolates. Oh, and she drank two litres of fizzy water, straight from the bottle, every night. (Sometimes, I would slip into her room to steal the dregs of this water; the taste of half-stale fizzy water is still oddly comforting to me.)

Puddings were obligatory on Sundays, but they were always shop-bought. Pancakes happened once a year, and were very clearly something that was done for my and Maddy's benefit rather than for the joy of it. Baking was

49

simply unheard of. When I was six, she gave me an Usborne cookery book for my birthday, perhaps not fully perceiving the role she would have to play in the execution of the recipes. With one aborted attempt at profiteroles – which ended with us tipping what looked a lot like a selection of dried prunes into the bin – any possibility of a burgeoning passion for baking was snuffed out, and no one was particularly bothered about rekindling it.

Because she didn't relish it, I think of her as someone who couldn't cook. But this is unfair. She had learnt how to cook through necessity when she was a teenager, when her mother had a hip operation. And there were some things she did brilliantly. I know I'm not alone in making this assertion, but my mother made the best roast dinners in the world: her Yorkshire puddings, as befits a Yorkshire woman, were second to none; her roast potatoes were superlative, and her carrots, blitzed with criminal amounts of butter and black pepper, were exquisite. The stuffing and gravy both came out of a packet, but for whatever reason, I've never been able to get them quite as good.

I loved her vol-au-vents, filled with a mixture of tinned tuna and Campbell's condensed cream of mushroom soup, which were as delicious as they sound disgusting; I never appreciated how old-fashioned they really were until I turned up to a New Year's party in my early twenties with a tray of them to a room of confused faces. She made leek and potato soup, coq au vin, boeuf bourguignon, and a Greek-style pasta bake topped with cheese and yoghurt and eggs, which blackened as the savoury custard cooked, filling the house with its deeply cheesy scent, drawing the family from our different rooms to congregate around the oven door.

Mum was very much of the 'life's too short to stuff a mushroom' school of thought. My mother was part of that generation that came of age in the 70s, and fell in love with supermarket convenience. The speed and ease which was once only the realm of Fray Bentos pies suddenly became possible for moussaka! And spaghetti carbonara! And, above all, fish pie!

Specifically, she had a peculiar theory that it was perfectly acceptable to buy even basic items, if you *knew* how to make them. Almost every week, she would buy a prepared fish pie; according to her, this would be a great moral failing if she couldn't make a white sauce herself. But since she could, it wasn't a problem. According to this line of reasoning, you only had to succeed at any time-consuming or difficult culinary feat once. Only a fool made a white sauce or pastry or custard on a regular basis. I therefore grew up in a culinary no man's land, thinking both that people who couldn't cook were uncouth, and that people who did were awful try-hards.

My mother never got round to teaching me how to make a white sauce – or rather, I never got round to asking her to. I was too busy enjoying the wilderness of my early twenties, feeling like I was the first person ever to sit law school exams, or go on dates, or move away from home. And then, of course, it was too late. This left me in the first camp – the uncouth one – with no one to teach me.

In many ways, it was this that spurred me into action. If my mother had died without teaching me how to make a white sauce – I would have to teach myself. I recognize that, against the grand tragedy of suddenly losing a parent, losing their limited culinary knowledge may feel like a footnote. But I didn't dare think about the bigger stuff. So this became my focus.

For the first few weeks, I'd survived on those supermarket pizzas left by my housemates, supplemented by autopilot trips to the corner shop. Instant noodles. Baked beans (it's what Mum would have wanted, although I still can't stomach them cold). A rotation of the same three ready meals picked up on my way home from work. But one night, a fish pie mix caught my eye: they're a regular resident of the reduced aisle in supermarkets: a trio of fish – lurid yellow haddock, pale pink salmon, and smooth white cod. I put it in my basket and carried it like a talisman around the supermarket with me. What else did I need to make a fish pie? Milk, probably. Potatoes, I was sure. Cheese. One by one, and helped by a lot of guesswork, I filled my basket with the things I thought I might need.

When I got home, I unpacked my small haul, and set myself in front of our temperamental electric hob. Armed with a Googled recipe in one hand, and a wooden spoon in the other, I tried to teach myself how to make a white sauce. First, a roux: something I would have been hard pressed to describe. But actually, melting butter and sizzling flour into it wasn't so hard. I found a whisk belonging to Rachel, my housemate, in the back of one of the kitchen drawers, and stirred milk into the mixture, expecting lumps, but instead, to my surprise, finding it smooth out, and become silken. As I got half way through the recipe, I could see that – bloody hell – I'd made a white sauce! On my own! I then realized two things: first, that I could do this. And second, that I had always hated fish pie.

Mum never understood my dislike of fish pie. I was a good eater. I wasn't fussy or picky. But fish pie was the exception. I was, even as a small child, affronted by the possibility that I'd be asked to eat it. I'm not sure whether my mother would collapse in laughter or tears if she were to learn that the first proper dish I tackled was, of all things, fish pie.

So I stood over the stove, proudly admiring my silken sauce, while pondering the fact that I was pretty much committed to making and eating a dish that I had hated for twenty-five years, which for reasons I couldn't unpick at that time had suddenly become terribly important to me. I spooned the sauce on to the fish. I mashed the potatoes, spread them on top, and put the dish into the oven.

And then I ate the fish pie. And it was delicious. When did fish pie start being delicious? How on earth could I ever have disliked this? But more importantly than that, something strange had happened. The act of making – and eating – a meal with my own two hands had anchored me. Calmed me. I hadn't climbed out of my grief bath, exactly, but it was as though someone had poured in a kettle of hot water. So, maybe not the next day, or the day after that, but some time later, I continued cooking. I kept returning to that fish pie, to the most hated dish of my childhood, that I found myself longing for on a regular basis.

The English Bar, for all its attempts at modernization, remains archaic in its structure. Entrance to the profession requires its own set of exams – like medicine or accountancy – but also your attendance at a series of elaborate dinners, featuring gowns and toasts and graces. Once you've managed that and been called to the Bar, you have to find a set of chambers who will take you under their wing as a trainee or 'pupil' barrister. When you become a barrister – you've passed all the exams, you've jumped through all the hoops, you've bought the wig and gown – you have to spend at least a year as a pupil in a set of chambers. As a pupil, your life is dictated by your pupilmaster or pupilmistress: they tell you where to be and when; they set you work and mark it, and ask you to prep or summarize papers. Your opinion will be sought on strategy, questioning, pleas; you will be tested on procedure, and correct steps to be taken, but when the client is present, you are seen, not heard. You are a note-taker. You sit quietly. You get coffee.

Barristers may pride themselves on their self-employment, but as a pupil, you're stuck with whichever cases your pupilmaster or -mistress takes. If they work solely in messy, dull VAT frauds, then for twelve months, so will you. And there's nothing you can do about it. My first case was about Viagra fraud, which, if possible, was even less glamorous than it sounds. I spent two weeks sitting in Harrow Crown Court, doing precisely nothing, as an investigator who inexplicably feared for his life gave evidence on the intricacies of counterfeit drug manufacture. It was to *The Wire* what *The Office* is to *The Wolf of Wall Street*.

In the wake of Mum's death, a trial that dull and unemotional would almost have been a blessing. Instead, a month after the funeral, my supervisor took on a murder. And not just any murder: a three-handed torture murder, with cut-throat defences, meaning all of the defendants had turned on each other. It was going to last six weeks, and take place at the Old Bailey. My poor co-pupil found himself stuck for a similar amount of time in the wilds of Essex on a case about the illegal disposal of waste televisions in Nigeria. I wasn't terribly gracious in my good luck.

The Old Bailey is the most old-fashioned of all courts. It sits just behind St Paul's, the entrance hidden down an unassuming side road, right in the heart of London. There's something special about the Old Bailey, and it's not just that it deals with many of the most serious cases in England. You have to justify your presence there. Defendants and witnesses are not allowed to roam freely through the corridors like they are at other courts, but have to give their name to security, and then wait in an anteroom until their barrister comes and collects them, like a child at nursery. Unlike pretty much every other court in the country, the Bailey has a separate entrance for the public, restricting them to closely patrolled public balconies and even then, no handbags or mobile phones are allowed. To see inside the inner sanctum, you have to be one of a select few: a defendant, a witness, a juror – or a barrister.

It's also one of the most handsome buildings in London: vast sweeping staircases, vaulted ceilings, and marbled floors leading up to huge, domed skylights. Even the courtrooms are grander than those of the other Crown Courts, boasting wooden panelling as far as the eye can see, balconies from which the public can watch, proper pews for counsel (the first row reserved for Queen's Counsel, even when none are present), and veritable thrones for the judiciary. Not for the Bailey the modern interiors of Southwark or Woolwich Crown Courts.

The Bar mess – where barristers are able to kick back, read their papers, eat lunch, or haggle over pleas – is appropriately grand, with chaises longues in place of the moth-eaten, ageing sofas of other courts, on which moth-eaten, ageing barristers can often be found snoozing. Even the food served is on a different level to other courts: if it weren't already a coup to receive a Bailey brief, the real treat is being present for the Bailey breakfast, where the eggs are cooked to order in front of you, like a West London hotel brunch. Behind the mess is a library, where barristers beaver away or, possibly, just escape the inevitable horse-trading that goes on in the mess.

In fact, everything at the Bailey is a little different. There is a separate robing room for male QCs (not for female QCs, of course, they have to slum it with us junior counsel riffraff). Instead of the small client consultation rooms of other courts, there are long oak tables, with straight-backed chairs around which barristers, solicitors and clients huddle, strategizing and plotting. The judges wear different robes, and are referred to differently: look closely at the blue notebooks of very junior counsel, and you might just be able to make out 'MY LORD' written at the top of every page, and underlined heavily, with multiple exclamation marks. For all its peculiarities and frustrations, there is nothing better on this planet for making you feel glamorous and important than clipping down a Bailey atrium, gown swinging behind you, the looped tails on the back of your wig bouncing.

I started working on the case on a damp, drizzly Friday afternoon. Sitting in our small room in chambers, which made up for what it lacked in size and grandeur with an absolutely perfect view of Temple Church, my supervisor handed me a thick stack of booklets, then started to pack up. 'These are the photos for the murder case. I'm going to go home. You can go once you've had a look through these. Just so you know: in autopsies they have to peel the skin away to look at the bruising from the underside.' I blanched.

Photobooks in violent crimes often lure you into a false sense of security: the first thing they will show you is the approach to the scene, which often presents as innocuous. Each page takes you one step closer: it's like a video game, edging ever nearer to the target, unable to tear yourself away, although you know danger is close. Slowly, depending on the crime scene, spots of blood appear, or signs of a struggle. Often, crime scenes are cleaned up before the police get to them: forensics teams have to search for the telltale signs missed by the perpetrator: communal bins are emptied, eagle eyes search ceilings and skirting boards for the tiniest spots of blood, ultraviolet lights are needed to identify traces that have been attacked by cleaning products. But not this one.

The case was obscenely violent. The Crown's case was that three members of the homeless community had lured a fourth homeless man back to a squat in South London where, over a twenty-four-hour period, they tortured him to death. The motivation, as so often is the case, was revenge: the ex-girlfriend of the first defendant, Dan, had had a short-lived fling with the victim, and Dan had concocted a plan to lure the victim into a flat, and get his own back. But this was also one of those hideous cases where one person's idea becomes a reality, and those around are carried along on the swell of adrenaline and violence. A mob mentality. A *Clockwork Orange* kind of case. Over the day, Dan invited friends and acquaintances to come and witness the torture. One after another they turned up, witnessed what was going on and left. One of the most powerful pieces of evidence in the case was a piece of audio, made by a builder in one of the other flats in the building who heard something strange – although he severely underestimated quite how strange it was – and began recording on his iPhone. It was clear from what could be heard that while the torture was going on, a Blondie greatest hits album was playing at full volume. It had been my job to transcribe the tape. Like a Tarantino film come to life, the violence ebbed and increased alongside the tracks: as the music moved from 'The Tide is High' to 'Heart of Glass', and finally 'One Way or Another', it was possible to hear the trajectory of the attack.

I sat looking at those photo books, slowly turning the pages. I hadn't thought I was naive entering this side of the profession: I'd known what I was letting myself in for, surely? I'd read the textbooks, I'd done the mock trials, I'd ticked off the work experience. But flicking through a series of photos that baldly, unemotionally chronicled the brutal death of a man, it hit me like a freight train. The absolute, unseating horror of it all. And I thought: was this really where I wanted to be? Was this really what I wanted to do? I'd fought fiercely to get this far, and already, I was a wreck. I felt like a fraud.

There isn't some threshold of distress we have to reach before we're allowed to be upset about something. Sadness isn't criterion-referenced. We all have that friend who, when we complain about our broken-down boiler or our burnt coffee, reminds us that there is a civil war raging in Yemen. But that's not how sadness works.

Sometimes, I am upset about my freezer-burnt pork. Sometimes, I feel as though the world is going to cave in because I just missed my bus. And sometimes, at the same time, I am upset in a deeper, if quieter, way about war, poverty and suffering. When you experience trauma, the equation changes a little. To most people, you are firmly in the 'legitimate complaints' column. But if you are a criminal barrister, you will still, every day, meet people whose suffering wholly eclipses your own.

As a criminal barrister, you are obliged to look at

photos of a dead person and recognize that the suffering –
not just their suffering, but their parents', their children's,
their friends' – may be worse than yours. And then you
have to leave it behind: you have to go home and make
supper and live your life, accepting that, however deep
their sadness, and any other sadness, yours is still legitimate. Women are systematically oppressed worldwide, the
victim was brutally murdered, the pork has freezer burn,
your mother is dead. These all co-exist, and they all hurt.

I left chambers feeling disillusioned and angry. Angry
at myself. I was better than this – wasn't I? I tried to
examine my feelings from different angles, prodding at
them like a tender spot that may or may not develop into
a bruise. I should've been over the moon to be in chambers,
with interesting cases, so why wasn't I elated? Trailing
dejectedly around the supermarket, I picked up a pack
of lemons and half a dozen eggs on my way home.

I stood over the hob, stirring the pan, waiting for the
moment when the lemons and eggs transform from a pale,
insipid liquid to a thick golden ribbon, leaving fat spoon
trails. There's something very therapeutic about making
curd: it's a slower, quieter, more delicate process than making jams or jellies. The temperature you need is much lower
than jam temperature, there's no molten sugar spluttering
and splattering everything in sight. Your only job as curd
maker is to control the heat, and to stir: stir until the sugar
dissolves and the liquid sloshes in the pan; stir until you are
convinced something has gone wrong, that you've mismeas-
ured, that you'll have to start again, that it will never work;
stir until suddenly, out of nowhere, the mixture thickens,

and becomes in one breath glossy and lustrous; stir until the smallest of blips bubbles through the mixture, and you have curd. It is an exercise in patience and faith. And as I stood there, stirring, stirring, stirring, I realized I wasn't thinking about the case. I wasn't even thinking about my overreaction to the case. I was just thinking about curd.

*

Lemon curd is, I think, the perfect preserve. It's the first I ever made, and, unlike jam, can be made in small quantities so, if you wish, you can make even less than the below – just enough for a small jar to keep in your fridge – by halving the ingredients.

This curd is a joy: zingy and zippy in flavour, and satin smooth on the tongue, the sharp scent hitting you as you unscrew the jar. It's looser than the thick chemical-stuffed shop-bought stuff, so it falls in drifts and waves on to hot toast.

Lemon curd

Makes: 250g of lemon curd
Takes: 15 minutes on the hob

3 lemons
100g sugar
2 eggs
50g butter, very soft but not melted

1. Fill a small saucepan half-full with water and place over a medium heat. Place a glass or metal bowl on top of the saucepan. Zest and juice the lemons into the bowl and add the sugar. Heat until the sugar has dissolved, then sieve to remove the zest, and return the sugar and juice mixture to the bowl – use oven gloves or a thick tea towel; the bowl will be surprisingly hot.

2. Whisk the eggs into the sugar and juice, breaking them up. Once they're incorporated into the mixture, switch to a small spatula and begin stirring, allowing the heat from your pan of hot water to gently cook the eggs. The key here is to be slow and steady: the curd will thicken, but it will take time, and you need to be stirring and keeping an eye throughout. Once the mixture visibly thickens and feels heavy on the spatula, remove it from the heat, sieve gently, and set it to one side.

3. Allow the mixture to cool enough that the bowl does not feel warm to the touch, then whisk in the very soft butter in small inclusions, until there are no streaks.

4. Spoon the curd into a sterilized jar, seal it and refrigerate. Spread it fridge-cold on to thick slices of hot toast, sandwich sponge cakes together with it or dunk shortbread or still-warm madeleines into it.

4

No trial begins life in the Old Bailey, not even the biggest ones. Criminal cases take place in one of two courts: the Crown Court or the Magistrates' Court. The Crown Court hears the most serious cases, pretty much anything which can carry a prison sentence over six months; here the cases tend to be longer, and will be heard by a jury, who decide the facts of the case, and are presided over by a judge in robes, who makes decisions on the law and the sentence. Then there's the Magistrates' Court for the less serious offences; these rarely last more than a day, and are presided over by a district judge in a suit, or a panel of three civilians ('lay magistrates'), who've done some training, but don't have any legal qualifications. Whether it's a district judge or three lay Magistrates, they make judgments on both the facts and the law. But in the first stage of all cases – the triage stage, the first appearance – they will be heard at the Magistrates' Court, where ultimate location will be determined. Every criminal case starts in a Magistrates' Court, even murders and terrorism, and that's where barristers of my terribly limited experience come in. Some of these court buildings are still very beautiful and old, like the loveliest town halls, with mezzanine public galleries, and big, carved old doors; even their cells are quietly impressive. Most are not like this. Most are tired, run-down places where the ceilings leak and everything else is made of concrete.

Of course, even among the concrete, being a barrister can be exciting: the tension, the intrigue, the *stakes*. But, for me, the dress was probably the *most* exciting part. And being fitted for your wig and gown in the first place makes you feel quite glamorous. You visit a little shop on Chancery Lane – robe makers and tailors since 1689 – and walk beyond the tailored suits and shirts at the front of the shop, into the rear, where the legal dress is situated and wig tins line the walls. The wig makers themselves sit on the floor below, in a little basement workshop, making the wigs that every barrister requires. The wigs we wear are hand-stitched and made of horse-hair; a simple barrister's wig takes up to a week to make. At the time of writing, the full get-up will set you back over £700, and that's before you succumb to the black and gold wig tin hand-painted with your name on it, or the thick blue cloth drawstring bag for your gown, embroidered with your initials. But for this steep sum, you do get to feel like you've slipped into Diagon Alley to pick out your wand. Or at least spent some time in Madame Malkin's robes shop.

All of this probably seems ridiculous, but the wig and gown serve a specific purpose. There's something pro-tective about wearing a wig and gown. It's supposed to make you anonymous. As a barrister, you have *permission* to ask the questions that society normally prevents us from asking. You demand intimate details about strangers' sex lives, you allege affairs, you ask about previous convictions and indiscretions, you accuse others of lying or violence, often in the midst of traumatic evidence. Doing so in a uniform means that I ask these questions not as Livvy Potts, twenty-five-year-old idiot, but Miss Potts of Counsel. It sounds like a supercilious distinction to make, but it's an important one. It identifies you as part of a system. You might feel like a bit of a berk as you straighten the wig on your head, but as you step out of the robing room, you're costumed and playing a part, you're in disguise. And it works: a client that I'd spent four days representing in a fairly serious assault trial, with whom I had spent hours in small rooms discussing the merits of his questionable alibi, wholly failed to recognize me when I slipped past him wig- and gown-free. It certainly made standing at bus stops next to people you'd just accused of shagging the postman easier.

Sadly for me, you don't wear the wig and gown in the Magistrates' Court, which, as a baby barrister, is where most of my cases were heard. The Magistrates' Court is where most British justice is done: 94 per cent of criminal defendants will have their case dealt with solely in the Magistrates' Court. Getting through these cases is a logistical and administrative feat so enormous as to be almost completely overwhelming, particularly given the governmental slashes to funding and workforce. One of the ways the Crown Prosecution Service deals with the sheer number of cases is by instructing independent barristers (usually, very junior barristers, like me) to prosecute 'lists' for them. These lists are whichever cases have been assigned to a particular courtroom on a given day; whatever comes into that courtroom, that barrister deals with. More often than not, these are not only lists of trials, but the stickiest, most underprepared trials that the CPS have to deal with on that day. If you're lucky, you will receive those trial files the night before; if you are unlucky, they'll be waiting for you when you're allowed into the court building at 9 a.m., an hour before you are expected to begin prosecuting them. If you're really unlucky, they won't have arrived before you do, and you'll have to hope you can survive on your wits that day.

But, let's assume you're lucky: you will have a handful of trials to prepare. Sometimes only four, but on the worst days, up to ten. The way cases are listed in the Magistrates' Court means that you have no idea which will take priority, and therefore be heard. You can guess, of course: it looks like the first one has a reluctant witness, so that might well collapse, whereas the third one down involves a vulnerable child, so that will shoot up the list. But the fourth trial has a defendant in custody, which means custody time limits apply, and you can see that time is running out. The second has been relisted twice already, but that's probably not going to be enough to get it heard against these more urgent cases. Naturally, any decision you make on which is your best bet for a trial that actually gets up and running is exactly that: a bet. It's quite possible that that reluctant witness does show up to court, and she's eight months pregnant; that the defendant in custody has now effectively served his time and pleads guilty rather than going through the rigmarole of a trial. In order to prevent public humiliation, and to satisfy the absolute minimum requirements of your professional obligations, you need to prep all possible trials.

If, as a baby barrister, the Magistrates' Court is your domain, Saturday Court is the Magistrates' Court on steroids, and pupils reign supreme. Saturday Court does what it says on the tin: it is a court that sits on a Saturday, and it exists for those defendants arrested and charged on a Friday night after the courts have finished their week's business.

No grown-up barrister or solicitor wants to schlep to Uxbridge Magistrates' Court at seven o'clock on a Saturday morning. None of them wants to answer a phone call from their senior clerk in the pub in the late hours of a Friday night saying, 'Sorry, Miss, case for you at Hastings Mags tomorrow, big client, wants bail, don't screw up.' So it falls to the pupils. Pupils who spend their time trying to prove themselves reliable and eager and who, more importantly, aren't actually allowed to say no to Saturday Court. To call it organized chaos would be to put a gloss over the entire debacle that it doesn't deserve. At Saturday Court the liberty of every defendant is in the collective hands of a bunch of newbies.

If you're lucky, you're bustled out of the clerks' room at 6 p.m. on a Friday with a scrap of paper bearing a name, and false promises of how this assault hearing in Hendon Youth Court will be the gateway to bigger, better things: murder trials, privately paying solicitors, a better desk location in chambers, or guarantees that the client is an important one, *he held up twenty policemen at gunpoint, and you'll get the trial, Miss!* If you're less lucky, the call comes at six o'clock on the morning after your best friend's birthday party.

The first challenge is to get yourself to the court on time. You throw on a black dress (probably the one you discarded the night before), brush your teeth, and pick the remnants of kebab out of your hair. The sheer logistics of getting to any one of the forty-five-odd Magistrates' Courts in the south-east is a feat in and of itself. It involves the sort of convoluted maths that reminds you of GCSE exam questions: if Sally leaves home at 7.16 and it takes her ten minutes to walk to the station and the train is travelling at 160 miles an hour, what time will she arrive at Aylesbury Magistrates' Court? You know the truism that men of a certain age, given half the chance, will discuss the pros and cons of a particular driving route for an implausible length of time? Baby barristers are like that with public transport. Tell one that you're off to Southend for a hen weekend, or mention that you took the overground line to Harrow, and they'll happily tell you not only the best routes, but four inferior possibilities and offer you a postscript on why you should NEVER take the overground to Harrow (trust me: it's really not worth it, just wait for the mainline train).

Once you've made it to court – congratulations, and I hope you managed to find a Sausage McMuffin and an extremely strong coffee on your way – you're likely faced with something more closely resembling *Lord of the Flies*.

Pretty much by definition, your client's going to be in the cells (at least, assuming you've been sent to the right court, and the prison van has arrived, and your client was actually in it . . .). The cells on a Saturday morning at a Magistrates' Court can contain anyone. Absolutely anyone. Murder defendants mingle with teenagers who drunkenly thought it would be a jape to steal a traffic cone, and then that it would be a good idea to argue the various merits of their actions with the attending policeman. None of them have seen their family since arrest, and those families are likely to be upstairs, confused and angry.

It's hard to convey accurately the smell of Magistrates' Court cells on a Saturday morning, but I'm going to try. The stench of sweat is overpowering. Underneath, you can detect the sickly-sweet smell of alcohol leaching from pores. There's a faint undertone of toilets. On top of this is the smell of instant coffee, and the plasticky, porky, beany tang of the all-day breakfast ration packs they feed the defendants. This smell clings. It lingers. It is indelible. I've defended in Saturday Court, gone home, showered, changed, and hours later, out with friends, been convinced I can catch wafts of that breakfast ration pack. Of baked beans and rubber. A friend of mine ended up stuck in a cell with her client one Saturday morning, when something had gone wrong elsewhere in the court building, and all the prisoners had been placed on lockdown. Her client had, in a fit of generosity rarely seen in the Magistrates' Courts, shared his breakfast with her. She told us this story over drinks and all I could think was, *God, it would have been a greater kindness for him to keep it to himself.*

When you've managed to locate your client, you have to explain their predicament to them. At the Crown Court, they will have had time to come to terms with their situation; if they're there for trial or sentencing, they'll probably be in their Sunday best, surrounded by loved ones. But not here. Not at Croydon Magistrates' Court at 7 a.m. on Saturday. When you step into the cells – a corridor of rooms locked with large old-fashioned keys, carried on the waist of the cell staff – they will be shell-shocked, and anywhere from cataleptic to disbelieving to just plain furious. Your aim is to get out unscathed, without being shouted at by the judge or your client. Bail is a bonus. If, despite whispered warnings to please let you do the talking, the defendant shouts at the judge, go straight to jail, do not collect £200.

Grief should be painful. Of course it should. You are processing the death, the absence of someone you loved. You have to navigate your place in the world without that relationship. But this pain that I could almost see in my peripheral vision, could feel creeping up on me, was so enormous, so insurmountable. I couldn't possibly look at it straight on. I had loved her so hard it made my throat ache to think of it. So I stopped thinking about it. I had turned away from it in an effort to organize the funeral and the admin, and that had worked out for me; perhaps I could simply continue now in the same vein, until it ebbed, or at least shrank to a manageable size. I spoke to Dad and Maddy regularly on the phone, far more so than I had before Mum died – although Maddy and I tended toward the emotionally easier WhatsApp, where the risk of voices cracking, or difficult pauses, was mitigated – but we avoided talking about the Big Stuff. I thought about them constantly, wondering how they were coping with this bizarre Uncanny Valley that was our newly shrunken family, but I didn't ask. We grieved individually, privately. This suited me just fine. Every time a thought of her welled up in me in anything but the most anodyne way, I switched to thinking about something else. I just turned off the thoughts. I became quite adept at this. I could talk about her. Make jokes. But alone, when I lay in bed awake, or sat at my desk staring into space, my cup of tea cooling, when those thoughts threatened to fill me up, I scooped them out, until I felt hollow and clean. Good, I thought, this is coping. This is moving on.

After a little while, people stop asking you about the death. At first, this is an overwhelming, almost physical relief. No longer do you have to retell the story, which you've told so many times you now have it down pat. The relief is visceral, euphoric. Personally, I was glad I would no longer have to talk about my life in socially acceptable euphemisms. I hated them. It's no secret that people don't really know what to say to you after someone has died. Perhaps understandably, they work around this social anxiety by using softer, flimsier, flowery phrases. Slipped away. Passed away. Passing on. In another place. In a *better* place. Sleeping. Sleeping with the angels. Sleeping with the fishes (OK, not that one). Even 'RIP' drove me mad.

How did you know she was peaceful now? Or resting? The woman was *dead*. My mother was *dead*. Of course, I never said that. I thanked people for their kind words, words that denied my reality, words that made my teeth itch. Which is why, when people stopped talking to me about death, I breathed a little easier.

But at the same time, I wanted to shout about it from the rooftops. Death is such a pedestrian occurrence, happening all the time, all around us and making pretty much everyone suffer the same mind-dissolving desolation, so world-changing that, like the first time you ever fall in love, or experience the rush of uninhibited lust, it feels to each and every one of them like no one has ever felt this way before. It seems incomprehensible that those around you can't feel the seismic shift that's occurred, are oblivious to it. 'HELLO?!' I wanted to yell. 'Are you aware that *everything has changed*? That it can never be the same again? That she's *gone*! You can't just carry on like nothing's happened!' Although that, of course, is exactly what I was trying to do.

It's not entirely true to say that before my mother died I had no interest in cooking. I once queued to get Jamie Oliver to sign a cookbook that I never used, save for his recipe for hot chocolate. I owned *Nigella Bites* as a teenager and read and reread it, turning down page corners, memorizing the photos, until each was as familiar to me as the posters on my bedroom wall. But I never cooked from it; though my mother didn't exactly delight in cooking, our kitchen was solidly her domain, and one which was not to be messed up, or infiltrated. At university, cooking was actively discouraged. My meals were all catered: the dining hall was characterized by the ever-present smell of boiled white rice. For the first term, I was so nervous I couldn't bring myself to eat in hall anyway, surviving on my nerves and endless chocolate Bourbons, plus the occasional slice of Marmite on toast. Microwaves were the only kitchen equipment provided, and, as the terms wore on, I developed a questionable taste for microwaved poached eggs and salami cheese toasties (also made in the microwave). After I graduated, I moved to London, where my culinary education continued to crawl, if not stand completely still. I lived in Bloomsbury, in a minuscule flat near Russell Square with a brown-plastic fridge, the size of a minibar, that dated back to the 1970s, and an oven of a similar vintage, which required you to stick a match into its depths to light it, at which point it would erupt in flame. For eighteen months, I had no hair on my right arm, despite only really using it to cook frozen fish fingers. Despite these practical hurdles, my flatmate, Pablo, was a good cook, and would throw extravagant dinner parties, where I would occasionally be appointed 'sous chef', which was a euphemism for 'washer-upper'. At the time he was going through a lengthy gelatine phase. Two weeks after I moved in, it was my birthday, and he presented me with a birthday breakfast that consisted of a perfect golden, shivering, saffron-scented blancmange. The following year, he made me a gin and tonic jelly which wibbled and glowed in the dark. I thought he was a wizard.

Now, in this post-mortem, post-fish-pie world, I too

wanted to be a wizard. I wanted to be a domestic goddess. I wanted to impress Sam, no longer vegetarian, with my superlative Sunday roasts. And though my mother had never actually enjoyed her position as our family's appointed cook, I wanted to take her place. To get started, I did what any good millennial does: I consulted the internet. I read recipe after recipe, not having any idea which ones were good, which ones were bad. But I figured if I threw enough mud at the wall, something would stick, so I just kept cooking.

High from the success of my lemon curd and fish pie, I decided to run before I could walk. Having only ever made one meal for one person – the fish pie I made for Sam – I went ahead and invited three friends round for dinner, and, equating richness of dishes with sophistication, I planned my menu. I would make pâté to start, and then a lasagne accompanied by a totally unnecessary four-cheese focaccia. And to finish, the *pièce de résistance*, I would make a perfect chocolate tart. I followed the tart recipe to the letter: I weighed out every ingredient in advance and sieved the flour, I'd even bought a new, perfect fluted tin for the occasion. The pastry was impossibly sticky. It hung off my fingers, and stuck to my worktop, no matter how much flour I added to it. I bundled it up into some cling-film and shoved it into the freezer, thinking that might solve it. Two hours later it was still the texture of Polyfilla, but marginally more usable than before. I just about managed to roll it out and press it into my brand new tin, patching and mending as I went. I tipped baking beans – another new acquisition – into the pastry and shut it in the oven, feeling proud of my first ever attempt at blind baking, and prouder still that I'd remembered to use baking beans to weigh the pastry down, and prevent it puffing up as it baked. But I couldn't leave it alone. I can't leave anything alone. Ten minutes later, I crept back into the kitchen to peek at my masterpiece. It looked odd. The pastry had puffed up, but that wasn't the real problem. I'd missed the instruction telling me to line the pastry before adding the baking beans and it had puffed up *around* the baking beans, and the beans had baked *into* the pastry. Panicking, I removed it from the oven, and began picking scaldingly hot ceramic beans – hundreds of them – one by one, from my sad, pockmarked pastry. The day before, I'd watched *Junior Masterchef* on TV, and seen an eight-year-old turn out perfect soufflés. Yet I'd managed to screw up a simple pastry case. But, weirdly, I wasn't terribly despondent. I put the divoted pastry back in the oven and cooked it; I poured in the filling and let it set. It didn't look anything like the picture in the cookbook, and the shell was peculiarly inflated, and cakey, but it made me feel extraordinarily proud nonetheless. I kept sneaking back into our small, grubby kitchen to look at it, sitting awkwardly on a plate on top of our greasy microwave. And when I served it, I felt invincible. Of course, after the pâté, the lasagne, and the one-thousand-cheese focaccia, no one could manage it anyway. But it didn't matter. For days afterwards, long after it was past its best, I would cut slices from it, eat it straight from its serving plate, and marvel that I had made a chocolate tart.

Soon, I found myself sitting in court, waiting for my case to be called, half-listening to magistrates warbling away about something which didn't concern me, and making lists of things to cook as soon as my case was over. Court hours meant I would often get back home before my house-mates, and in those quiet late afternoon hours, I would cook. Almost every day I would cook or bake something. The results were mixed, to put it mildly. For every successful lemon curd, there was a curdled custard, a sunken cake, pastry that could have been used as an offensive weapon. I didn't understand why these things were happening, and I was momentarily sad about them. But they didn't deter me.

In May, for Sam's birthday, I decided to make cake pops. I have no idea why. Have you ever eaten a cake pop? They're cake crumbs stuck together with buttercream, moulded with sticky fingers into little spheres, then dunked into coloured, low-quality white chocolate before being allowed to set on a stick. They are intensely unpleasant: extraordinarily sweet, and oddly textureless, like a cupcake without any of the benefits. But I'd set my heart on making them for him, and what was more I was going to make them look like foxes. Sam loved foxes! My plan was flaw-less. I set about making perfect little cupcakes that I would then rip apart for the cake pop interior. The cupcakes were beautiful; I should have quit while I was ahead.

I burnt my first batch of white chocolate. I hadn't pre-viously known that this was a thing you could do. I ran to the corner shop to get another bar, then soldiered on. I glued the cake crumbs together with buttercream — buttercream which I had dyed neon orange — manipulating the mixture into rough rounds, my hands sweet and greasy. You're supposed to use lollypop sticks, but I only had kebab skewers, which probably says a lot about me. The mixture immediately slid down the long, thin, sharply pointed sticks and broke apart. I carefully re-formed and replaced them, but they slid off again. Halfway through this struggle, I pushed a strand of hair back from my face in annoyance, swiping a streak of bright orange buttercream across my cheek. I could save this. Maybe I just needed to stick the mixture together a little more. If I dunked them in chocolate *first*, before putting them on the stick, they'd surely hold. I thought of my chambers profile – 'Olivia prides herself on problem-solving under pressure' – and felt rather smug.

The mixture still slid down the stick. And this time, it settled, flattening at the bottom, and leaving a greasy orange smear. Finally, I decided I would simply embrace this flatness and assemble them upside down, and put them in the fridge like that to set firm.

Half an hour later, I brought them out of the fridge. They had darkened as they chilled to an unappetizing rusty brown. Each was an uneven, acorn-shaped blob, rather than the perfect sphere it should have been. Most were also inexplicably, bafflingly grainy. But they had set – they had *set*! I attached flaked almonds for ears, and chocolate drops for eyes. I also stuck little fondant beards on their chins, in the hope that this would make them look more like foxes. I surveyed my last two hours of work. They looked like angry bears with flat heads, apart from one, which was grinning at me. I compared the image I'd Googled to the monstrosities in front of me; they bore no resemblance either to the picture, or to each other, or to foxes. My housemate Suzy, who had taken up position as sous chef halfway through this process, was on the floor incapable with laughter, surfacing just once so she could take a photo of herself with my 'fox pops' for posterity. I never made a cake pop again.

But it didn't really matter if I made a mistake: baking took the whole 'there's no point crying over spilt milk' to new levels of literalism. The stakes were low – so much lower than my day job – and though I've focused on the worst bits, there were successes along the way. I made credible honeycomb on my first attempt, gobsmacked as it whooshed up, just like it was supposed to. I made a treacle tart, and this time remembered to line the pastry before adding the baking beans. Very, very slowly, I started to get a little bit better.

Sometimes the cooking I did was meditative: simmering marmalade, waiting for the setting point as the strands of peel bobbed in the glowing amber jam. Sometimes enlivening: toasting spices, coriander and mustard seeds popping, cumin and fennel crackling in the dry pan, filling the kitchen with the promise of the coming dish. Sometimes it was exhilarating, like the moment you flambé crêpes Suzette, the orange-scented flame licking the pan and the pancakes. And some was pure joy: the moment that honeycomb billows, climbing up to the top of the pan in an opaque golden cloud. Some required concentration, some simply muscle memory. I loved all of it.

There was something calming about recipes – a set of instructions that, if followed properly, would result in a predictable outcome, even if my end product didn't always match the glossy photographs. Everything around me was dissolving into uncertainty, but here, consequences followed neatly from actions. I put something in the oven at 180°C, and twenty minutes later, it was done – it was golden-brown; it was piping hot; it had risen – just like the recipe told me it would. In these circumstances, I favoured the strictest recipes I could find. I therefore gravitated towards baking, where temperatures mattered, and ingredients needed to be precisely weighed. You know where you are with baking. You know exactly where you are.

I should say now that when it comes to food, Sam's repertoire and interests are peculiarly old-fashioned. When he informed me that he was running late for one of our early dates because he was 'waiting for his marmalade to set', I was charmed (if a little irritated). How many twenty-four-year-old men in London know how to make marmalade? It's probably relevant that I find myself attracted to any person who possesses skills that I do not, which I assume is some kind of evolutionary adaptation, to round out the limited package I can offer. (This meant that, for almost twenty-five years, I lusted after any person who could drive a car, and to this day shouldn't be left in the same room as someone who can play the piano.) It probably goes without saying that when he (eventually) turned up at my door, bearing a sticky jar of still-warm marmalade, I was smitten.

But marmalade-making was just the tip of the *Good Life* iceberg. He was obsessed with fruit cake: the old, dry, treacle-bound, currant-laden type, the domain of wedding and Christmas cakes, encased in marzipan and royal icing. Until he went to university, he thought that birthday cake was in fact fruit cake, in the same way that when we say Christmas cake, we mean fruit cake. No Colin the Caterpillar cake or giant Millies' Cookie cakes for him. I thought he was mad. He loved porridge and homity pie and corned beef, and didn't think that serving curry with desiccated coconut, sultanas and chopped bananas was, well, bananas. One hot summer's day, he informed me that he very much wanted to make lardy cake – the heavy, pig-fat-based cake that no one has made or eaten since about 1930, and with good reason – and set about doing exactly that. But irrespective of his strange tastes, he was willing to put time and energy into cooking, a concept which I'd previously never, ironically, had the time for. I had been very much of the instant gratification school of thought: work days are long, life is short, this pasta can be ready in three minutes. But Mum's death gave me a new sense of time, or perhaps simply more of it; I didn't much feel like going out to the pub, or to the cinema, or anything else. Instead, I stayed home, and watched butter brown in a pan, or pressed pastry into a quiche dish, while refusing the lardy cakes Sam kept offering me.

He did have some better ideas. One night, he arrived at my house after work clutching a large Tupperware container. Inside was the pizza dough he'd made early that morning and stored in his work fridge all day, gently proving, so we could make pizzas that night. I'd never handled pizza dough before. In fact, I'd never touched any kind of bread dough. I knew you could buy pizza *bases* from supermarkets and make your own pizza from those, but frankly, making your own dough at home was a whole new level of commitment to pizza. It was pale and cool, despite enduring a Victoria Line Tube journey and rather too long in a rucksack. And when I pressed it with a finger, it kept the indentation, but didn't collapse. I watched Sam knead it into a circle – he'd worked in a pizza restaurant as a teenager, and even if he'd ever let you forget this expertise, the burn on his hand, where it was once accidentally shut in the door of a pizza oven, served as a reminder – and tried my best to copy. He made it look easy, but as I stretched the dough away from me with the heel of my hand, imitating his movements, it kept springing back. He waited a polite amount of time before taking over. We topped our pizzas with anything and everything we could find – anchovies, olives, an egg – and placed the lopsided ovals into the oven. They were perfect.

*

When Madeleine and I were very little, our favourite treat supper was pitta pizzas: brown pitta breads (healthy!) spread with ketchup and dried oregano, then scattered with shredded wafer-thin ham and bagged, grated mild Cheddar. I can still taste them now, and the smell of dried oregano and tomatoes is enough to transport me right back to our kitchen table. When I asked my sister recently what her most powerful memory of Mum's cooking was, this was it. (Mum, I'm so sorry: your coq au vin was exquisite.) It seems right, then, that pizza formed the culinary foundation of mine and Sam's relationship. And this wasn't a one-sided relationship, either. Because, just as he introduced me to homemade pizza, I introduced him to takeaway pizza. Can you believe that, before he met me, he'd never had a proper dirty takeaway pizza? A Domino's or a Papa Johns or our now-favourite, Pizza GoGo? I'm always comforted by the fact that no matter what happens in our relationship, I'll always have brought this small, distinct joy into his life.

Don't worry, I'm not giving you a recipe for a take-away pizza, although it's fair to say that there's nothing terribly authentic about this one. It's a bit of a hybrid, between a Neapolitan and a New York-style pie, for the simple reason that that's how I like it. This dough crusts up nicely, and the slices can just about support their toppings, but it also has that satisfying, doughy bite. I use the no-knead method, which is about as simple as making dough can get: you combine the ingredients in a bowl, and leave them to ever-so-slowly prove in the fridge – a cold ferment – for five whole days. As well as being incredibly low effort, this produces excellent flavour, and the aforementioned soft texture.

The key to getting a decent bake on a pizza – where the edges of the dough bubble and bulge into what Italians call the *cornice* ('eaves') – is *heat*. Proper eye-watering, mascara-melting heat. In restaurants, they have pizza ovens which are kept red hot all day, so the pizzas can cook in a matter of moments. At home, this is best aped using a cast-iron skillet pan and the grill. Preheating the skillet so that it is properly hot when the dough hits it means you're able to get good colour and texture on the base of the crust; transferring it to the grill not only bubbles the cheese and sauce, but puffs up the dough at the edges, blackening and burnishing it, creating those perfect *cornici*.

The tomato base is a bastardization of Marcella Haz-an's famous sauce where she stews tinned tomatoes with an onion and a whole heap of butter. Here I add garlic cloves as well as a little bit of sugar (and a little less butter). Where Marcella discards the onion, I leave it in, cooking it with the garlic until they're soft, then blitzing the whole thing until it is thick, smooth and pale. It is ridiculously easy, and probably the nicest tomato sauce I've ever eaten.

Pizza

Makes: 4 pizzas (serves 4 with salad, or 2 greedy people on a date)
Takes: 5 days, including proving time
Bakes: 20 minutes

For the pizza dough
500g strong white bread flour
350ml water
6g instant yeast
1½ tablespoons olive oil
13g salt
15g sugar

For the tomato sauce
1 x 400g tin of plum tomatoes
6 cloves of garlic, peeled
½ a medium onion, peeled
40g butter
1 teaspoon dark brown sugar (caster sugar is fine
    if you don't have dark brown)
Salt, to taste

To finish
200g mozzarella cheese
A handful of fresh basil leaves
½ teaspoon dried oregano (optional)

1. Mix the flour, water, yeast, oil, salt and sugar and
   bring together to form a dough. Place in a lightly
   oiled bowl, cover with clingfilm and refrigerate
   for 5 days.

2. Remove from the fridge and divide into 4 equal
   balls, placing each in a separate, clingfilmed
   bowl or ziplock bag to prove for a couple of
   hours at room temperature.

3. To make the tomato sauce, tip the tinned
   tomatoes into a pan. Squeeze the tomatoes to
   break them up, but do this with them submerged
   under the sauce, and wear an apron, as they can
   spurt. Add the garlic, onion, butter and sugar.
   Bring to the boil, then reduce to the lowest
   possible heat and cook for around an hour, until
   the garlic cloves squish when pressed with a

spoon – top up with water if it begins to look too dry while cooking. Using an immersion blender, blitz the tomato sauce until thick and smooth. Add salt little by little, tasting as you go.

4. Turn your grill on high, and place a cast-iron skillet on the hob, on a medium-high heat. When both are preheated, take a ball of dough and stretch it out to a round the size of the skillet – it should be thicker at the edges than in the middle. Drop this on to the skillet, and top with a heaped tablespoon of the sauce and 50g of torn mozzarella.

5. Once the base of the pizza has taken on a good, dark colour, move the whole skillet under the grill – use a dry tea towel to lift it, as the handle will be very hot!

6. Leave the pizza until it has bubbled and charred to your liking – around 5 minutes – before removing the pan from the grill.

7. Top with freshly torn basil. If you're feeling truly nostalgic, add a sprinkle of dried oregano.

5

I was not coping with work. Or rather, I was coping outwardly: I could turn up on time and do my job. I could sit at my dining table each night, surrounded by the following day's files, doing the necessary preparation. I could advise clients and ask all the appropriate questions. But inside, I was falling apart.

And to top it all, my tenancy decision drew near. I had a new date: 7 June. Originally, the decision had been scheduled for March, just a few weeks after Mum's death. When I'd returned to work, my chambers had asked if I'd wanted to push back the decision, and I'd gladly accepted, having no idea whether it would help either my tenancy chances or my chaotic head, but grateful for the deferral nonetheless. After almost two years in chambers as a pupil barrister, my fate hung in the balance, and I had two months to (finally) impress my colleagues. But two extra months still felt like no time at all.

The first few weeks back at work had been easy. I'd relished the distraction; the more boring or involved a case, finickety a judge, or tricksy a client, the better. For the first time in my brief career, I was actively seeking out work, calling the clerks and asking where they could send me, which cases they could pass my way, whether they could fill any more of my time. It didn't last. A month later, my anxiety had become overwhelming. Every phone call made me jump, every email made me panic.

Anxiety had been part of my life from a very young age. Many of my earliest memories are of undiluted panic at losing small, unimportant items. Aged three, I broke my patterned hairband at nursery school, and no one could console me for the entire day. When I was four, I was driven to distraction by losing a half-eaten packet of apricot throat sweets at school. When I was eleven, I misplaced the small crucifix necklace I had been given for my confirmation, and my guilt was so overwhelming that for the following decade I refused to eat the supper my mother had served me that night, or allow her to serve it to anyone else (an Asda meat feast pizza, for what it's worth. Until recently I had forgotten this detail, but it seems that for my sister, it's a grudge she will always bear). That weekend I begged to be allowed to go to confession to atone for my sins; my mother rolled her eyes and reminded me that we weren't Catholic.

I had absolutely no perspective when it came to this sort of thing; I couldn't keep small losses in proportion. Close on the heels of this loss anxiety was a preoccupation with death. Aged five, I became obsessed with the idea of drowning or being drugged, even by those who loved me. I was particularly scared of eating Rolos, for fear they had been tampered with. Ironically, given her own set of neuroses, the only person who could talk me down from my whirring guilt and worry was my mother. Without her, panic bloomed.

Before my mother died, we would speak every day on

the phone. This habit began at a weirdly young age: even in my first years at senior school, long before I had a mobile phone, I would call her at lunch or break times, sometimes both, queueing for the payphone, just to check in with her.

In my first year at university, I was so desperately homesick that I would call her every day, sometimes several times. To me, there didn't seem anything odd in this, and even if it alarmed my mother initially, we soon settled into a pattern, talking as often as if we lived under the same roof. This continued long after I'd stopped wanting to run away from college. The conversations themselves were nothing special: we talked about what I'd eaten, what she was reading, what I was studying, how well we'd each done in yesterday's episode of *Pointless*. Later, when I was a pupil barrister, I would phone her on these long walks to and from provincial courts. I didn't mind them so much when I had my mother for company. After she died, there was nothing I missed more. I was forced to walk alone.

Late April, a spring day. Two months after she'd died and one month until my tenancy decision. I was walking across Cambridge on my way to the Magistrates' Court, and thinking about a book we'd both read. I couldn't recall the title, and, since I could barely trace the outlines of the plot – something about some women who cooked together in the Second World War – Google wasn't my friend. But she'd know. I instinctively reached for my phone, and froze with it halfway to my ear. Even as my mind knew she was dead, my body betrayed me. Old habits, you know?

Muscle memory is a funny thing: it overrides even what you consciously know in the very same moment. Fifteen years of daily phone calls – literally thousands and thousands of phone calls – were programmed into my movements. I thought constantly about my mother's death, and yet my own body had tricked me into forgetting. That day in Cambridge was just one example. It happened over and over again.

It happens all the time, of course, not just in grief. We give taxi drivers our old addresses, and call new partners by old partners' names. It's funny, and occasionally embarrassing. The moment of realization is jarring, but we laugh it off, struck by the disconnect between our conscious minds and our reflexes, marvelling at how our brains can betray us, as though a beam of light, glancing at an odd angle, has revealed the puppet strings we never saw before.

But when you forget your mother is dead, and then remember, it's like the floor has suddenly dropped from under you. That night, I told the story to Sam over a drink in a bar, laughed it off. But my laughter felt hollow.

However trite, it is true to say that when someone you love dies, it physically hurts: it's not for nothing that we talk about broken hearts. For me, it wasn't quite heart-based, but it was at least in that general area. I can best describe it as somewhere between acute indigestion, and that heavy feeling of indignation or injustice that you feel when told off for something that wasn't your fault. A physical lump sat high in my chest, a constant presence, a pressure. There were certain things that would cause the lump to rise higher, to swell, take over my entire throat. I missed her touch.

My mother wasn't a tactile person, but when we were together I would touch her constantly, my sister and I sitting too close to her on the sofa (often to her feeble protests), holding a hand each, or looping our arms through her elbows. Even as an adult, I would fiddle with the rings on her hands, and stroke her arms. Never terribly maternal before she had children (or indeed afterwards), she had a tendency to appear stern. But to me and Maddy, she was a puddle of warmth: a pair of open arms, with a clavicle and chest I could draw with my eyes closed. I didn't see the body – her body, after she died. It was my father who found her – too late – who phoned for the ambulance, who waited with her, with the body, with *her* body. By the time I made it to Newcastle some six hours later, she had been taken away. I never touched her. I never got to hold her hand or kiss her or just . . . touch her.

I look at my hands and arms now and I see them turning into hers. The first sign of wrinkles when I move in a certain light, the skin just starting to thin, and I touch them, because it's the closest I can get to touching her. I can't bear the fact that I'll never touch her again.

I don't think I'm a particularly angry person. I hate confrontation, so any fury is limited to politics or occasions where I've accidentally drunk too much white wine. But now I was consumed by anger. A special feature of sudden death, according to John Bowlby, an eminent grief process psychiatrist, is an increased need to understand, to search for meaning, to find cause and attribute blame. And boy, was I keen to attribute blame. But her cause of death made it hard to do that, so my anger swirled without target. I was ashamed of how angry I felt. How angry I was with her. I was furious with her for dying. For leaving me, for *abandoning me*. I wasn't ready to live without her. Of course, I was doing a good job of hiding this anger from everyone, including myself, pressing it down, refusing to allow myself to feel anything.

Armchair grief counsellors – or really anyone you meet within the first twelve months of bereavement – will inform you that anger is a natural response to grief, but more importantly, it's a phase! It's just a phase! And you have to go through it ultimately to reach acceptance. It's *good* to be angry. Except it's not. And the idea that it is, is predicated on nonsense.

The notion of the five stages of grief was first set out by Elisabeth Kübler-Ross in 1969 in her book *On Death and Dying*, and is one that every film or TV show you've ever watched that involves death took to its heart. The theory was pretty quickly and comprehensively rejected by the academic and practitioner community, and in fact, wasn't actually supposed to deal with the effect of death on the bereaved, but rather the effect of death on the *dying*, those with terminal illnesses. And even then, it wasn't really meant to be a linear timeline of grieving – *and* was based on anecdotal evidence – but that hasn't stopped the Western world adopting it as such, and ignoring Kübler-Ross's many attempts in her subsequent years of research to clarify. We continue to trot out those stages as a universal experience, nodding sagely when someone bereaved exhibits anything that can be dropped into one of the five grief buckets. It places a nice little narrative over grief: it's neat, and it suggests a clear end point.

It's not surprising that we cling to this discredited theory: the only thing that is truly universal about grief is that it is entirely chaotic. Most people will experience the whole gamut of emotions, including the famous five, and it's natural that – as an outsider especially – we would want to reassure those going through it, would want to impose some kind of structure on the whole sorry spectacle. So we recite, we chant the five stages of grief, as if the mantra alone will bring us closer to that final, healthy stage: denial, anger, bargaining, depression, *acceptance*; denial, anger, bargaining, depression, *acceptance*. But that's not how it works. For me, it was more: shock, numbness, anger, numbness, anger, anger, anger. So far, I was elbow-deep in anger, and it didn't look like I was going anywhere soon.

As strongly as I felt it, I wasn't articulating or externalizing this rage. I felt as though I had absorbed it into my very bones, that it zipped round my body, that I was powered by it.

Grief theory and practitioner methodology have moved on a lot since Kübler-Ross's influential book. In the 1980s, J. William Worden set out a pragmatic approach to dealing with grief, which took Freud's idea of 'work' in bereavement and broke it down into something more practical. According to Worden, there were four tasks a griever had to complete:

1. <u>Accept the reality of the loss</u>: First, you need to accept that reunion is impossible. The person is dead. Most people manage this – genuine 'failure to accept' has only really been documented in those with psychosis or those who are both eccentric and reclusive. It more normally manifests as calling out for the dead person, retention of possessions, or misidentification of people in the street for the dead person. Those that struggle with this stage might well try to reframe their relationship with the dead person as being less important than it was. Rituals help here as they externalize the reality of the death.

2. <u>Work through to the pain of the grief.</u> Next, you have to open yourself up to pain: it's not possible, Worden says, to work through grief without opening yourself up to the vulnerability of pain. Avoiding or suppressing the pain is likely only to prolong the course of mourning.

3. <u>Adjust to an environment in which the deceased is missing.</u> This means coping pragmatically without the deceased. As one grieving person described it, it's not about how to find an answer to the death, but how to live without one.

4. <u>Emotionally relocate the deceased and move on with life.</u> The last of the four stages requires the griever to foreground themselves: to find a

way of living their life that doesn't revolve around the deceased. Accepting not only the death of the person, but also life as it now is; that life goes on.

Failure to carry out this work, these tasks, can lead to 'incompleted grief', which can further arrest growth and development, in the same way that incomplete healing from a wound can lead to future weakness and complications.

Two months in, my development had arrested somewhere between stages 1 and 2. Stages 3 and 4, and with them any chance at freeing myself of the brambles of arrested grieving, seemed so far off as to be fictional. But that's not what I thought at the time. As far as I was concerned, I'd skipped stage 2 and jumped straight to 3 in a staggering and entirely unconcerning feat of efficiency. I struggled to see mourning as anything other than self-pity, weakness. I didn't want to be vulnerable; far from recognizing that it was an essential feature of engaging with any part of this process, I thought it was the road to ruin. So I didn't. Bowlby had a grim prediction for what this meant: 'Sooner or later, all those who avoid all conscious grieving break down – usually with some form of depression.'*

You don't want to remember – but even more, you don't want to forget. I was becoming frustrated by the imprecise nature of my memories of Mum. They became hazy,

* Bowlby, John, *Attachment and Loss: Vol III, Loss: Sadness and depression*, New York, Basic Books, p. 158.

shadowed. Almost everything I encountered still reminded me of her, but even physical prompts were starting to wane: a keyring she'd bought me – a small, silver barrister's wig – was lost along with my keys when they fell out of a hole in my tote bag. A jumper she gave me for Christmas shrank in the tumble drier. Soon after that day in Cambridge, back up north, I found a flimsy leopardskin-patterned cardigan at the back of her wardrobe, and it smelt of her, of her skin and her hair. I brought it home with me and tied it up in a plastic bag. I rationed the smelling, partly because I convinced myself that the smell was finite, and if I sniffed too much, it would be quickly used up. I bought her cleanser, her face powder, her perfume, her nail varnish, trying desperately to recreate that smell on my skin and my clothes. It didn't work. So I tied the plastic bag that contained the cardie tighter and, like everything else, tried not to think about it.

As much as Mum was hazing over in my memories, at night she was brought to life. I'd been having nightmares since Mum's death. Not sporadically, but every night. Vivid nightmares and sleep paralysis, featuring huge looming figures. I couldn't remember how my mother sounded or looked, but the moment I'd fall asleep, my mind would immediately conjure her. My mother was alive, we'd made a mistake, she was alive, and I was so *relieved*, only to realize that she hated me. I woke up every morning exhausted from my mind turning the same ideas, the same images over and over. Every night, the same. I was a cliché, waking up panting, drenched in sweat. I forgot the details as quickly as they had arrived, and was left only with the feeling of guilt and anxiety that hung around me in a fug like a hangover until mid-morning, when a shower and a coffee and the heaviness of an insistent email inbox pushed away the forehead-prickling, breath-quickening images, until it was night-time again.

I kept on walking, day after day. Over those three months, I tramped from Willesden Magistrates' Court to Neasden Tube station, from Woolwich to Plumstead, from Hammersmith to Barons Court. I walked along motorways, under bypasses, over bridges; I skirted kerbs, sunk my heels into grass verges, and dragged my battered wheelie suitcase over miles of gravel and cobbles and tarmac. And because I had to do *something* and no longer had her phone calls, because I had to fill my brain with something other than memories, I made up a game. It was called Grief Top Trumps.

Grief Top Trumps is easy to play. All you need is one dead relative. There are various categories: how close you were to them; how suddenly they died; how old you were when it happened. For each one, you get a score out of ten. You're playing against me – against my scores out of ten. And here's the most important rule: because it's my game, I choose the category.

As I walked, I played this game in my head against everyone I knew: friends from college, girls from school that I hadn't seen in fifteen years, people on the news, fictional characters in whichever book I happened to be reading. No one was safe. A friend from school lost her father to cancer – a horrible drawn-out death. She scored a 9 on Pain, and an 8 on Age When It Happened. But she couldn't beat me on Suddenness. 1–0 Olivia.

Someone I went to college with had lost his grandmother the day before his wedding, which scores highly on Logistical Nightmare and Emotional Poignancy. But I'm not stupid. This time, I played Closeness. 2–0.

True, the deck was stacked in my favour, but even so I was very good at this game. If I was struggling to win, I could always add a new category. A younger, more formative death lost out because I had to give my mother's eulogy, and choose the coffin, and decide what her mourners would like to eat at the wake. I could even beat my own mother, whose father died when she was thirteen: the loss of her beloved, kind, funny father paled when his death was set against the administrative burden I'd borne from hers. The most traumatic and unpleasant deaths could be minimized, turned round to ensure my triumph. I felt a perverse victory in being able to win something with the hand of cards I'd been dealt. Grief Top Trumps is easy to play, but hard to win. Unless you're me. In this game, the house always, always wins.

My pace would increase as I played Grief Top Trumps, my pulse quicken; I felt like I was vibrating with anger. I had entirely lost the ability to feel compassion. Most of all, I was viscerally, incandescently angry with just about anyone whose mother was still alive. For me, they now fell into two camps: those who didn't appreciate their parents, who took them for granted, and those who threw the continued existence of their parent in my face, who crowed about their love for their mothers. I hated them both equally. And if someone had the temerity to use the words 'shocked' or 'heartbroken' when someone in their eighties died, I would steam with rage. Those who mourned grandparents were contemptible to me. There were no limits to my scorn.

While I hadn't exactly been planning to patent and market Grief Top Trumps, sell it to schoolchildren, get it stocked in newsagents, when I discovered Emily Dickinson had got there before me with the idea of the one-upmanship of loss –

> I measure every Grief I meet
> With narrow, probing, eyes –
> I wonder if It weighs like Mine –
> Or has an Easier size.

– I threw myself into researching her grief to ensure that I did in fact suffer more than she. Calmed by the thought of trumping Emily Dickinson, I ignored the fact that perhaps she bore it with better grace than I did. What I knew was this: my suffering was worse than anyone else's. No one had ever been through anything as horrific as this before. It didn't matter that on the odd occasion I could zoom out from my own life and see that this was clearly, rationally untrue. In my heart, it was all I could feel.

I sought death out: memories, magazine articles, news reports, and consumed them greedily, each time inducting them into my little game. I felt manic in my pursuit of it, greedy, like the Hungry Hippo of grief: mine, mine, mine. But also, it sought me. I saw death and grief all around me, both in those I knew and those I didn't. Around this time, I went to a hen weekend where four – *four!* – of the other hens had lost parents in a range of traumatic ways. I was flabbergasted that I hadn't guessed, couldn't tell as soon as I looked at them; I assumed I now had some kind of sixth sense – that I could see dead people by proxy, through those who mourned them. I couldn't stop thinking about these four hens. When the wedding came around, I watched them from afar, like museum exhibits.

Sam did his best in adverse circumstances. Faced with a woman who insisted she was coping, but would at the drop of a hat descend into frantic, furious grief calculations, he learned quickly not to liken my pain to anything he had experienced. I didn't want empathy because no one could possibly empathize. Sympathy was permissible, so long as it didn't tip into pity, which was absolutely forbidden. He was walking a tightrope, but, for the most part, he kept his balance.

For better or worse, my work anxieties were something he *could* address. He latched on to that, and, as my tenancy decision approached, and I wound myself tighter and tighter, he suggested we take a long weekend away from London. When I proved reluctant he *insisted* we take a long weekend away from London. My reluctance wasn't feigned – it's not really the done thing for pupil barristers to take holidays, especially at short notice, and certainly not just before a tenancy decision. It smacks of caprice and unreliability or, worst of all, a disregard for the whole process. But I was exhausted, and just about clinging on to enough rationality to know that I was doing myself no favours by acting the martyr and working an extra day and a half.

The moment we stepped off the train in Lyme Regis, I felt my lungs loosen. For all the Grief Top Trumps, the tenancy reckoning, I had truly believed I was coping. My belief, at least, was not feigned. But breathing in the sea air made me notice that I'd been holding my breath for a very long time.

So much of the time Sam and I had spent together over the previous four months had been frenetic, laced with the administrative details of death, or the endless, circular talking that goes hand in hand with it. As far as I was concerned, my mother's death was my entire life at this point. And for Sam, it really was my whole life as he'd known it. And yet, somehow, he had managed to rise above it.

We walked for hours along the Jurassic cliffs, and ate cheese and bread and a pork pie under a tree. We signed up for fossil hunting, and turned up to find we were the only adults there without children. I discovered a hitherto unknown talent for finding ammonites. Sam had a simple tactic for dealing with me when I trailed off, or stared into the distance, or welled up: he carried on with whatever we were doing at the time. On the second day, we were in a pub. He tried to engage me in a crossword while I stared into space. 'Liv, come on. 13 across: Anonymous nude man sculpted, seven letters. I've got two N's, and it ends in a D.' I rolled my eyes: he'd brought this cryptic crossword with him, torn from a paper he'd bought at the train station as we embarked on our trip. I hated cryptic crosswords. I didn't get them. I looked at him wanly, feeling sorry for myself. He waggled his eyebrows, and I smiled in spite of myself. I sighed dramatically, taking the crossword from him, as if I were doing him an enormous favour, when really it was him doing the favour for me.

We ate with abandon: thick-cut brown bread sandwiches, spilling out crab and mayonnaise, and bags of scampi and cones of chips, doused in salt and vinegar, and inhaled on the beach. Sam, after some serious consultation, doubled back to the beachfront chip van, queueing patiently, before returning to the stone wall boundary cradling his first ever pickled egg, showing it to me reverentially, as if it had come from one of those Jurassic animals whose bones peppered the coastline.

On our last night, we walked along the beach together. I looked at Sam. This was the man who had fed me pancakes as he listened to countless drafts of my mother's eulogy. The man who had made me laugh, let me cry, hadn't made a big deal out of the fact I was an almighty mess, and played along with the pretence that I was keeping it together. This man had made up stories for me until I fell asleep next to him, brought me loaves of bread instead of flowers, and taught me how to make pizzas from dough he had got up early before work to make. Sam had let me be a person, rather than just a victim. And on the beach I realized I'd fallen in love with him.

It surprised me. It felt like a betrayal to have found love while I was so consumed by loss. But in among all that bitterness, there had been a surprising measure of sweetness.

I turned to Sam, the words forming on my lips, and stopped. I didn't need to say anything at all; not saying something to a person you love doesn't invalidate how you feel. The moment is enough. This moment was enough.

The following day, we went to a bakery-cum-café: simple but charming, with only toast and jam available for breakfast, and homemade soup and fat doorstops of bread for lunch. We sat on one of the trestle benches, and noticed a little poster revealing the place was up for sale. 'You could do that,' Sam said to me.

'Oh, sure,' I replied. ''Course I could. Look, if tenancy doesn't work out, I'll just jack it all in, and become a baker, OK?'

I kept thinking about that bakery after we came home, as tenancy swirled around me like a dark drifting fog. I imagined a life that revolved around flour and slow proofs and making things for other people, rather than custody time limits and angry clients and scolding judges. And even as I acknowledged it as a pipe dream, I baked soda bread, and hoped for something better.

*

Soda bread uses normal soft flour that you would use for baking cakes or making a roux, as opposed to the strong, protein-rich bread flour we normally use for making 'real' bread. Soft flour doesn't give yeast enough food to create a good rise, but will support bicarbonate of soda reacting with buttermilk, producing a soft, tender crumb and a crisp crust.

Although soda bread may feel both inherently Irish, and as old as time immemorial, bicarbonate of soda – integral to the rise of soda bread – didn't actually arrive in Ireland until the 1830s. Moreover, the Irish probably weren't the first to pull this trick; there is evidence of Native Americans using pearl ash (potassium carbonate) to leaven their bread in the eighteenth century. But soda bread was adopted so wholeheartedly by the Irish that it has become an indelible part of the national identity.

If you're nervous about yeast, soda bread is a great introduction. When I first began baking, I dismissed it as a cheat's route to bread. Which is, obviously, exactly what it is. But that's also why it's such a gorgeous bread to make. Soda bread is impossibly easy, with no instructions really needed beyond 'mix wet and dry ingredients and shape'. It's great for using up yoghurt or milk that is slightly past its best. Because this is a no-yeast quick bread, it doesn't need any proving time. I've changed the more authentic and traditional soda bread by shoving handfuls of mature Cheddar into it. Of course, you don't have to do this, the bread will work perfectly well without it, and will taste delicious. But I love the combination of the natural sourness of the bread alongside the strength and sharpness of the cheese.

Cheesy soda bread

Makes: 4 individual buns
Takes: 5 minutes
Bakes: 30 minutes

200g plain flour
150g wholemeal flour
50g oats
10g salt
15g baking powder
½ teaspoon mustard powder
100g mature Cheddar cheese
280ml buttermilk
15g honey

1. Preheat the oven to 180°C fan/200°C/gas 6. Line two baking trays with greaseproof paper, and sprinkle with flour.

2. Combine the dry ingredients in a large bowl. In a jug, measure out and mix the buttermilk and honey.

3. Add the wet ingredients to the dry and mix immediately, using your hands. You need the dough to come together cohesively, but to work it as little as possible. The dough won't be smooth or elastic, so don't worry if it looks a little scraggy.

4. Divide the dough into four, and briefly roll to form balls. Place on the baking trays, spaced well apart and – using a knife or dough scraper – press in a cross stretching the length and breadth of the dough ball. This should be deep: you want to stop just short of dividing the dough ball.

5. Bake for 25 minutes, until golden and cheesy-smelling. Cool for 15 minutes before carefully peeling from the paper. Eat warm, if possible, but these will also keep for at least a day, and toast up well.

6

I sat on the top floor of a pub on the Strand, waiting for the phone call to tell me whether I'd succeeded in what I'd been working towards for over a year and a half – double that, if you include law school. Despite everything I'd been through in the last three months, I really wanted this. I needed this. I'd felt so directionless since Mum died; I thought success would provide me with some kind of certainty again, a purpose.

Sometimes, the decision of whether or not to offer a candidate tenancy is easy, and the pupil is either approved or dismissed unanimously within minutes of the meeting beginning. Other times it is fraught, with debate and negotiating, wheedling and politics that go on for hours. The discussions are secret, even after the decision has been made. In some chambers, it's a simple procedure: any pupil who wishes to apply for tenancy puts their name forward, and if no one blacklists them within a week or so, they're in. Others elect a tenancy committee to make the decision on their behalf. But often there are multiple pupils fighting for one or two places, and most decisions go to the vote.

The etiquette for tenancy decisions is that you get out of chambers early. Reports on your conduct and progress are available for voters to peruse, along with a portfolio of work. Pupilmasters or -mistresses are available for interrogation. Members tend to congregate about an hour before the decision takes place, keen to get the low-down from those who know the pupil better than they do, to try to persuade those who remain on the fence, to gossip. So, the pupils, who up until this point have taken advantage of every occasion to have their faces seen before and after court in chambers, clear out. Traditionally, all the pupils would go for a drink together somewhere nearby, to await their fate. But on this occasion, I was the only pupil up for tenancy. My former co-pupil had been rejected after twelve months, and the other pupils still had six months to go. It was just me.

I'd been here before. Just before Mum died, just before I'd met Sam, chambers had voted to give me another six months to prove myself – a 'third six' in barrister parlance – on the basis that I was 'rough around the edges', but 'showed promise'. It's not unusual, but it had been a big blow to my pride. I'd been given a new pupilmaster for this third six, Miles, who spent most evenings on the phone to me, alternating between good cop and bad cop. Tenancy was within my grasp, he would tell me, I could do this, but it was down to me now. Only I could make this happen.

I was sitting in the pub with Sam, clutching a pint of lager, trying not to look at the mobile phone that lay between us. It was still early – barely even 6 p.m. The meeting had begun at 5.30 p.m. We probably had another hour to wait, minimum. Sam got up to go to the loo. The phone rang: it was Miles. 'Are you sitting down?' he asked, ominously. 'Yes,' I replied, testily, thinking, *Come on, get on with it.* 'You're in.' And that was that.

Sam came back from the loo, drying his hands on his jeans. 'I'm in,' I said, as soon as he got within hearing distance. 'Dryer doesn't work,' he replied. I looked at him. 'Wait, what?' 'I'm in,' I repeated. 'Oh!' he replied. 'God, I wish I hadn't agreed to go to my reading group tonight now.'

I didn't quite feel euphoric, but I was sure it would come. This was all I'd wanted. And now I had it. I went home to Sam's flat without him, ate an enormous packet of cheese and onion crisps and fell instantly asleep.

Sam came home from his book group late that night and slipped into bed beside me. I lifted myself up until I was resting on my elbow and looking at him: 'I love you, you know?' I told him. He laughed: 'I know. I love you too.'

Fast on the heels of finally securing tenancy came my first Crown Court trial.

Your first Crown Court trial is a big deal. As described earlier, while minor offences – like low-level theft, and careless driving – are dealt with in the Magistrates' Court, Crown Courts see murders, serious assaults – what you could call the juicy stuff. They're decided in front of a jury, who haven't sat through dozens, maybe hundreds of trials before. This is probably the first time they've seen cross-examination, or heard a closing speech. They aren't jaded or hardened. Your audience is pristine.

In the old days, you'd be doing Crown Court trials almost from day one as a barrister, but times have changed:

fewer criminal cases receive government funding in the form of legal aid, so fewer lawyers are needed, and those that do receive funding get less of it, which means that more barristers are fighting for Crown Court cases. After hundreds of hearings and Magistrates' Court trials, and twenty months on my feet, I was finally going to be let loose on a jury. 'You're up, Miss,' Dan, one of my clerks, told me over the phone. 'Trial tomorrow. Public order case. It's at Croydon. No, sorry.' He paused for a second. 'It's now at the Bailey. You're D1, and Miss Daniels is D2. Papers are in the clerks' room.' When a court is overbooked, their cases are redistributed to other nearby courts. Which meant this incredibly low-level public order case which should have taken place in Croydon, and had somehow been entrusted to me, had found its way to the hallowed halls of the Old Bailey. Court 2 of the Old Bailey no less.

The charge was intentionally causing harassment, alarm or distress, contrary to Section 4 of the Public Order Act 1986. It was alleged that this had happened in a way that was racist, meaning that it carried a maximum of two years' imprisonment. I'd dealt with plenty of cases like this before, but none at the Crown Court, and definitely none at the Bailey. I should have felt reassured by my experience doing these types of offences, but I didn't. Instead, I sat up late that night, with the papers spread around me. When you're taught advocacy at Bar school, you're instructed not to write out your speech in full, but to write bullet points instead. That way, you'll cover all the points you need to make, but you'll be natural, rather than scripted. You'll look at the jury rather than staring at your sheet of paper. I'd followed that advice countless times at the Magistrates' Court, and been pretty good at it, too. Advocacy had always been my strongest suit, and it was definitely where I felt most confident; I'd done advocacy exercises and exams, I'd competed in mock trials; I'd given so many speeches in front of Magistrates, often without the choice of whether to prepare or not, so limited was the brief, or so last-minute were the client's instructions. That night, nerves got the better of me, and as I pictured myself freezing up in front of a jury at the Old Bailey of all places, searching for just the right phrase, I ignored the advice: I wrote out my closing speech in full. Every word.

The next morning, I turned up at the Central Criminal Court, aka the Old Bailey, feeling the familiar jangle of nerves I always felt here, even when I just came here as a pupil for cases with my supervisors.

I hauled my files up to the Bar mess to look for my opponent. He was nowhere to be seen. Nor was Alice, my co-defending pal from chambers. It was only while I was up there, nursing a coffee, watching calmer, more experienced advocates nonchalantly queueing for full cooked breakfasts, that I realized I'd been given the wrong time. The case had been put back to the afternoon, giving me even more time to wind myself up into a frenzy of nerves. When my opponent finally showed up, I could see that he was significantly more senior than me, and clearly thought the case – not to mention his opponent – was beneath him.

It should have been reassuring that I was co-defending with Alice, but it wasn't, because, though she was every bit my superior, I was D1 – representing the first defendant. That meant I would be asking all the questions first. If I did well, she could just adopt my questions; if I didn't, she would have to make up for my shortcomings. Either way, there was nowhere to hide.

I clopped down the stairs to find my client, Marcus. Marcus was easy to spot: barely out of his teens, and this being his first time in court, he was clearly overawed by his surroundings; filled with empathy, I had to stop myself blurting out that this was my first Crown Court trial. (In my experience, clients like, as a bare minimum, to think you've spent more time in the courtroom than they have.)

The case itself was a tale as old as time. The police officer claimed that the defendant had behaved badly in public in a fairly mild, but nonetheless criminal way, that he had intentionally caused harassment, alarm or distress, and done so in a racist way. The defendant said he'd done no such thing – and in fact, that the police officer had been the aggressor.

So many court cases, up and down the country, every day, come down to that: one person's word against the other. The verdict depends on whose account the panel of magistrates or – as in this case – twelve jurors prefer. For the vast majority of cases, it's not like television: there's no star witness, no dramatic 'Aha!' moment, no chance of an independent inquiry. Typically, there's barely any police inquiry. There's very rarely CCTV footage, or forensics, or cell-site analysis. Blood spatter patterns, reenactments, fingerprints? You should be so lucky.

I wasn't feeling terribly optimistic about the case. I held no illusions about the power of a police officer's word. Juries are less susceptible than magistrates (they don't, for example, refer to prosecution witnesses as 'our witnesses', or try to convict before they've heard the defence case). But it can still be hard for a bunch of people unfamiliar with the justice system to treat a member of the establishment's word with adequate scepticism. One person's word against another's should almost never result in a conviction, police officer or not. The reality is, it often does.

Here, my job was made even trickier: this was not simply one person's word against a single police officer's: there had been several police officers in attendance, all singing from the same hymn sheet. A suspiciously similar hymn sheet if you're a cynical criminal defence barrister; a deliciously convincing hymn sheet if you're not.

I began cross-examining the police officers, running through all the details of their story, pointing out gaps and inconsistencies. All the usual stuff. I didn't have a hope in hell. Then the police officer who claimed to have been assaulted took the stand. In his statement, he'd described being so intimidated by my polite, slight young client that he suffered fear, harassment, or distress. I fought back a huge sigh as I got to my feet, straightening my robe, which never wanted to hang properly from my shoulders, and gave it a shot. 'Officer, you didn't actually feel fear, harassment or distress from my client, did you?' 'No, your worship,' the officer replied, managing the double whammy of police officer evidence – he deliberately ignored the barrister asking the question, addressing himself to the judge instead, and screwed up the correct address to boot. Wait, what? I did a double take. For this offence, if the officer didn't *feel* intimidated, the Crown didn't have a case. Emboldened, I chanced my arm: 'It's right, isn't it, that it wasn't even Marcus who made racist comments?' 'That's right,' the officer agreed with me. For a moment, I was stunned into silence. I was standing in Court 2 of the Old Bailey, cross-examining a police officer, and the Crown's case had just fallen around its ankles. Somehow, I suppressed a whoop, and instead muttered, 'No further questions, My Lord,' then sat down with only the smallest of flounces.

The judge addressed the prosecuting barrister. 'Well, Mr Childs, it looks like your witnesses might have decided the case for you.' Childs prevaricated. He said that he would continue with the case and leave it to the jury. The judge was having none of it. 'If you don't take instructions, Mr Childs, and drop the case, I will be inviting submissions from defence counsel, and I think we all know how that will go.' Chastened, Mr Childs offered no further evidence, and Marcus was formally acquitted.

I couldn't believe it. I'd won my first Crown Court defence trial, at the Bailey no less, even if it was by default. I folded up the copy of my speech and slipped it into my suitcase, along with my wig and gown. I walked back to chambers, along past St Paul's Cathedral and down Fleet Street, turning left into Inner Temple and across the cobbled courtyard that led to my set of chambers.

I decided not to mention the result to my colleagues hanging around chambers. It wasn't exactly something to shout about. I was just gathering up my bag and coat to leave when Adam, a member of chambers a couple of years senior to me, caught me: 'I heard you smashed it in the Old Bailey today! Alice just told me.' 'Oh!' I replied, wrong-footed. 'Um, well, yeah, not really: the Crown offered no evidence in the end. I didn't even get to do my speech.' 'Hey, a win's a win,' he retorted, and sloped off.

But my bizarre and unlikely work triumph contrasted with – well, everything else.

'Tell me what happened,' the therapist said.

I examined the far wall diligently.

'In your own time,' he prompted.

I was here because of my 'severe morbid anxiety' – or, to put it another way, because I was really, really terrified that my loved ones were about to die. I was sure that I wasn't here about grief, or Mum. I'd dealt with that, I explained. I just needed to take the edge off the anxiety that was with me every moment, getting under my feet, tripping me up, stopping me dead in the street. My GP had referred me to a psychiatrist, who had in turn referred me to a therapist.

Now, here I was.

The truth is, I have always catastrophized. It truly struck me as a profoundly sensible way of moving through life. As the saying goes, the pessimist is never disappointed – if you assume that the worst thing possible is going to happen, and it does, you're as prepared as you can be, and if it doesn't, it's a bonus. CBT, or Cognitive Behavioural Therapy, essentially tries to talk you out of this. It's one of the most widely used of all psychological therapies – and really, it's incredibly simple. The therapist will help you identify irrational beliefs and then challenge them. Its aim is to embed new thought patterns, so you can identify when you are being irrational. CBT encourages you to look at the worst possible scenario and then acknowledge how unlikely that in fact is to happen. Unfortunately for the proponents of CBT, and my therapist in particular, I'd spent ten years anticipating the very worst thing I could imagine every time the phone rang, only ultimately to be proved right. 1–0 Livvy.

At the end of each session, my therapist sent me away with a little photocopied handout. It prompted me to imagine bad things, then come up with reasons as to why they might not be bad. It would end up scuffed and ignored at the bottom of my handbag until half an hour before my next session, when I'd reluctantly fish it out and try to divine what healthy answers would be, scribbling them in, leaning the sheet of paper on my knees on the Tube. We never really got to grief in those sessions: all I could talk about was work. And even when I'd exhausted work, I talked about it some more, simply so as to avoid the elephant in the room. I'd tried so hard to carve out time away from court so that I could go to these sessions, and then I spent my whole time talking about being there.

'When patients come to see me, saying that they want to leave their job or their partner, these things are never the answer to their actual problems,' my therapist told me, leaning back in his chair. He was clearly pleased with this observation. I could see him rolling it over in his head, wondering how he could turn it into an even snappier aphorism. I'd never said to him that I wanted to leave my job.

Law is in my blood. My mum, dad and maternal grandfather were all solicitors. My dad still is. I'd grown up with him dashing off to the police station on evenings and weekends to serve as the duty solicitor, with discussions around the dinner table of wills and trusts. I'd spent my teenage summers filing papers according to whether they dealt with vibration white finger or emphysema. When I was sixteen, I spent the holiday working at Dad's firm. Dad sent me into court to take notes for one of the firm's other lawyers. Within minutes I was hooked. It was my first real exposure to criminal law, something Dad hadn't practised since I was little, and it was intoxicating. Newcastle Crown Court sits on the quayside, surprisingly grand and imposing for a court built in the 1980s: the scene was set for a young, impressionable, gobby girl to fall in love. The lawyers I saw in court weren't immersed in paperwork. They were quick-witted and glamorous, swishing about in their wigs and gowns. And although they addressed judges in deliciously old-fashioned terms, when they turned their attention to the jury they were telling stories, even jokes. They were turning half-facts and vague possibilities into compelling argument. They were locking horns with their opponents, inviting you to believe them.

A career in the law seemed like something of a foregone conclusion by the time I got to university, at least to me. My parents weren't keen; they hoped for something more exciting, more creative, perhaps, than the jobs they'd had. They convinced me I should study literature, which I did. And then in my final year, I surprised them, if not myself, by declaring that I would be converting to law, and wanted to be a criminal barrister.

I'd gone into it for all the right reasons, done my due diligence. I'd shadowed judges, done countless mini-pupillages. I'd done mock trials and competed in mooting competitions (like mock trials, but without the thrill, focusing on legal argument and paperwork, rather than swishy dramatic cross-examination). I knew that criminal barristers didn't make any money. I'd fought through the miserable process that is getting pupillage, round after round of personal statements and interviews and fake bail applications and pretend pleas in mitigation in front of countless members of different chambers. Most Saturdays that summer were spent in pubs near the Inns of Court, candidate after candidate trailing into the pub, one after another, to drown our sorrows and lick our wounds after interviews. Even if I got a pupillage – and many didn't – I knew my chances of ending up as a fully qualified barrister were slim (about one in three). But it was a triumph of stubbornness, blind hope, and possibly a good dose of youthful arrogance.

I also believed in the justice system. I believed that everyone was entitled to representation, to have their case heard in court; I believed that representation should be free if they couldn't afford to hire a private lawyer. I believed in the adversarial system, in the English Bar, in its independence. I truly believed these things. It was the single exception to my hatred of earnestness. And I loved being able to say that I was a barrister. Perhaps it was just my own inbuilt snobbery, but it always felt like more than a job title, like being a barrister said something about me – not all good, maybe, but some of it.

So why, ten years later, after going through everything I'd gone through to get here, after surviving pupillage and securing tenancy, after building up a varied practice that ranged from blood-and-guts crime to white-collar fraud to parole boards, after being surrounded by good colleagues and clerks, loyal instructing solicitors – why was I so lost?

I'd always been anxious, but this was new territory. The prospect of a trial in my diary was enough to set me on edge for weeks leading up to it, and I would spend whole days obsessing over whether it would fall apart on the day, praying for witnesses to be no-shows, or clients to change their minds at the last minute.

I tried not to care – and sometimes, that wasn't so hard. When a client berated me for not getting him off a fine he'd incurred for deliberately speeding, I would struggle not to roll my eyes. When a father told me that the drugs charges his daughter faced would destroy her dream of being a quantity surveyor, I had to bite my tongue. No nineteen-year-old girl in the history of the world has dreamed of being a quantity surveyor.

But for every unsympathetic case, there were ten that

felt monumental. Every week, I would spend hours with families – whether they were perpetrators, witnesses, victims, or some mixture of those – ripped apart by these charges, by these alleged crimes. One client, who had already lost four of her five children to social services, stood in the dock, trembling and crying. Beside her stood her partner, the co-accused, the man who had beaten her to a pulp earlier that week. As I pleaded for leniency on her behalf, trying to give the judge a flavour of the difficult life she'd lived with this man, that her failure to care for her children had been temporary, it put my own tribulations into perspective. Another client I represented at his parole hearing. He'd been pulled back into prison after he was accused of a new offence. He was acquitted of that offence, but the parole board inexplicably still refused to release him. I'd always been gently reprimanded by judges for wearing my heart on my sleeve, but these injustices felt burned into my soul.

I was losing my patience with the system. I'd been briefed to represent a man named Gerry in his trial for assault at City of London Magistrates' Court on a dreary December morning. I took instructions from him in the cells: we talked through the offence. As is sometimes the case, it turned out he didn't in fact have a defence in law – she'd started it, he said, but he had retaliated in anger, rather than fear – and when I explained this to him, he told me he would plead guilty. Gerry was more worried about his cat, anyway, who'd been left alone in his house since his arrest a few days previously. We came for sentencing before a notoriously harsh and unsympathetic judge, who sentenced him to two weeks in prison – just long enough to make sure he wouldn't get out in time for Christmas. I went down to see him in the cells, and his only concern was his poor cat, that someone go to his house and look after her. I phoned the solicitors multiple times, I wrote notes, I asked them to please, please deal with this. Nothing was done. No one cared about the cat. I don't know what happened to it. Inside I raged: this wasn't my job; why was I the only one who cared?

Or there was Robbie, who pleaded guilty to blackmail. We'd been on a rollercoaster ride, the two of us, over a period of two months and various court hearings. We'd gone from him thinking he was going to get a slap on the wrist to understanding that he was facing serious prison time. But in that final sentencing hearing, I'd given it my all. I was on my feet for almost an hour speaking on his behalf – far longer than I would normally be. I threw everything at the case, just hoping that something would work to stop this sad man from going to prison for the first time. Of course, it didn't work. He went to prison anyway. I went down to the cells afterwards, a courtesy call really, as we'd both said everything that could be said. 'Thanks, Miss. You did everything you could. Can you call my parents, and tell them I'm not coming home?' My stomach dropped. 'They don't know you're being sentenced today?' I replied in shock. 'No,' he replied. 'They don't know about . . . any of this stuff. They don't know I've been in court at all.' Jesus Christ. So, as I left court, I had to call the extremely elderly and disabled parents of my client, parents who could not care for themselves or each other, nor had any other care systems in place, and break the news to them that not only had their son been accused of a very serious crime, but that he was going to prison for several years, all while they wept down the phone to me. I walked to the train station and all I could think was: 'Fuck: this isn't my job.'

Then there was the time I turned up at Hammersmith Magistrates' Court to represent Jessica, who was up for a fairly straightforward assault charge. I went down to the cells and signed in. 'There aren't any free conference rooms, Miss. Do you mind seeing her in the cell?' This wasn't unusual, and normally sped things up, because you didn't have to fight your way past everyone being processed and discharged. I was escorted to Jessica's cell. When the door was closed, I gave her the not-terribly-pleasant news that, in my professional opinion, she too didn't really have a defence. She told me she understood and would plead guilty. It was clear from her manner that she was vulnerable; she was moving and speaking erratically, unable to look at me, and spoke of paranoia, voices. I made a note to raise the possibility of a psych report, then rang the bell for someone to unlock the cell. No response. Irritated, I rang it a few more times, making awkward small talk with Jessica. Still nothing. Eventually, a member of the cell staff walked past me carrying a sandwich, and I managed to flag her down thanks to some extreme arm-flapping through the letterbox slot in the door. She released me, and I headed back upstairs, thinking little of it beyond my time being wasted. When I got into the courtroom, the legal advisor handed me a sheet of paper. 'Handcuffs application,' she said grimly. She saw my face drop. 'Didn't you know?' A handcuffs application is made when a defendant poses such a risk to court staff that the only safe way for them appearing before the court is to do so in handcuffs. It is only made in very exceptional circumstances, because of the obvious concern that a defendant in handcuffs looks dangerous, and is therefore unlikely to get a fair shake. I reviewed the application. The defendant had made disclosures that she wished to harm the judge and her legal representative. She was also known to regularly secrete blades and fashion them into makeshift weapons.

All the breath went out of me. And then surged back in. I was suddenly furious. The cell staff knew this when I went down there. They must have – they were the ones who'd handed the damn thing into court. But thanks to laziness or negligence they'd locked me in a room with this woman who was so dangerous she had to wear handcuffs in court, who probably wanted to knife me. And then they hadn't even come when I'd rung the bell.

I filed a complaint with the court staff, then called my clerks and asked them to put a cautionary note on the file for future counsel. This wasn't their fault, but I was so cross, I had to stop myself from exploding at them, 'How the fuck is this my job?'

I couldn't shake cases once I was done with them. I just rolled them around in my head, like a marble in an empty jar, terrified I'd made a mistake. I told myself over and over what I needed to do – that I should go in, do the job as well as I could, then wash my hands of it. But

I couldn't. A good lawyer needs to look at a case dispassionately, then argue it with emotion. But with my emotions pinging around like my mind was a pinball machine, I could do neither.

I felt battered and bruised as I traipsed from courtroom to courtroom. I felt messed around, blamed, overworked. I was so, so tired. I was tired of representing domestic abusers who breached bail conditions and court orders to intimidate their partners. I was tired of victims who went back on their statements when they took the stand. I believed, as I always have and always will, that everyone deserves their day in court. But I was less and less sure that I wanted to be part of it.

Around this time, I met up with some friends from law school for a drink. I listened as they discussed their cases. One had had a gnarly sentencing that morning, another a serious assault trial with a demanding client. I felt sick at the prospect of their cases falling into my own diary. But they seemed happy. They seemed *delighted*. When they talked about their cases, you could tell they were playing through the emotions, like a musician recalling a melody in their head. The thrill of a closing speech. The rush they felt as the jury returned a verdict. For me, these moments were ones of utter panic followed by, at best, a wave of relief that the whole thing was finally over. I listened to my friends and for the first time, I understood: it wasn't the Bar that was the problem. It was me. I needed to leave.

*

And then, all of a sudden, it was Christmas.

The passage of time after death is weird. Everyone will tell you that you have to get through each first season without that person: experience their birthday, your birthday. Mother's day. Summer holidays. Sunburn. Kids going back to school. The leaves falling from the trees. Having to buy a new winter coat. Perhaps it depends on when the death falls as to what stings most, as that of course dictates how long you have been grieving for when certain dates arrive. But I think Christmas is the hardest. Christmas for us was a whole ten months after Mum's death; it felt like I should have grown a thicker skin by that point. Our Christmases had never been perfect before Mum died. But they were ours.

Maddy, Dad and I had decided to spend the day itself just the three of us, so I was readying myself to head up to Newcastle. One last trial before Christmas stood in my way, and I'd been messed around a lot on this one. It was a benefit fraud trial, at Inner London Crown Court, with a time estimate of a couple of days, and I was prosecuting. We'd made it through the trial, and the jury had been sent out to come up with a verdict. The jury had already been deliberating for longer than the length of the trial. The judge was cautious: slow to give them a majority direction, slow to pull them back in and ask whether they were able to reach a verdict. The clerks had told me it wouldn't run past its time estimate; now it was theoretically the last day, and the jury weren't showing any sign of returning. The train I'd booked home came and went. When a jury is deliberating, you need to be there, in case anything comes up. But if it doesn't, you just sit around, drinking endless cups of coffee, and trying to occupy yourself. I brought my knitting with me, but couldn't settle to it; I never got past a single page of the book in my bag. Most of the time was spent speculating with the other lawyers on the case about the possible verdict, followed by one of us inevitably intoning, 'Of course, you never can tell.' Sam went up to see his family. I was left to wait out the jury deliberations, armed only with Netflix and a family-size tub of Quality Street to fill my lonely evenings. In the end, on Christmas Eve, with the only courtroom in the whole court still sitting, even the Christmas bail applications having been and gone, the jury were hung, undecided, after four days. The judge reluctantly dismissed the case and sent them home. After all that, I had 'lost'. I should have been disheartened. But instead my heart soared as I headed straight from the court to King's Cross, to catch the next train to Newcastle.

I don't think there's any way we could have made that first Christmas easier. It was just something we had to endure. Mum wasn't in the kitchen filling vol-au-vents and prepping sprouts. When Dad made a mad dash to the supermarket late on the 23rd, he did so alone. And of course, there was no minestrone soup on Christmas Eve. And we always had minestrone on Christmas Eve.

We did what we could to mitigate the gaping loss: we hunkered down, just the three of us, as if by making ourselves as small a unit as possible, we could protect ourselves and each other, share body heat. We deliberately eschewed anything that could be considered normal – anything that would underscore Mum's not being there. We ate goose, and played Trivial Pursuit, both of which Mum scorned. Madeleine and I took on the cooking. We laughed. We laughed a surprising amount. We took photos! We never took photos! But the house was dreadfully quiet, still without her presence. The kitchen was empty without her standing by the sink, Radio 2 on, cigarette in hand. The biscuit tin was unstocked. Her bedside table lacked its characteristic pile of books. I hadn't noticed her presence until it was an absence. Her soft body, that seemed moulded to mine, on our golden sofa. Her glass of wine in the garden on the garden bench. Her handbags hanging from the door, smelling of leather, and coins, and her perfume.

It was the first time I'd spent any period of time in my home, the place where Mummy had died, since her death. While we were there, Madeleine and I were determined to face up to a task we'd put off for as long as we possibly could: clearing out Mum's belongings. We sorted through drawers and wardrobes, cupboards and bureaux; we emptied her dressing and bedside tables. We were desperately efficient; almost completely without emotion. It took us less than an hour.

Mum was an excellent present-giver, and would squirrel away gifts all year round ready for birthdays and Christmases. Once upon a time, these gifts would be secretly placed in various hiding places around the house, to mitigate the risk of curious children discovering them. This practice ended one Easter when Mum only remembered that she'd hidden the Easter eggs in the hot trolley *after* she'd preheated it for lunch. After that, gifts went in a designated drawer in the spare room (whose sanctity we were by then old enough – and scared of Mum enough – to respect).

Now, Madeleine and I looked in that drawer for the first time in our lives. It felt like trespassing. Inside, we found a host of tiny gifts: miniature shampoos, and a couple of nail varnishes, a set of highlighters, and a bejewelled notebook. Nothing of consequence, but every one of fresh importance.

For as long as I could remember, my Granny – my mum's mum – had been obsessed with divvying up her possessions before she died. Granny was morbid, it's true, convinced that death was just around the corner, even when I was young and she was in good health. She'd walk me round the house, pointing at items: 'That's for you, you should take that when I'm gone. But this one's for your cousin Emma, she's already got dibs on that.' Mum and I had rolled our eyes at her, sharing scorn for this ghoulishness. But now I found myself wishing Mum had had more of a proclivity for this kind of allocation.

We threw away almost everything. I bagged up her clothes for the charity shop with wild abandon, divvied up her jewellery as mementos for others, threw away her makeup and toiletries. I didn't take a memento for myself, sure I was immune to the sentimentality that others indulge in. But I descended on her books like a jackal – her Anne Tylers and Margaret Drabbles and Helen Dunmores and Mary Wesleys and Elizabeth Jane Howards and Margaret Atwoods. I couldn't stand the thought of them being given away or lost, or of me missing out on a book she had read and loved. They felt like a key to her, one that I couldn't lose.

I took her Le Creuset casserole pot, too (my luggage for the train ride home ended up being rather unwieldy) – not the pretty duck-egg one she'd recently invested in, but the dark blue one. The one with the chipped lid and interior discoloured by countless bologneses, in which she'd made chilis and soups for us all. And to accompany it, I took her small collection of cookbooks.

Only a couple of her recipes were actually known to me. I'd made her pineapple fruit cake – her single concession to proper baking – for Christmas, based on a handwritten recipe Dad had sent down, though it wasn't in Mum's handwriting, but an unknown friend's, their identity consigned to the vicissitudes of time. I knew her bolognese by sheer exposure, and by this point, I'd reverse-engineered her Greek pasta bake.

In this new cache, I stumbled upon her pineapple jam bread and butter pudding. I thought it was lost to the aeons of time until I found a slim pamphlet hidden among the hardbacks, produced by the Cleadon Ladies' Lifeboat Circle – a fundraising group that Mum had joined when she gave up her job after giving birth to my sister. The recipes therein were all products of their time, none more so than Mum's other contribution: a frankly inexplicable gelatine-set tuna mousse. The bread and butter pudding has held up rather better (so to speak), and I was delighted to have it.

But this wasn't my hobbyhorse. I had become obsessed by a soup. Whenever I was poorly, Mum would make minestrone soup. She would sit opposite me at the kitchen table, watching quietly as slowly, spoonful by spoonful, I ate it, and then she would walk me equally slowly, quietly around the garden. If I'd known she was going to die, I might have asked the important questions: what do I need to know about childbirth? How do you get curry stains out of a white shirt? How do you make your minestrone soup?

I had never once asked for the recipe, and now it was too late. I needed to recreate this soup. The entirety of my mother's cooking and love seemed bound up in minestrone. So I began trying to make it from memory. I knew it involved tiny pasta, and bacon and a lot of vegetables. I knew that those vegetables were diced precisely. Over and over again I bought pasta and bacon, and I diced vegetables precisely. All year, I'd been trying to recreate this soup. I'd fed Sam dozens of minestrone soups. Over Christmas, I asked Dad and Maddy about it, though I'd asked them before. They had no idea, nor did they really understand why I cared so much. My first attempt was wrong. So was my hundredth. I could get close, but it was never quite right. It was never my mother's soup. I turned to the internet, and spent nights gazing at search results for soup recipes, eliminating possibilities: no, no, no. Of all dishes, minestrone must be one of the hardest to recreate. There is no such thing as a definitive minestrone; God, why couldn't she have just written the damn thing down?

This was the true impetus for lugging her cookbooks back down to London. But after much searching, I gave it up for lost. And then, one night, when I was on the hunt for something new to cook, I found myself returning to those cookbooks. I flicked through book after book, idle and uninspired. I almost didn't spot it. But as soon as I began reading, I could see: this was the recipe. This was my mother's minestrone soup. I studied the method, line by line, and pictured my mum dicing, frying, stirring, the intricate ballet of her perfect soup. I closed the book and looked at the front cover. It was Delia's *Complete Cookery Course*. My mother's minestrone soup was Delia's minestrone soup. I had been searching for this recipe, experimenting, testing this recipe for months only for it to be in one of the most famous cookery books ever published.

I felt elated and also like a total fool. How could I have missed it? Why didn't I guess? I made the soup, not completely believing that I'd finally found the recipe I'd been seeking for so long. It was perfect. It was Mum's soup. I made it in the dark blue, chipped Le Creuset, and came the closest I'd managed to conjuring Mum since her death.

*

This isn't identical to Delia's recipe: I use tiny little pasta shells where Delia uses macaroni, courgette where she adds cabbage, and I don't think Mum ever added basil, although the recipe called for it. It turns out that even when I found the recipe that comforted me the most, that felt like an untouchable family institution, I couldn't resist fiddling with it just a little.

Mum's minestrone soup
(with apologies to Delia)

Makes   4 hearty portions
Takes   10 minutes of chopping, plus 2 hours simmering on the stove

25g butter
1 tablespoon olive oil
4 rashers of streaky bacon, snipped into lardon-sized bits, or 100g of lardons
1 medium onion, finely chopped
2 sticks of celery, finely chopped
1 large carrot, finely chopped
1 x 400g tin of chopped tomatoes
1 clove of garlic, finely chopped
Salt and pepper
1 litre chicken stock
2 leeks, finely sliced
1 courgette, finely chopped
75g tiny pasta shells
1 tablespoon tomato purée

1. Place a large saucepan or casserole dish on a medium heat. Melt the butter and add the oil. Add the bacon and allow it to colour and go slightly golden. Turn the heat down to low and add the onion, celery and carrots, and cook until just softened.

2. Add the tomatoes, garlic and a pinch of salt, and leave on a low heat for 20 minutes, occasionally stirring to prevent sticking.

3. Add the stock. Bring to a gentle boil, pop a lid on, and leave to simmer for an hour.

4. Add the leeks and courgettes and pasta and continue to simmer for another 30 minutes.

5. Stir in the tomato purée and cook for a final 10 minutes, then taste and season with salt and pepper.

7

There is a recklessness that grief brings. It's not so much that it puts things into perspective, but almost that it does the opposite: perspective is so skewed, everything is so upside down and inside out, that you feel utterly unconstrained by the life you had before. Grief gives you licence, whether you want it or not. It's no surprise that death changes you. It happens in glaringly obvious ways, like weight change and ill health. It strains relationships that seemed rock-solid; for some, it can act as a catalyst to start a family. For others, death brings a manic embrace of life, a desire to make hay while the sun shines. These people run ultra-marathons and travel the world. Others find their faith, or lose it.

These are the big shifts – the ones everyone notices. But death also changes people in much more subtle ways – ways you would never discern unless you looked very closely. I doubt an old acquaintance who met me in the year after Mum's death would have found me a drastically different person. But inside, something had shifted. I had recalibrated. My world had been thrown into uncertainty, and that had established in me a new feeling that was both paralysing and exciting: my future was in my hands.

I had this thought at the front of my mind as I sat

awkwardly on a bench in the atrium of the Old Bailey, waiting for my Head of Chambers to get out of his big trial.

'So, what's up?' he asked.

I took a deep breath. 'I have to leave.'

Because cooking hadn't really been part of my child-hood, I had little in the way of gut feeling for it. That's why I loved rules and recipes. I wanted there to be a right way and a wrong way; if there wasn't, how did I know if I was doing it right? The problem was, each recipe stood alone. I could make meringue, but meringue-based macarons eluded me; I could make a jelly using gelatine, but not a gelatine-based mousse. I couldn't work out where I was going wrong. However many books I read and YouTube channels I subscribed to, it felt like I wasn't really learning anything at all.

When I asked Sam for recipes for things he cooked for us, he looked at me blankly. He knew recipes through osmosis, through cooking for twenty years, through a family that was always in the kitchen, through not relying on supermarket pasta for all of his adult life to date. He knew how to throw a dish together based on the contents of his fridge and cupboards. I'd never seen him follow a recipe. And if he did encounter anything tricky, he'd call his mum and dad. He was, therefore, totally useless to me. One night, I decided to knock up the beef rendang I'd spotted on a blog. I'm not sure that I'd ever even eaten a beef rendang, but I'm a sucker for a good-looking recipe. It was all going swimmingly until the final instruction, which told me to fry the beef in the oil. Nowhere did it tell me to stir or in any way manipulate the beef, so I left it to its own devices. It began to smoke a bit, but that was probably meant to happen, right? Otherwise they'd have said something in the method. After fifteen minutes, the kitchen was filled with smoke. Sam came in and peered through the smoke at me. 'Liv, I don't think this is quite right.' 'No, no, I've followed the recipe exactly. It categorically doesn't mention stirring.' 'But the beef is burnt, Liv. It's obliterated.' And it was. Obviously it was. The smoke was now acrid; I don't know if you've ever smelt properly burnt beef, but it's truly, truly horrific. I dumped the charred remains into the bin, and then ten minutes later had to take the bin bag down to the outside bin, so bad was the smell. Suzy's freshly washed linen was hanging in the corner of our already too-small kitchen. It took three washes to get rid of the smell.

If I wanted to learn to cook, and learn fast, I was going to need some help. And I did want to learn fast: I was acutely aware that I was playing catch-up – although exactly what or who I was trying to catch up with, I wasn't sure. I just knew that it was important that I did.

Quietly, for the last few months, I'd been Googling cooking schools – idly at first, but then more compulsively. I sat on my bed, opened my laptop and began to type the same URL into the bar I'd been typing every time I'd opened it for the last three months: the Cordon Bleu website popped up, and I immediately felt calmer. I knew the page off by heart: its pictures of lines of students in pristine white uniforms, topped with sweet little caps, the odd tall chef's hat rising among them.

Looks of concentration as they iced sponges and glazed croissants. Precisely plated dishes bearing single petals of onion and perfect rectangles of what I guessed might be duck. The text offered up myriad different programmes, and testimonials praising every inch of the institution. I'm not sure when the idea first came to me, what drew me to it. But I knew I was smitten.

This was not the first of my madcap schemes. I'd gone through a period where I'd obsessively researched the ins and outs of Harvard Law School, largely because Elle Woods in *Legally Blonde* had a good time there, and ignoring the fact that attending Harvard Law School wouldn't help me practise law in the jurisdiction in which I lived. Even before I'd fallen for cooking, I'd briefly harboured an idea of throwing in the legal towel and becoming a butcher. Despite my utter lack of upper body strength, I thought I'd probably be quite good at it, and it made me sound unusual and practical. But *this* felt different. Even if I found my justification hard to put into words, the idea gave me an energy I hadn't felt in a long, long time. However crap I currently was at it, I found solace and fascination in baking and cooking. Being in the kitchen made me feel grounded and calm. But I wanted so much more. I wanted to learn how to make perfect éclairs and beautiful brioche; I wanted to understand chocolate, and be able to put something on a plate in a way that suggested something other than 'compost heap'.

When I told Sam, he didn't laugh in my face. He didn't gently swerve the conversation to another topic. He took me seriously. We talked through the pros and cons, the not-inconsiderable logistics. Quite apart from the tumult of leaving my career, the full-time pâtisserie course is expensive; but Mum's death meant that for the first time, this wasn't a complete barrier. It didn't matter what spin we put on it: the outcome remained the same.

I was going to go to Le Cordon Bleu.

When my practice had dwindled to a few cases, Sam expressed an interest in coming along to watch before it was too late. A key tenet of our justice system is that it is open and public – in most cases, anyone can spectate. He'd never seen me stand up in court, and now here was his chance. He'd chosen a good one: this was undoubtedly the biggest case I'd had to date. Section 18 wounding is the most serious kind of assault you can be charged with – the next rung down from murder. In theory, it can carry a life sentence, although here it was likely to be more in the region of a handful of years in prison. My client was accused of having been the ringleader in a broad-daylight gangland stabbing on a London high street, committed when he was sixteen. I'd spent ages working on my mitigation, determined to drag this young man's sentence down to one that could be served in the community, because I knew all too well what happened to young men from rough areas when they went inside. I had worked and reworked my notes, searching for the most heart-wrenching (and judgment-changing) phrases I could muster.

I deposited Sam outside the courtroom and went to get into my robes. When I returned – in wig, gown, and the clacking heels that I never wore outside of court – Sam looked anxious. 'What do I do when we go into the courtroom?' he said. 'Where do I sit?' 'Just in the public gallery,' I replied. When he continued to eyeball me, I clarified, 'Back left.' It's easy to forget how strange and intimidating the court system can seem to an outsider – even to someone who was there merely to watch, and who had heard me bang on about it for ages.

My client was late, despite extremely explicit instructions that he must, must arrive in good time. I began to feel nervous, pacing back and forth in front of the courtroom, trying to look calm and composed. By the time he sauntered in precisely two minutes before the case was due to begin, I was ready to haul him over hot coals. The usher popped his head round the door. 'Judge is coming up,' he informed us. There was no time to discuss our plan of action. I hustled my client into the courtroom and, as he entered the dock, settled myself into the advocates' bench, stealing a glance at Sam. I was glad he was here, despite the stress of the case. I might have decided to leave this career, but it still made me proud, deep down, to stand up and represent the most vulnerable in society. Plus, I looked great in a wig and gown, and it would have been a shame for him to miss that.

The judge entered and we all stood up. 'Miss Potts,' he began. 'Your honour,' I replied, readying myself to launch into my carefully structured mitigation, taking a breath. 'I have looked at your client's pre-sentence report,' he continued before I had a chance to address him on the finer points of sentencing practice, or the deep injustices my client had already borne in his young life. 'I am minded to suspend his sentence, with a curfew requirement. How does that sound?' I was floored. Where was my glorious, soaring mitigation? Where was the moment where I spoke so movingly, so eloquently that those in attendance could see the hard-nosed, world-weary judge visibly soften? 'Just one question,' the judge said, drawing me out of my incredulity. 'What hours does your client work? Just so I can ensure that the curfew hours aren't unworkable for him.' My mouth goldfished. This is an exquisitely predictable question in sentencing, and most mitigations will focus heavily on the defendant's job as a synecdoche for his contribution to society, his stability, and unlikelihood of recidivism. Obviously I hadn't asked him. 'Could I . . . could I take instructions, your honour?' I asked, a formal way of saying, 'Sorry, judge, I have no bloody idea.' 'Of course, Miss Potts, but before you do: what does your client actually do?' Nope, I hadn't even got that far: 'I'm going to have to take instructions on that too, your honour.'

I trotted to the back of the courtroom to speak to my client. I was so flustered by the turn of events that my client ended up calling out his answers to the judge directly. My contribution to his exceedingly generous sentence? Absolutely bloody nothing. I changed into my civvies and Sam and I walked out of the building. 'About that case,' I began. 'Yeah, I'm guessing it wasn't your best performance,' he replied. He took my hand and we walked away from court together.

Later that week, after not having exactly covered

myself in glory at Snaresbrook, I found myself at chambers tea. Chambers tea is a tradition generally reserved for sets of barristers' chambers whose practices don't rely on them being at a different far-flung court every day of the week. It can otherwise prove tricky to round people up for tea and cake mid-afternoon. But thanks to equal parts stubbornness and generosity on the part of a particular member of my chambers, we persevered despite our criminal bent. As well as being a much-needed break from whatever hours of CCTV or binders of phone records are occupying your day, it's an opportunity for anecdote, one-upmanship: dispatches from counsels' row. Who can present the most outrageous, hilarious, or horrifying story from their week of work?

By this time, news had begun to get round about my plans to fly the legal nest, although not everyone knew the specifics. I braced myself for a few more editions of the 'So you're leaving law to bake cakes?' conversation. Actually, I'm being unfair: almost everyone had been incredibly kind and supportive on hearing my news, but now I was stuck talking with Scott, an older barrister, who thought we were closer than we were, certainly close enough that he could make scathing comments about my career choices. 'You're just leaving the Bar because your mum died,' Scott said to me, baldly, sipping his fancy loose-leaf tea, as if he hadn't just said something potentially devastating. 'That's . . . that's not true,' I said, pathetically. I excused myself politely from the conversation, and decided I'd had enough. He's wrong, I thought angrily as I stomped up towards Blackfriars Tube station.

How *dare* he? He knows *nothing* about me, or my bloody mum. He couldn't be more wrong, I fumed. I didn't want Mum to be the reason that I left the Bar. To do that would be to turn her tragedy to my benefit, would be to undermine it, to reframe the whole bloody thing around *me*. Wouldn't it?

Grief becomes part of your identity after a while. I felt like it should be on my chambers bio: *Olivia studied English at Corpus Christi College, Cambridge, and attended City Law School. She was called to the Bar in 2011 by Gray's Inn. She practises in fraud and serious crime, lectures in trading standards, and her mother died three years ago.* If I were on a dating website, it would say: *Livvy, London, 26. Curvy brunette, GSOH (gallows sense of humour), in denial about death of mother. WLTM fellow bereaved who understands that their pain is subordinate to hers.*

Dead mothers are a trope as old as time. They litter fairytales and fables, from Hansel and Gretel to Beauty and the Beast. Victorian writers were obsessed with plucky young men and women navigating the world without the guiding hand of a loving mother: Eliot used them to great effect in both *Daniel Deronda* and *Middlemarch*. Wilkie Collins was a fan of this plot device, too. Dickens couldn't get enough of it: *Bleak House*, *Great Expectations* (Pip *and* Estella!), *David Copperfield*, *Oliver Twist*.

And the obsession with dead mothers didn't end with the picaresque sentimentality of the Victorians, as you quickly discover if you have recently lost a parent and are feeling vulnerable. We continue to be obsessed with them in modern media. You can't move for dead mothers. Take almost any animated film you can think of. In *Finding*

Nemo, Nemo's mother Coral is eaten by a barracuda before we even reach the title sequence. Quasimodo's mother in *The Hunchback of Notre Dame* is killed by Frollo, the man who ultimately brings him up, on the steps of the cathedral. In *Lilo and Stitch*, Lilo's parents are killed in a car crash before the film begins. In *Snow White*, and *Cinderella*, the death isn't even explained in the barest terms; it is simply an established fact, a springboard from which the plot can jump. And, well, most viewers of *Bambi* would struggle to remember anything other than the scene in which he watches his mother get shot by a hunter, followed by one of the most brutal lines in cinema: 'Your mother can't be with you any more.'

The mothers are all dead, or at least absent. There are exceptions, but they're few and far between. The reason for this is simple: narrative arc. Dead mothers are a plot point; they deliver motivation. The dead mother represents an adversity to be overcome for our beloved protagonist. It places a slight question mark over their identity, their origins, leaving them free to find the right path for themselves, which will, ultimately, deliver the happy ending we all crave. The conceit is that the mother's absence is necessary for emotional growth, for self-determination; that it creates a space for identity to develop.

Rose-tinted memory allows these mothers to appear as two-dimensional paragons of virtue, who are only ever described in the context of their relationship to our protagonist. But I didn't want this. I didn't want to fictionalize my mother. I didn't want to turn her into a legend, made of words. She was a real person. It's so easy to mythologize the dead, and even easier to see your mother as no more and no less than that: a person who only existed in relation to you. Put the two together, and in my mind, she quickly became a character in my life, rather than a person in her own right. And that wasn't how I wanted to think of her. As Hilary Mantel puts it in her essay for the *Guardian* on grief, 'The dead person recedes, losing selfhood, losing integrity, becoming an artefact of memory.'*

Ruth Potts was a three-dimensional, complicated woman whom I loved more than I thought possible, and mourned with equal ferocity. Her life was curtailed, cruelly. She is an absence in my life, and my father's, and my sister's, as well as in those of her friends. But she was more than that.

She was a little girl who once hid her vegetables in the posh cutlery drawer, so that her mother didn't find them until it was too late. She was the child who, after a drinks party her parents hosted, went around quietly drinking the dregs from all the glasses before declaring, 'Well, it's been a lovely day!' and over-enthusiastically flinging the glass she was holding through the closed French windows. She was the young woman who captained netball teams and was fiercely competitive at air hockey. She was a woman who'd fallen in love and married, who'd paid bills and written shopping lists. She was the young mother who played 'libraries' in the garden with her bookish daughter, hauling her entire book collection

* Mantel, Hilary, 'Hilary Mantel on Grief', *Guardian*, 27 December 2014.

outside, just so that she could choose six (no more: without rules, there is only chaos) and pretend to stamp them with her fist. Her attention would light you up from the inside out.

She would cry without fail at 'Away in a Manger'. She was a grown woman who loved Marks & Spencer, Robert Lindsay, menus, dogs, hazelnut yoghurts, sherbet lemons and really posh soaps. She was a mother who would get stage fright on her daughters' behalf, having to leave the room whenever they mounted the stage for one of countless verse-reading or public-speaking competitions, but who wouldn't let this diminish her competitive edge ('You have to enter the Bible-reading category, no one else does! It's like shooting fish in a barrel!'). She was a middle-aged woman who'd been ill, for a long time. She was someone who battled anxiety, and called her daughters 'Angel Cake' and 'Lovebird' and 'Pet Lamb'. She was a person before I came along, and continued to be one afterwards, even if I hadn't been able to see her that way until it was too late.

I had been on the cusp, I think, of understanding that she had selfhood beyond being my long-suffering mother. But I was in my early twenties, and selfish, and self-obsessed. I never got to know her as a person. I'm sort of angry with her for dying before I had a chance to redeem myself; to become the balanced, empathetic, generous-spirited daughter she deserved. I felt so guilty, and it was all her fault.

I tried to figure out the reasons *why* I was doing this. Not the proximate ones – wanting to be able to make nice croissants and custards – but the ones that sat behind those. Maybe I needed a new start. Maybe I needed to turn my life upside down and shake it, just for a bit. To see what stuck. To see who I could be. Maybe I wanted to work hard. Or do something with my hands as well as my brain. Maybe it was exhaustion and exasperation at the state of the criminal Bar: underfunded, anxious-making. Maybe it was as simple as wanting my life to revolve around something sweet rather than something bitter for the first time in what felt like forever.

I was going to culinary school because my mum had died. Of course I was. But I was also going for all the other reasons – because I was unhappy at the Bar, because I wanted a new start. Because I wanted to see if I could do it. Because of me.

A couple of weeks later, I made a new friend, Kate. Kate had recently left her job in theatre for cookery. It was our shared career change that had led to us meeting up. I was nervous; it felt like a first date as I waited for her in a Hackney bakery. As we drank coffee, and then cocktails, we began to get to know each other. Happiness shone out of her as she told me about her decision to leave the career she'd trained for and excelled in: her love of food was obvious, and we talked over one another to share our excitement and enthusiasm. I told her about my plans, about my hopes and anxieties. I waited for her to express reservations, or question my sanity. 'Oh my God, Liv,' she said, 'you have to go. You are *so lucky.*' And she was right! I was *so lucky.* Screw Scott and anyone else who tried to psychoanalyse or deter me. I was going to go and study cookery for nine months. I was *so lucky*.

I took a breath and clicked 'Apply'. The form required a motivation statement. I rattled through my recent history in brief terms: dead mother, started baking, quit job. I drew tenuous comparisons between courtrooms and professional kitchens, and listed skills I wasn't sure I actually possessed. And then I wrote the most true thing that I could think of: that baking brought me joy and brought joy to others.

The decision between studying cuisine or pâtisserie was never really a choice for me. I loved what I thought of as 'proper' cooking: grilling and roasting and sautéing and poaching, standing over a flame with a pan and a piece of meat. But it wasn't what I wanted. I wanted the rigours of pastry.

Having looked at the cuisine syllabus, it seemed to be a case of – once the very basics of stocks and filleting and turning vegetables are established – stuffing increasing numbers of meat products inside animal skins, until you're left with the meat equivalent of Russian dolls that wouldn't look out of place at a Tudor banquet. But I'm quite sure that someone whose heart skipped at the idea of consommé could be just as scathing about the pastry syllabus's predilection for making laborious, edible structures that are never intended to be eaten. Each to their own.

Pâtisserie is about precision. It's all about control. You can stand over an open flame, sweat dripping, but unless you learn how to slow things down, until you can control your actions, and the effect they have on a batter, or a custard or just piping a single line of chocolate, you'll never succeed. You learn to develop muscle memory, until those things come naturally, until that control, and that precision, is part of you. The roots had been ripped out of my world unexpectedly. Now, I wanted to deal in certainties. I wanted my actions to have consequences for which I was 100 per cent responsible. That's pâtisserie. Also, I rather liked the idea of knocking seven bells out of a ball of dough.

But it was also about pleasure. Pastry is pure pleasure to give and to receive. It is almost always a celebration, even if it's just a small one. I know several people who routinely eschew puddings on the basis that they're pointless: that they're empty calories. But this seems to miss the whole point. They're indulgence and escapism. They require creativity and invention, technique and effort. They should delight. We have to eat to live. We don't have to eat puddings to live. We don't have to eat them at all. Puddings aren't sustenance. Puddings are joy. The squidge of a hot syrup sponge, coated in thick, cold custard; the knife's first slice into a cake. Ice cream scooped at the perfect temperature. Your first taste of caramel, and the revelation that something bitter can also be sweet and the best thing you've ever eaten. The snap of precisely tempered chocolate. Beautiful macarons in every shade of the rainbow. A single doughnut splurging with scarlet raspberry jam. A gravity-defying soufflé; is there anything more magical?

Puddings are emotional. They are bound up in memory and nostalgia. Sacrilege it may be, but the Colin the

Caterpillar cake is not an inherently wonderful cake: grown men and women of my generation continue to love it because it recalls their childhood. It represents celebration. I don't make rice pudding for nutritional balance; I make rice pudding to remind me of the way my grandma's house smelt and tasted. Do you remember the first time you cracked a crème brûlée with the back of a spoon? The magic of the immaculate, brittle shell shattering to the smoothest vanilla custard beneath. I do. I was nine, maybe ten, and in Normandy on holiday with my family: I tried so many new foods that summer. But it was the crème brûlée that really stuck. And all of this is something you can create, something that can be produced by your hands if you just manipulate eggs, sugar, butter, cream, chocolate.

But I couldn't fit all of that on the application form, so I went with 'joy'. And joy, it, turns out, was enough: I was in.

Le Cordon Bleu translates literally as 'the blue ribbon'; originally this referred to a literal blue ribbon, from which hung a diamond-encrusted medal that was bestowed by kings, starting with Henry III in 1578 after he set up l'Ordre des Chevaliers du Saint Esprit (Knights of the Order of the Holy Spirit). The knights of this order were part of the King's innermost circle, and the story goes that this bemedalled group became known for their outrageously extravagant dinners, each more lavish than the last. During the Revolution, 'the blue ribbon' became a byword for fancy dining, and survived the death of both the monarchy and the Order.

The modern Cordon Bleu began life as the first French culinary magazine at the end of the nineteenth century, *La Cuisinière Cordon Bleu*, set up by Marthe Distel. It concerned itself with classic recipes and tips for entertaining. Free cooking classes were introduced in an effort to increase circulation – some in the kitchens of the Palais Royal, no less – but their popularity soon surpassed that of the magazine. Classes were taught by the most eminent chefs of the day; Henri-Paul Pellaprat, a disciple of Escoffier, led the school in its early days.

In 1933, former students of the Parisian school, Dione Lucas and Rosemary Hume, were given permission to open a school in London, L'École du Petit Cordon Bleu. It grew quickly. By 1953, despite having been closed during the war, the school was eminent enough to cater Queen Elizabeth's Coronation luncheon, for which Hume invented the famous Coronation chicken. The dish was a solution to the difficulties of the gig. There were 350 guests, sitting in two separate areas, which meant hot food was out of the question. The waitresses were all amateurs – students who'd been roped in. Perhaps most significantly, the guests came from all over the Empire, and their 'varying and unknown tastes' (LCB principal Constance Spry's words, not mine) could only be guessed at. A relatively bland chicken dish fitted the bill nicely.

In 1984, Le Cordon Bleu was bought by André Cointreau, descendant of the Cointreau and Rémy Martin dynasties. The school quickly expanded to – at the time of writing – fifty branches in twenty countries. Over 20,000 students pass through their doors every year. The school now offers a variety of courses – everything from boulangerie to wine diplomas – but the two most prestigious qualifications remain the Diplôme de Cuisine and the Diplôme de Pâtisserie.

And I was going to go.

Sam and I went on holiday a few weeks before I was due to start the course. We flew to Tuscany for the wedding of two friends. It probably wouldn't have been Sam's first choice; we'd been on holiday to Tuscany two years before, and he likes to visit new places and see new things. But the wedding was in Florence, and it seemed silly not to extend the jaunt into our summer holiday. I, meanwhile, was quietly delighted. While I like seeing new things, I like sitting in a pretty Tuscan town square – ideally the Piazza del Campo in Siena – drinking Campari and eating olives even more. I successfully lobbied for us to return to Siena over my birthday. I was ecstatic.

Though Sam packed meticulously for this trip, he had left his subtlety at home. At the airport, on the flight, and every few hours during the first few days of our holiday, he told me that I was not to touch his rucksack, since it contained my birthday presents. As we were leaving the apartment in Florence, Sam forgot himself and called behind him, asking me just to double-check for passports. I reached down into the hidden pocket at the back of the bag where I knew he kept them. I felt the passports, and then my hand hit something else: something small and square. Something ring-box shaped.

Sam's holidays normally proceed at a steady clip and

on a strict timetable. He likes to take in at least two museums and one church or cathedral (or mosque or temple, when we were in Indonesia) a day. It drives me mad. But on my birthday, with great personal anguish, he allowed this schedule to loosen. We had a leisurely breakfast, read our books and drank coffee, then went to a lunchtime tasting of Tuscan red wines, meats and cheeses. I was suspicious, but didn't say anything – not wanting to ruin a possible proposal, and if I was wrong on that one, for fear of alerting Sam to our weirdly chilled-out day. Every time he knelt down to tie a shoe-lace, my heart raced. At one point he disappeared for ages to 'get a better angle on a photo', and I stood semi-patiently, faux-nonchalantly, awaiting what I assumed was the inevitable flashmob, making sure that I was giving my best angle to any surrounding photographers. After fifteen minutes, I got bored and went to find him. And there he was, crouching by a bollard, and aiming his camera squarely at the Duomo, rather than me.

By evening, I was starting to doubt myself, even after he'd uncharacteristically offered up an opinion when I'd asked whether I should paint my nails before we went out for dinner. We sat outside a bar at the edge of the Piazza del Campo, facing the Duomo, drinking Americano cocktails and playing Trivial Pursuit. Sam seemed remarkably laid back for a man I was certain was going to propose. Was it possible I'd misunderstood? Was bringing me here on my birthday a red herring, a feint? Was the small box actually, say, a sewing kit? (If that seems implausible, know that Sam carries some kind of craft project almost anywhere.)

We walked down a quiet, unassuming alley towards a restaurant we'd been to on our previous trip. Our last meal there hadn't been fancy, but it was memorable: big plates of hand-rolled pici, too much wine, fat cantuccini dunked into tiny glasses of Vin Santo. I'd loved it.

When we were alone in the alley, Sam suddenly stopped. 'Would you like your final birthday present?' he asked. Before I had a chance to reply, he pulled a thin rectangle from his rucksack and began unwrapping it. *Rude*, I thought. He held a sheaf of prompt cards in his hands. The prompt cards had familiar-looking lines on them, but he wasn't looking at them. He was looking right at me. He started speaking in a very deliberate way, as if each word was imbued with heavy meaning. But he was talking nonsense, comparing me to broccoli and a turkey dinner. I wondered, for a moment, what on Earth he was talking about. Had he chosen the worst possible time to lose his mind?

Then I realized: he was reciting 'You're The Top', a silly old Cole Porter love song, from the musical *Anything Goes*. It's a duet – the singers compare each other to various superlative things, from Greta Garbo's salary to Cellophane to, well, a turkey dinner. We sang it at home to each other all the time, taking the two different roles in the song, dancing round the kitchen together. He reached the end of the first verse and thrust the prompt cards at me. 'Now you!' he hissed. He'd written out my part on the cards. Wait – did he want me to join in? I began reading the words aloud from the cards, pushing down the slight feeling of affront: I was . . . doing my own proposal? It could never just be *simple* with Sam, could it?

He reached – or rather, *we* reached – the end of the song, and with the final line, he dropped on to one knee and brought out the ring box I'd found two days before (and – in a fit of unbelievable self-control – hadn't looked inside). It held a pale, pale blue sapphire surrounded by diamonds. 'Will you marry me?' he asked. 'Yes,' I replied instantly. Then I added, 'Obviously yes.' We walked the last few steps to the restaurant, and ordered exactly the same dishes we'd ordered last time, marvelling at how much had changed in those two years.

*

Cantuccini are Tuscan biscotti and, although they have the same basic composition as their non-Tuscan brothers, they are typically shorter and squatter. They are traditionally flavoured with the golden Tuscan pudding wine, Vin Santo, and served alongside it for dipping. You can sub amaretto for the Vin Santo here, if you'd rather, as it's easier to get hold of, and goes so well with the almonds.

Cantuccini

Makes: About 30 small biscuits
Takes: 15 minutes
Bakes: 45 minutes

250g sugar
60g butter

Zest of 1 small orange
Zest of 1 small lemon
2 eggs
2 tablespoons Vin Santo or amaretto
½ teaspoon salt
400g plain flour
1½ teaspoons baking powder
150g whole almonds, skin on

1. Preheat the oven to 160°C fan/180°C/gas 4. Place the sugar and butter in a bowl and add the citrus zest. Cream the mixture together until pale and fluffy.

2. Add the eggs one by one, and mix thoroughly. Stir through the amaretto and salt, and mix in the flour and baking powder, then the almonds. Turn out on to a floured surface and knead very briefly to bring the dough together and distribute the almonds evenly.

3. Line a baking sheet with paper and divide the dough into three even portions. Roll these each out into sausages about 5cm wide and 4cm high and place on the baking tray, leaving space for them to spread.

4. Bake for 20–30 minutes. The sausages will have spread slightly and should be firm but not hard. As soon as they're cool enough to handle, and using a bread knife, cut slices on the diagonal about 2.5cm wide.

5. Set these slices out on a baking tray (you will likely need a second tray here), cut side up. Return to the oven for 10 minutes. Turn each of the slices over and place back in the oven for a further 5–10 minutes. The biscuits should be golden but not brown, and feel hard but not brittle; they will harden as they cool. Allow to cool completely. Place in an airtight container, where they will sit happily for a week.

8

Chef whites look ridiculous on me. I probably discovered this too late in the day, as I sat down in the demo kitchen of Le Cordon Bleu for the first time, clutching my obnoxiously large folder of recipes and theory to my chest, and looked around me. The first thing I noticed was that my cohorts all looked born to the uniform. My head was too big for what I had been told was the largest size of hat, a little cotton beanie that refused to sit flush against my forehead and, as I would discover as time went on, would shrink an inch every time you washed it. The chequered trousers seemed, impossibly, both too long and too short. I was extremely conscious of the thick, crinkly, terry-towelled waistband, and of the fact that I was wearing trousers with a Velcro fastening for the first time in twenty-five years. My classmates, on the other hand, all looked like they had made good use of the hemming tape overnight, while I had been eating takeaway and talking with my mouth full about my new knife kit. The necktie we had been given, supposedly to stop stiff necks resulting from heavy sweating in hot kitchens, only fanned the flames of ridiculousness. The teaching chef had shown us how to fold, wind, and tie these triangles into perfect knots, which would make us look smart, professional, if also a little old-fashioned;

mine looked more like an all-white version of a boy scout's neckerchief and woggle.

And as for the chef's jacket, with the eponymous blue ribbon and school name embroidered on the left-hand side, it's safe to say that they are not made for women with an ample bosom. Mine strained at the press-studs across my chest and hips, despite swamping my shoulders, neck and wrists. The clogs I had so proudly bought from a specialist shop a week earlier now felt like clown shoes. I lumbered up the stairs in them, like Godzilla. Everyone else looked like they could tap dance.

I'd come in the previous day to collect my uniform and knife kit, and had decided to take the scenic route to Bloomsbury, in an attempt to get a hold on my nerves. If my plan was to embrace my fresh start, I couldn't have chosen a worse path. I walked up past the Old Bailey and on to Fleet Street, where I skirted the door in the wall behind which lies the secret domain of lawyers: Middle and Inner Temple, housing my old chambers. Up Chancery Lane, and along High Holborn I passed my Inn of Court, Gray's Inn, where I'd studied for the Bar, taking exams, doing mock trials, where I'd heard speeches and eaten dinners. On the way to start my new life, I had accidentally taken myself through the potted highlights of my old one.

I rounded the corner into Bloomsbury Square, and the school came into view. Le Cordon Bleu sits behind the British Museum, an elegant Georgian townhouse, its dark blue and white flags thrusting forward into the square. The building is made up of four levels, each holding two teaching kitchens and a demonstration kitchen. Each is named after a significant figure from the food world: Julia Child is the name of a cuisine kitchen, Brillat-Savarin a pâtisserie kitchen, and Cointreau is the top floor demonstration classroom. A herb and vegetable garden sits on the roof, and there is a café on the ground floor that is open to the public.

A queue stretched almost the length of one sidearm of the square, hundreds of people waiting to register for courses. My feeling of being unique and special, with an unusual dream, ebbed away. I joined the end of the queue, and over the next half-hour, slowly edged closer.

The queue gave me the chance to take in my fellow students: the vast majority were women, and most quite a bit younger than me. A couple of them were complaining of severe hangovers. One woman brazenly queue-jumped me, and I immediately made a mental note to make her my nemesis. I tried to guess whether those around me were destined for the cuisine course, or the pâtisserie, or the Grand Diplôme, which combines the two into one nine-month stint. The queue continued inside the school, all the way up the four floors of staircase. We walked along the final corridor. Black-and-white photos of the teaching chefs lined the walls, all looking severe and vaguely naval in their toques – the tall hats that chefs traditionally wear. We shuffled into an already crowded room and collected big binders full of school rules and procedures, were handed uniform bags and knife kits, held in thick, rectangular bags, and shuffled out again.

I headed to the locker room to try on my uniform. It

was seething with people: a whole room of writhing women trying to force their way into ill-fitting whites. I tried on one of the jackets I'd been given, and began to half-heartedly hitch a pair of the chequered trousers to my waist, before thinking better of it. I threw my civvies back on, and decided to make a break for it.

But that was yesterday. And now here I was, actually sitting in the Cordon Bleu demo kitchen, about to begin the Diplôme de Pâtisserie. The demo lecture room is beautiful. At the front is a gleaming chrome professional kitchen, with an open counter so students can see in. Three cameras are trained on the teaching chef, including one that can zoom right in on the chef's hands to show in high definition what he is doing at any given moment. The images are broadcast to four large television screens around the room. There is an angled mirror above the demo bench that reflects the entire cooking area, so students can watch as chefs debone fish, turn mushrooms, or spin roses out of molten sugar. Everything is, of course, spotlessly clean. Too nervous to talk to those to either side of me, I turned to the pages assigned for this demonstration: stages of cooking sugar, fruit salad, and meringues. So far, so doable, although I was surprised to note that the recipe folder only included a list of ingredients, rather than any kind of method. In fact, looking through the rest of the folder for this term, I couldn't find a single recipe.

The teaching chef arrived and a hush descended. 'Good morning, ladies and gentlemen. I am Chef Nicolas,' he began, in a mellifluous French accent. He was a small man, made taller by a large toque perched on his head, which managed, unbelievably, to look less stupid than my tiny hat. The chefs' hats are made of paper so that, in the event of them catching light, they whoosh up like amaretti paper, immediately turning to ash rather than burning the head of the chef.

Chef Nicolas began methodically taking us through the thirty-three-item knife kit. 'Approximately one third of you will cut yourselves today,' he warned, matter-of-factly. I glanced up at my fellow students, who seemed oddly unmoved by this revelation. Meanwhile, I was frantically running the numbers. There were about sixty of us in the room. At least twenty of us would cut ourselves. I did not fancy my chances.

There are knives for boning and filleting and cleaving and breaking bones, which he dismissed quickly. Everything imaginable is in there, right down to a teaspoon (a chef's teaspoon!) and a nailbrush (a chef's nailbrush!). There were knives I'd never seen before: the turning knife is curved like a tiny sickle, and used for shaping vegetables into perfect rugby balls, or carving mushrooms into intricate spirals. This too was dismissed by Chef Nicolas. Again and again, he emphasized the sharpness of the knives: 'This one,' he said, picking up another seemingly identical blade, 'is *very* sharp.' As he picked up the trussing needle, he wore an even more severe expression. 'This is for sewing little creatures back together.' He paused. 'Do we use that in pâtisserie? No, we are not animals.'

We then got on to the main business of the practical.

The 'basic term' is self-explanatory: taking students from an assumed point of no knowledge to one where they are confident with a plethora of techniques and basic recipes (pâte sucrée, crème anglaise). So we were starting at the very, very beginning, with fruit salad. The chef proceeded to turn an enormous pile of fruit into an array of perfect shapes: identical cubes of mango, intricate waves of pineapple, spheres of pear, coins of strawberry, wafer-thin slices of apple, jagged little half-grape crowns. I was aware he was making it look easy, but I was not worried: who can't cut up fruit? Looking up, the chef saw us all scribbling frantically. 'No need to write a book,' he said gently. 'You just have to cut up an orange and an apple.' I blushed. I had already made six pages of notes.

As we moved away from fruit and on to the next item on the agenda – meringues – the curious case of the missing recipes was solved. Chef Nicolas explained: Le Cordon Bleu does not do recipes. That's not to say they don't believe in a 'correct' way of doing things; indeed, it would soon become clear to me that Le Cordon Bleu's teaching staff have very strong ideas about what is and is not correct. But the theory is: as soon as students are presented with a recipe, they tune out and stop listening. By giving just an ingredient list, and making us write up the recipes ourselves, they are ensuring that we pay attention, or fail. It also has the added benefit – and I'm with them on this – of ensuring that recipes are written in a way that the student understands, irrespective of native language, linguistic level, or base culinary knowledge.

All very commendable. But on day one, it just filled me with panic.

Each demonstration was to be paired with a practical; three-hour demo, three-hour practical. In the practical, we would be expected to reproduce exactly what had been shown to us in the demo, using the recipes we'd noted down. Often, achieving what we inept, inexperienced amateurs could be expected to manage over the course of three hours left the teaching chef with far too much time on his hands, so we'd be treated to an extra dish or two that we wouldn't have to replicate. But, basically, it was a case of monkey see, monkey do.

Demo over, we made our way to the teaching kitchen. The chef arrived, marching down the corridor, and past us huddling awkwardly together. This chef was new to us, different from the one who'd given the demo, and had been absent during our induction. Chef Olivier. He stood at the door, with arms crossed, unsmiling. He looked much stricter than Chef Nicolas, and I felt a wave of nerves ripple through me. 'Take a number, and go to your numbered station. Put your knife kits on the bench and do *not* open them,' he instructed. We did as we were told.

The kitchen itself is cool – nothing like the sweaty, fiery kitchens you see on television. In big restaurants and hotels, the pastry station tends to be a cooler place, literally and figuratively, than the cuisine kitchen. Often, it is an entirely separate room, away from the flame and flambés of the meat and veg sections. It's in the pastry chef's interest to keep things cool: cream splits if too warm, hard caramel melts, butter seeps out of pastry, and tempering chocolate becomes an absolute nightmare.

Our practical kitchen smelled of hot sugar and butter and eggs, as if the aroma of baking brioche was being piped into the room to get us in the mood. (I later learned that these kitchens hid a smaller kitchen behind them, where the real baking – for the Cordon Bleu café downstairs – took place.) A huge bread oven stood in the corner, braced with Heath Robinson scaffolding that enabled many loaves to be baked at once. Unlike the cuisine kitchens, where each student had their own oven, there were just two large ones here, bookending the kitchen. Around the edges of the room, there were eight sets of hobs, one between two; in the centre, there was just one enormous marble work bench. Bins of flour and sugar flanked the space. Sitting alongside the kitchen, through a constantly swinging door, was the potwash area, where we would dump our used pots and pans, and where they were washed by hand at a fiendish pace and high temperature before being returned to us.

Chef Olivier stood at the end of our bench, at the teaching station: 'OK, *now* you may remove your knives. And remember! They're sharp!' We slowly, painstakingly, unloaded our knife kits, carefully removing each sheath warily, the warnings from the demonstration ringing in our ears. (*A third of you will cut yourselves* had become *You have a one-in-three chance of losing a finger* in my head.) I looked wildly at the contents of my kit: I realized that despite three hours of rapt attention and thorough note-taking, I had absolutely no idea which knives I needed or, really, what I was doing here. With the subtlety of a brick, I did what students have done for millennia: I watched those around me, and copied them, selecting three knives and placing them on the silver tray in front of me.

I gathered a haphazard array of fruits from the enormous fridge: some grapes, an orange . . . redcurrants? Who cuts redcurrants? Who *eats* redcurrants?

It swiftly became apparent to me that my fellow students were not new to cutting fruit. They got to work like they were in a kung fu movie, chopping, skinning, dicing. I, on the other hand, started to feel like I'd never encountered a fruit before. What is a pear? Can you eat its skin? Are bananas real?

I gingerly sliced an apple into uneven flaps, and put it in my bowl. It looked like the fruit you get with a McDonald's Happy Meal. I glanced left and right. Those around me didn't seem scared of their knives at all. I wanted to scream at them, 'A third of you will lose a limb today!'

A sharp intake of breath came from somewhere to my right, audible amid the quiet concentration of sixteen people trying to cut fruit. I looked up and saw a pair of big, shocked eyes, and a wobbling mouth. 'All right, all right, come up and get a plaster,' Chef Olivier called.

Unnerved, I picked up a weighty chef's knife and topped and tailed an orange, then began cutting it into segments. It's fair to say I didn't manage the deftness the chef had demonstrated earlier. Approximately half my orange ended up as pulp, which I discreetly binned. Meanwhile, my peers were carving grapes into crowns. Did you know you can carve grapes into crowns? Did you know that this is something people *still* do in the Year of our Lord, 2016?

I tried to copy them. I zigzagged my paring knife clumsily around inside a grape, then pulled the two halves apart. I peered at it in the way you might peer at the innards of an ungutted fish. Actually, it wasn't that bad. It was a bit uneven: it looked more like a set of teeth on a wild dog than a crown. But it *was* kind of crown-shaped. I looked up, flushed with pride, only to see that now someone had carved a swan out of a fucking plum.

But at least I hadn't cut myself yet! Already, three of my classmates had had to take the walk of shame to the head of the kitchen, where Chef Olivier continued to stand, looking severe, to ask for blue plasters for various wounds. Some surreptitious tears had been shed.

But the worst was yet to come. Next, we had to cook sugar.

Cooking sugar changes the way it behaves. It's a very simple way of showing a bunch of over-eager pâtisserie students the importance of precision, and of controlling heat. These temperatures are *very* specific: at 110°C, sugar will form little strings that hold; at 116°C, soft balls can be formed. At 121°C, those soft balls become hard; and cooked further to 148°C you will hear a sharp crack as it cools. The names of these stages are deliciously uninventive: thread, soft ball, hard ball, crack.

There was an instant-read thermometer in our knife kits – one with a long, trailing wire to ensure that you needn't trail your fingers into whatever you're measuring the temperature of. But apparently, we weren't allowed to use it today. We were cooking sugar to exactly 116°C, 'soft ball stage', to make a syrup for our salad – but we were to do this in the traditional way. First, we numbed our hands in iced water, then we plunged them into boiling sugar. If we found ourselves able to remove a small piece of sugar and mould it into a pliable ball, we'd achieved the right temperature.

The theory here is that if you don't have a thermometer, or it breaks, or runs out of battery, or isn't calibrated correctly, you can still cook your sugar. A chef should be able to use their eyes and nose and ears and hands to identify when something – anything – is ready. Fine. But the thermometer was right there, and my hands were the soft, gentle hands of a lawyer. Standing in front of a pan of boiling sugar, I rejected the theory. Just carry two thermometers. Carry three. Put some spare batteries in the pockets of your chef's trousers.

But, I am an orders-follower. So I diligently plunged my fingers into the ice water as instructed, then into the syrup, and pulled out a blob of sugar, before plunging straight back into the ice. *I'm alive!* I thought. I squeezed the sugar ball to make sure it was still soft, as it should be, and the molten sugar burst out on to my supposedly numb fingers. 'See?' Chef Olivier said, circling the room. 'Not as bad as you thought, eh?' I winced as the pads of my fingers throbbed, and silently nodded at him.

Next up: meringues. I looked at my sprawling notes, and hoped that at least these wouldn't cause me physical harm. I'd done this dozens of times: I'd made roulades and pavlovas, and little Italian nubbly meringue cookies. But then, I'd also cut up an apple before, and that hadn't stood me in great stead. I cracked egg whites into a metal bowl, and immediately dropped yolk in there too. Nobody seemed to have noticed, so I surreptitiously tipped the spoiled eggs into my food waste bowl, and began again. This time, I used both my hands to crack the eggs, rather than attempting a weird and unnecessary one-handed nonchalance. I whisked the sugar in, bit by bit, and piped it out into simple rosettes, feeling grateful that at least here I wasn't expected to turn this product into crowns or swans.

At the end of the practical, our efforts were marked. Each practical is judged by the teaching chef on a scale from 1 to 5: 1 is extremely poor, 5 is no meaningful criticism; we were told not to expect to see 5s. Our marks would be added up to form part of our final grade; every practical counts.

Chef moved around the room, assessing the efforts: I tried not to look like I was eavesdropping, but I definitely was. Most were getting mediocre feedback: fine fine fine. The girl who'd made the plum swan was praised, and irritation – no, pure jealousy – bubbled up inside me. The student next to me had her efforts dismissed as 'disappointing', and I suppressed a melodramatic gasp. This was the first practical; clearly Chef Olivier wasn't going to be pulling any punches. I looked back at my plate: my fruit salad looked like the walking wounded. It was all present and correct, but pretty lacklustre. Even so, I was feeling OK: the meringues were glossy, and I had arranged my motley collection of fruit pieces neatly on the plate. I'd made a grape crown, for God's sake! I held my breath as the chef appraised my creations. 'This is fine,' he said in a tone that suggested it was extremely not-fine. 'But your knife cuts are unadventurous.' *Unadventurous.* Who wants their knife cuts to be adventurous? What would an adventurous knife cut even *look* like? And isn't that how you wind up cutting yourself? I was about to ask him what he meant, but he had already moved on to the next student. That was it. That was my feedback. I didn't need to see my mark to know that it wasn't going to be an impressive one.

I slung the fruit into my small plastic box. It sloshed in its syrup. I abandoned my plan to proudly photograph my first creation, because who wants a photo of an unadventurous fruit salad? I wasn't cross or sad, just underwhelmed. How was I ever going to prove myself if these were the parameters? And how was I going to learn anything worthwhile if we spent two and a half hours making a bloody fruit salad?

'Well,' Chef Olivier said once he'd finished marking. 'How do you think that went?' A few of the more confident students voiced enthusiasm, which was tempered by a combination of floor-staring and mumbles from the rest of us. 'You should be proud of yourselves,' he declared, at which the morale and chins of the group seemed to lift. 'You have accumulated more cuts than any of the other groups. That means I win the chefs' bet. You can go home now.'

*

Meringues were the only part of the practical that didn't fail me. I kept them in a washed-out butter box on the bench in my kitchen for over a month until I eventually realized how ridiculous I was being, and threw them away. Meringues alone may be beautiful, but they're not delicious. They just taste blandly sweet. But with soft whipped cream, and zipping-zinging fruit, they are transformed.

When we were little, there was one dish apart from her pineapple bread and butter pudding that my non-pudding-making mother *did* occasionally make: pavlova. We were barely allowed to watch it while it cooked, so keen was the fear of cracking. When it came out, little fingers weren't permitted to pry or poke. Then it was crowned with cream and accoutrements, and placed in the back porch – desperately tempting, and absolutely forbidden. I thought it was the most impossibly glamorous pudding.

We were never present for the grand unveiling. Pavlova was strictly a dinner party indulgence; we were pyjama'd and tucked in long before it emerged. But leftovers were always promised, and usually forthcoming (the one time they weren't, I didn't speak to my mother for three days).

Mum's pavlovas were either fruit-based (truly grown up), or filled with chocolate and marshmallows (a child's dream; how dare it be wasted on adults?). This one combines the two. Passionfruit and milk chocolate is a surprising but heavenly combination: the tart tang of the fruit alongside the creamy richness of the milk chocolate. The curd is a dream, and if you have any left over, you'll have to lock the fridge to stop others smearing it on anything in sight.

Passionfruit and milk chocolate pavlova

Makes: A dinner-plate-sized pavlova, enough for 6
Takes: 2 hours
Bakes: 1 hour 15 minutes

For the pavlova
1 teaspoon lemon juice
3 egg whites
250g caster sugar
1 teaspoon cornflour
1 tablespoon vinegar

For the passionfruit curd
5 passionfruit
2 large egg yolks
75g caster sugar
50g butter, soft

For the milk chocolate Chantilly
350g whipping cream
85g milk chocolate, chopped into small pieces

For decoration
1 passionfruit
50g milk chocolate, for shaving

1. First, make your pavlova. Preheat the oven to
   180°C fan/200°C/gas 6. Wipe the inside of your
   bowl with the lemon juice, using a piece of
   kitchen paper. Using a stand mixer or an electric

whisk, whisk the egg whites gently on a low speed until little bubbles appear, then whisk vigorously until they reach stiff peaks. You can use a normal whisk here too, but it requires strength of arm and spirit.

2. Add the sugar bit by bit, each time beating the mixture back to stiff glossiness before the next addition. Add the cornflour and vinegar, and briefly rewhip. Spoon into a piping bag, if using.

3. Draw a large circle on a piece of greaseproof paper (I draw round a dinner plate). Fix this to a baking tray with a couple of small blobs of meringue, which will stop it moving around. Spoon or pipe your meringue on to the paper inside the outline of the circle, then fill in the rest of the circle. Pipe or spoon blobs in a second layer along the outside of the meringue circle to create a raised edge.

4. Place the pavlova in the oven and immediately reduce the temperature to 150°C fan/170°C/gas 3. Bake for 1 hour and 15 minutes. Don't open the oven during this period. When the pavlova's had its time, turn the oven off, crack the door of the oven open, but leave the pavlova in there to completely cool.

5. To make the passionfruit curd, juice the passionfruit, sieve out and reserve the seeds, and place the juice, eggs and sugar in a small bowl

over a bain-marie. Break the eggs up with a whisk, and heat, stirring continuously with a small spatula until the mixture thickens. It should just hold itself without collapsing when pushed to the side of the bowl. If you have lumps, push it through a sieve. Beat in the softened butter and return the seeds to the curd. Set to one side to cool.

6. To make the milk chocolate Chantilly, heat the cream in a small pan until it is steaming but not quite boiling. Place the chocolate in a heatproof bowl. Pour the hot cream on top and leave for 2 minutes. Stir until they are combined. Allow to cool completely before whisking until the cream forms stiff-ish peaks.

7. Pile the chocolate cream on to the pavlova base. Spoon dollops of the curd on top. Just before serving, squeeze the final passionfruit into a small cup and distribute, seeds and all, all over the pudding. Finish by shaving over fat curls of milk chocolate.

9

Three weeks in, and I was slowly beginning to find my feet at Le Cordon Bleu. I had just about embraced shouting 'Backs!' And 'Sharp behind!' when carrying hot trays or knives in the kitchen, even if doing so made me feel like a total idiot. I could locate my lecture room on the second if not first try, and I knew to avoid, at all costs, the coffee in the café. I knew how to tie my neckerchief, and I had discovered that I could escape the chefs' wrath by swapping over the press-studs on my chef's jacket to cover up the mess I'd made in a morning practical before I returned in the afternoon. But there was still a portion of the school that was a total mystery to me: cuisine.

The cuisine and pâtisserie kitchens are located alongside each other; they share a potwash area, and occasional forays are necessary to locate equipment. But, when the need arises to venture into the cuisine kitchen – for a mandolin, or a chinois, or, perversely, for a rolling pin – it's like entering a different world. The cuisine kitchen is, to the pastry student, a caricature of a real working kitchen: billows of steam greet you, scented with lemongrass and holy basil, or searing meat alongside softly cooking onions. Unlike in pâtisserie, where it feels like you never stop racing from the flour bin to your hob, peering hurriedly, worriedly into the oven on your way, cuisine students rarely move away from their stations. Their feet remain still while their bodies reach and pivot towards what they need, slowly transforming their various ingredients to neat mise en place, each in its own metal container. They are a model of efficiency, and make you feel clumsy and slow just looking at them.

There's a reason pâtisserie chefs dismissively refer to cuisine chefs as butchers: the flash of sharp knives cutting into meat is everywhere. But that's deliberately facetious, and does them a disservice. The work is faster, hotter, more brutal than in the pâtisserie kitchen. As much as I would never have admitted it to a contemporary, the knife skills of cuisine students are far beyond those of their pâtisserie equals. I can't imagine the horror of the cuisine students, let alone their teaching chefs, if they saw pâtisserie students using the blades of those sharp, sharp knives to do all sorts of ridiculous blunting activities, crimes against blades: scraping them on workbenches to form chocolate curls, running them around metal cake tins to release the sponges within, heating them on blowtorches to shape chocolate, and plunging them into molten sugar to create sculptures, cutting straight down through pastry on to marble worktops. Despite being equipped with a steel in our knife kits, I shall confess: I did not at any point during my nine months at Le Cordon Bleu reach for it to sharpen my knives.

But I was unlikely to need my knives today, sharp or otherwise, because we were beginning boulangerie. Boulangerie was taught by Chef Dominique, a man for whom the word sardonic (or perhaps sardonique) was invented.

Chef Dominique was a very tall, very thin man with a thick accent, and this was his domain. While he sometimes supervised other parts of the pâtisserie course, and was clearly a skilled and competent pâtissier, his interest was bread, and he did little to disguise this. There might be a croissant in the place his heart should be.

Despite Chef Dominique's not-so-gentle disdain for clumsy, basic students, I entered the boulangerie portion of the basic term eagerly: I was good at bread. I'd made lots of it, from soda breads to sourdoughs, and it seemed a lot of the people in the class hadn't even turned their hand to it. After fruit salad, it was clear I was never going to match their fruit-carving skills, so it was nice to be about to do something where I was ahead. Since Sam had entered my life clutching a loaf of sourdough and offering up Welsh rarebit, I'd decided I wanted to get the hang of bread. Less in a romantic way, and more in an anything-you-can-do, I-can-do-better way. But whatever my motivation, the effect was the same: I baked a lot of bread. Most weekends, I would try a different style of bread or yeasted dough, from granary loaves and milk buns to English muffins and naan breads.

We were starting simply, with a loaf of soda bread. The demo filled me with confidence; I'd done all this before. The recipe was a standard one, and I nodded along, making briefer notes than normal. Maybe this was it, I suddenly thought. Maybe bread was my calling. I pictured myself with an attractive dusting of flour on my nose, laughing, as a host of doughs in proving baskets surrounded me. I'm not sure how, but in this daydream, my bread had made me famous and universally loved, and perhaps secured me a prime time telly slot.

As we headed into the practical, I picked my station out of a hat (not, sadly, the chef's hat, but a less literal basket that contained the sixteen station numbers, and dictated where you would spend the practical session) and pulled one that meant I would be cheek by jowl with the chef. Normally, this would have made me nervous, but I was sure Chef Dominique and I were going to be famous friends, bonding over our love of gluten, our bready acumen. Surely if anyone could break through his Gallic insouciance to form a lifelong mutual respect laced with humour, it would be me.

To make bread, you need air. Normally, that comes from the biological reaction between yeast and the naturally occurring sugars in flour, but in the case of soda bread, it is from a chemical reaction between an acid and an alkali, creating carbon dioxide, which in turn creates the rise in the bread. The school's recipe for soda bread uses a combination of bicarbonate of soda and cream of tartar to cause this reaction rather than making one of the components in the bread the acid (like the buttermilk used in my soda bread in Chapter 5).

I weighed out my ingredients, keeping an eye on Chef Dominique, ready to slide into some gluten-based bonding should the occasion arise. Everything mixed beautifully, I put my soda bread into the oven, and set my timer. This was it. Finally, I would make up for the unadventurous fruit salad. It wasn't Chef Olivier judging me this time, but perhaps my soda bread would be so perfect that Chef Dominique would feel compelled to mention it over lunch. 'I have this basic student. She is *quite* the star. Olivia something, I think.'

'C'est bon?' Chef Dominique asked me as I stood next to my station, waiting for the bread to have its time.

'C'est bon,' I told him. And I meant it.

I crouched down to peer through the glass. Nothing was rising. But that was OK. I hadn't left it long.

Twenty minutes later, I was standing for marking, as I'd stood so many times in the past three weeks. There was a leaden ball in my stomach to match the leaden ball I'd pulled out of the oven five minutes earlier.

I don't really know what went wrong. I have my suspicions, but they rely on blaming others rather than my own negligence. I remember asking pals to pass me the bicarb and the cream of tartar. I remember adding them both. And then I remember my bread dough, lone among the sixteen in the class, failing to rise, sitting in the oven solidifying into a dense puck. When it came out, it was a peculiar shade of grey. There was nowhere for it or me to hide, so it sat sadly on my station, a little slate-coloured thundercloud beside fifteen plump golden loaves. One by one, we were called up to the chef's station for marking. 'What happened here?' asked Chef Dominique, his mouth twitching in mirth. 'I don't know, chef. I think I used two lots of bicarb or tartar.' I sighed. 'It went wrong,' I conceded. 'You can say that again!' he roared. I'd made him laugh, but not really in the way I'd been hoping for. As I walked away from marking, I dropped the loaf into the bin, where it landed with a clunk.

*

I suddenly had a lot of thinking time at Le Cordon Bleu. Life at court had afforded me little free time, and I'd leaned into that after Mum's death. It suited me perfectly. I couldn't dwell because there simply wasn't the time. Now, for the first time since her death, my days weren't filled from beginning to end, and it began to feel like there was a klaxon wailing in my head whenever I wasn't actively busy. Normally, when an alarm goes off, we leave the room. We evacuate if that's what we're supposed to do, or just move away from it. But have you ever stayed in the room when a really loud, discordant alarm is going off? It's surreal: it makes you feel hysterical, and it seeps into your limbs, into your brain and stops you thinking straight.

Although inside my head was a mess, outwardly I had become very, very good at talking about grief, without ever actually talking about *my* grief. *No, my mother died. No, it's fine! Well, it's not fine, of course it's not fine, but you know what I mean.* All of this I had down pat. It puts people at ease, I told myself.

I constructed a blurb for my life story, for what had happened. It featured the key points, the salient facts, but left out the messy, confusing bits. If I didn't stop to inhale halfway through, I could get it out in thirty seconds – more quickly, sometimes, than it would take my conversation partner, who had innocently asked a stranger at a Christmas party how they'd become a pâtisserie chef, to swallow their canapé. I retold the story over and over, honed it, rubbed off the edges until it was smooth like a pebble you find on the beach, until I could hold it in my mouth like a mint imperial. It was easy. Easy, and false.

In any event, this story doesn't set people at ease. Not even close. What this story really does is: it allows me to think about things less and less. I don't have to engage my brain. It clamps down my thoughts about Mum, puts them in a box, so they cannot drift.

I had fought so hard not to allow myself space to think about Mum's death, so convinced, so terrified that the moment I engaged with the pain and sorrow, I would drown in my own pathetic self-pity. But in doing so, I just languished in grief even more. And now, of course, I had far more time to do so. I read memoir after memoir, immersing myself in accounts of others' grief: Joan Didion, C. S. Lewis, *Fun Home*, *Grief is the Thing with Feathers*, *H is for Hawk*. I read it all. I read theory and practitioners' guides for grief therapy. I read scholarly articles, and I listened to podcasts. My jaw was permanently clenched, my shoulders like concrete. One day, sitting on the Tube, reading what must have been my fortieth grief memoir of that year, I realized I had bitten through my cheek. The tang of blood filled my mouth.

Talking allows your mind to process what has happened to you. It's stating the obvious to say that denying trauma, refusing to talk about it, does little to relieve it, and in all likelihood, entrenches it. But suppressing it was exactly what I'd worked so hard to do, ploughed my energies into for years. I rated my own acting skills so highly that I was convinced I'd hidden how badly I was coping from Maddy and Dad, but I'm sure I hadn't. Sam had broached the question again and again of me returning to therapy, but I was resolute. And now I faced the twin problem of having transferred my energies somewhere new, and having headspace, so much headspace, whether I wanted it or not.

There's something intoxicating about death, like putting your tongue against a battery. It zipped through me. A thrill. I wanted to drink it in. I'd become so good at denying my own pain that I'd become voyeuristic for others' grief, hungry for it. I was attracted to public outpourings of grief, fascinated by them, and found myself watching hours of footage of the aftermath of Diana's death, consuming every documentary and book I could find on the Hillsborough disaster. These deaths were so extraordinary, so plainly tragic, that I could let my Grief Top Trumps hand drop. My calculations paused.

The deaths of women around my mother's age, in particular, were an obsession. Grieving for them felt safe. When I was very little – maybe three or four – my mother's sister, my Auntie Jan, lived in Muswell Hill, in north London. My memories of that time are few, although I do remember encountering my first samosa, sitting at her breakfast bench, holding it between my two small hands. Jan lived near the actress Linda Bellingham, who had played the mum in the Oxo adverts. So familiar was she to our TV screens that every time Mum saw her on the street or in the local shop, she'd greet her like an old friend, before realizing in horror as they parted ways that, oh God, she'd done it again. Mum used to tell the story over and over, laughing at herself. Two years after Mum, Linda Bellingham died, and I couldn't stop crying.

Much later, Victoria Wood's death in 2016 hit me just as

hard. She had been such a part of my childhood, our household's unanimous favourite comedian, that she felt like someone I could reach out and touch, her scripts on our bookshelf, her routines in our video drawer. Her death felt like a physical blow. I didn't consider the people Victoria Wood and Linda Bellingham left behind; when I thought about them, I was just feeling sorry for myself.

'My life is almost entirely about cheese,' the lecture began. The speaker was a man who introduced himself, wonderfully, as Tom the Cheeseman. You could tell that he had given this speech many, many times before, probably word for word. But there was something captivating about him, and the truth of the statement was clear from his energy. He was very well-spoken, very slim, wearing a striped shirt, suit jacket, and a bow tie, along with a long Cordon Bleu apron tied at the waist, and he was as English and enthused as Chef Dominique was French and acerbic. He clearly cared more passionately about cheese than I have ever cared about, well, anything. He might be a visiting lecturer, he told us, but he was the longest-serving lecturer at Le Cordon Bleu.

Studying pâtisserie also means studying wine and cheese. Three hours each term were allocated to the study of cheese, and three to wine. You weren't going to catch me complaining. It felt like I'd been training my whole life for these classes. And it does make sense: in Michelin-starred kitchens, the chef de pâtisserie is often in charge of the cheese. And wine is where most restaurants make their money – it has far higher mark-ups than food, sometimes 500 per cent or more. Any students who wanted to run their own kitchens needed to know their wine.

However delighted I was, several of my classmates seemed surprisingly unimpressed that they were being made to devote three hours to cheese. To be fair, the lectures ran from 6 to 9 p.m., and it was a dreary, cold November evening. But still. Wine! Cheese! My classmate James, a cheese-denier, was positively lugubrious at the prospect. I strategically positioned myself in the seat next to his, hoping to be a good home for the samples that didn't interest him.

'By the end of this lecture,' Tom the Cheeseman continued, 'you'll think, "I'm going to have to get a cow."' 'No I bloody won't,' whispered James, glumly. Tom had supplied Michelin-starred restaurants and hotels with some of the finest cheeses in the world. He probably hadn't won over any critics in this class with his first offering, though, which was a dried-out camel cheese. Fortunately, we were not obliged to eat it – just to smell it. It was rock-hard – I assumed the same lump had served Tom for quite a few of his many lectures – but as pungent as a damp sock left to fester in the washing machine. Fortunately, the actual tasting started on more familiar territory, with a piece of ricotta. Ricotta is the simplest of cheeses, made from the whey by-product of other cheese-making. It's mild and creamy. As we worked our way up through the cheeses, the rest of the lecture passed in a lactic blur: Cashel Blue, Caerphilly, Brie de Meaux, Little Wallop, Emmental, Parmesan, and about half a dozen others. And this was just first term! I left feeling dreamily content, and Googling the price of a good milking cow.

As for the wine – well, I wasn't going to turn my nose up at what was essentially a free drinks party. The reality was rather more sober, however. We spent two hours and forty-five minutes sitting in the wine-tasting room without having a drop, being told about terroir, regions, tannins and sweetness. At the end, we got one tiny tasting glass of red, and one of white. Never has there been such a damp squib.

If you join the army, their job is to break you down before building you back up. Sometimes, culinary school feels similar. The teaching staff are on you from the get-go: if you're not wearing your neckerchief to lectures, they want to know why not. If you don't have the correct kitchen shoes, you won't be allowed in the kitchens, no matter how much you beg. Attendance itself was strict. Lateness was not tolerated, with students being sent away from practicals if they weren't prompt, and being marked as absent if they didn't arrive at lectures on time. The chefs didn't sugarcoat their words; plates were untidy, stations messy, students slow. So far I'd managed not to piss them off, but I faltered for the first time when it was my turn to be the classroom assistant.

Each group has its own weekly rota of classroom assistants. The responsibilities are many and mostly menial. Assistants help the chef prepare and distribute ingredients; they note down fridge temperatures, turn ovens on.

At the end of the class, they oversee the cleaning of work stations, emptying of fridges, and putting produce away. My position near the end of the register meant that I'd escaped that duty so far, but now my time had come.

I turned up outside the kitchen appropriately early, clutching my knife kit and notes. I dithered outside the door, peering in at the windows, where the chef was clearly moving around busily. I couldn't bring myself to stick my head inside. I'd spent five years addressing judges, accusing furious witnesses of lying to the court, and placating frustrated defendants when they'd been sentenced to a decade in prison. But this, this was beyond me. If Chef needed me, I told myself, he'd come out and ask. I knew I was kidding myself. With a minute before the practical was due to start, Chef Nick emerged from the classroom. 'Where are today's assistants?' he asked. 'I'm one!' I offered up meekly, hoping that the absence of my partner would mean I would be found favourably. Unfortunately it just meant the spotlight was on me. 'Well, why didn't you come in? You can see me running round like my arse is on fire,' he fumed. I began offering up excuses, but he'd already turned his back on me and stormed back into the kitchen.

Le Cordon Bleu prides itself on being international, which is borne out by experience in my class alone, with students from Peru, Chicago, France, Edinburgh, Stockholm, and Singapore. Nonetheless, the institution is proudly and indelibly French. I might even go so far as to say that the syllabus was *excessively* French: jalousie, pithivier, entremet ... My schoolgirl French had not equipped me for this. On day one, we were all given a lengthy French vocabulary list to memorize, but it was often oblique or unhelpful. It took me weeks to work out what I was supposed to do when I was told to 'fraiser' pastry, for example (turns out it means push dough away from you by smooshing it across the worktop using the heel of your hand; there is no word for it in English). Ironically, given its name, crème anglaise is Le Cordon Bleu's signature preparation, and, while the course would call for many more complicated dishes, we would still be required to produce a perfect crème anglaise in our final, superior exam.

They take all manner of custard seriously at Le Cordon Bleu. Of our eight-week-long basic term, two whole weeks were solely devoted to it. As I sat in the lecture room, waiting for our first custard demo to start, I flicked through the pages for the coming days in my folder. The mind boggled at the number of different types: crème anglaise, crème pâtissière, crème diplomat, crème chibouste, crème caramel, crème brûlée, crème renversée. I'd only heard of maybe half of them, and I thought I was pretty custard-fluent. To be fair, most of my custard fluency came from eating, rather than making. The first time I made custard, it was from a packet, and I still considered it a major achievement. There's a very particular joy to the thick, canary yellow – custard yellow! – custard that comes in a packet. And it has a rather charming backstory, too. It was invented by Alfred Bird, a chemist, as a custard-dupe for his custard-loving but egg-allergic wife, Elizabeth. He also invented baking powder because Elizabeth was allergic to yeast, but wanted to be able to eat bread. We owe a lot to Elizabeth's intolerance, and Alfred's chemical romance.

Anyway, for bakers, what makes 'real' custard tricky is the eggs. Eggs are fragile beasts, prone to splitting mixtures, curdling, and going lumpy, ruining an otherwise perfectly smooth sauce. But they are also the thing that makes (non-packet) custard magical – you apply gentle heat, stir, and suddenly, a thin liquid coalesces into a beautiful, thick, satisfying sauce. The risked alternative is as upsetting as the desired outcome is marvellous: in a heartbeat, the luscious primrose liquid can split into sugary scrambled eggs.

As well as learning how to make custard, our practical covered what to do with it. This was our first introduction to plated desserts, which are just as they sound: something arranged nicely on a plate, as opposed to something bought from a café. In many ways, the plated dessert is the cradle of modern French cooking.

The idea of individual plated dishes is relatively new, and completely changed the way restaurants and kitchens worked. Restaurants as we know them didn't really exist before the middle of the nineteenth century, and we have Auguste Escoffier to thank for the development. Prior to the French Revolution, dining took place in private residencies and inns, and the top chefs worked in people's homes, cooking exclusively for them and their guests. But following the Revolution, and the fall of the aristocracy, chefs were out of jobs. They began to open establishments that were open to members of the public. Escoffier, who was born in 1846, changed the style of restaurant service from à la française, where dishes were brought to the table together, to service à la russe (Russian-style), which divided the eating experience into ordered courses; he also introduced à la carte menus, allowing the diner to choose from a selection, as opposed to set menus. This style of dining called for a kitchen rejig. Escoffier brought the brigade system to professional kitchens – the system of organization that you'll find in virtually every restaurant and hotel kitchen today. It revolutionized working kitchens. Previously, dinners had unfolded over several hours for aristocratic men and ladies of leisure. Dishes were brought out when they were ready and shared among diners. Now, with the rise of the middle class, restaurants had to cater for those who had both money to burn and jobs to return to. And this meant that service had to be faster, more efficient; different dishes for the same table had to be able to hit the pass at the same time. The brigade system was based on military structure, with each member of the kitchen team having clearly defined roles and duties.

There were many more roles in Escoffier's kitchen system than we have today (you're unlikely now to find a chef making ice creams – a glacier – or inedible showpieces – a décorateur – who isn't also a general pâtisserie chef in even the largest modern kitchen), but the broad brigade system stands strong. And he is credited with inventing the crème brûlée (and, more famously, the pêche Melba) so it seems appropriate that for our first crack at plated, restaurant desserts, we'd be tackling crème brûlée.

All of which is to say that this felt a little more

professional than fruit salads and tiny piped meringues. I felt perversely excited, and a little bit nervous, at the prospect of plating pudding. What we'd made so far in classes had been slightly more refined, more technical, than the kind of thing I'd been doing at home, but essentially still stuff I'd already had a go at. Plating puddings was restauranty. It felt serious, like something that was training us up for real kitchen work. This was *proper* cooking.

Our practical was being led by Chef Nick – to be distinguished from Chef Nicolas, and known imaginatively as 'English Nick'. Although we'd been shown a variety of different plating options in the demo, we were plating up as we wished. This meant that for the first time, we were to be graded on our creativity, our aesthetic, rather than simply our ability to follow instructions. Having said that, each plate needed to have two types of coulis, piped chocolate, a sugar cage and a tuile on it. So we weren't making any Ferran Adrià creations today.

As we busied ourselves making coulis and tuiles, turning out crème caramels and brûléeing crèmes, ready to take pride of place on our carefully polished plates, one by one, each of us was called up to Chef Nick's hob, where he was stirring a big pot of molten sugar and wielding a ladle. Spun sugar was the order of the day, and we were making sugar cages to perch jauntily over our crème brûlées.

Chef Nick demonstrated for each of us individually, deftly flicking the sugar over a knife steel, and dragging even, delicate strands of sugar off the edge before snipping them neatly with scissors. Then he showed us how to swish it across the underside of a greased ladle, criss-crossing, and circling round to give the whole thing structure. He loosened it gently and off came a perfect sugar cage. 'Now it's your turn,' he said. Chef Nick held the ladle, and handed me the spoon with which to flick. My first attempt was gloopy and blobby, big splodges of hardening sugar, rather than the fine lines of the cage he'd shown. 'That's OK. Try again,' he said, with more patience than I would be able to muster in reversed circumstances. The second time, he guided my wobbly sugar-holding hand, while still gripping the ladle. It was like an unsexy, burn-risk-heavy version of that scene in *Ghost* as he guided my hand back and forth. This attempt was much better; the lines weren't terribly even, but they were at least lines rather than a sugar Rorschach test.

I assembled my two plates: on one, a sugar cage perched on top of my crème brûlée; on the other, with the crème caramel in the middle, I piped double helixes in chocolate on the plate, and then drip-dropped alternating raspberry and mango coulis into the gaps. On top, I balanced my slowly wilting tuile. Tuiles are little biscuits, used as decoration on plates: they can be piped or spread across templates before baking, so they can take interesting forms; taste- and texture-wise, they're similar to fortune cookies. When first out of the oven, they are soft, and can be moulded around different shaped objects before they set hard. My tuile had started life as a kite (why had I tried to make it look like a kite?), but had gently flopped into something more like a drunken swan. Chef Nick moved round the room, marking work, offering feedback. Eventually, he reached me. 'It was meant to be a kite!' I began, defensively, my voice an octave higher than normal, anticipating criticism. But it didn't come. 'Tuiles, nice. Piping, nice. Sugar cage, nice. Caramelization on the crème brûlée a bit uneven. Colour on the crème caramel, nice. Good set on the custard.' He liked my work. I compared it to the notes I'd made for myself: tuiles poor, piping poor, more work needed. I looked again at my plate, trying to see it through his eyes. My crème caramels had slipped out of their moulds neatly and sat perkily on the plate, the contrast between the buttermilk-coloured custard and the mahogany caramel just right. Sure, the plating was pretty old school, maybe a bit outdated, but then so is crème caramel. And sugar cages. And piping chocolate on to the plate. I could only work with what I'd been given. The dish looked like something you might actually find in a restaurant, albeit a provincial French restaurant from the 1970s with ideas above its station. I felt a little pinprick of pride.

After each practical session, we took home – if we wished – whatever we'd prepared. Juggling a box full of sloshing fruit salad or a rapidly melting buttercream-covered cake on a packed Central Line at rush hour was about as much fun as it sounds, and my spoils rarely arrived home in the condition they had left the school kitchens. Commuters would look resentfully at the cake box you were carrying, in the same way that I roll my eyes at those who refuse to remove backpacks or take up a seat on a crowded carriage with their shopping. I didn't have high hopes that the custards would survive, but nothing ventured, nothing gained, and anyway I wasn't terribly interested in the crème caramel, I'd just brought it home for Sam. I love crème brûlée, but crème caramel I've always wrinkled my nose at. When we went on holiday to France as children, Mum and Dad would buy the version from the supermarkets in yoghurt pots, uniformly sweet; slimy, rubbery, and scented by the plastic container. But, as I unloaded mine into the fridge, a combination of greed and curiosity won out. I dug my spoon into it. This was unlike anything I'd had before: wibbly and so softly set, complex and smoky from the caramel, mellow and fragrant within. If this was the kind of thing we were going to be making, I could get used to it.

*

Unlike crème brulée, crème caramel seems to have rather fallen out of fashion in England. Raymond Blanc describes it as 'the French national dessert', and it continues to enjoy rightful popularity in its home country, a regular feature on menus prix fixes. As well as the traditional vanilla speckling the mixture, I've infused the custard with saffron threads, which turns the pudding a bright gold, and complements the smoky nature of the caramel. It's warm and earthy, almost metallic, and elevates the custard into something truly special.

Using half milk and half cream, along with an extra egg yolk, makes the pudding irresistibly rich, and cooking it at a low temperature ensures that it will have the maximum possible wobble, while still holding itself. Make sure to refrigerate the pudding overnight, as this will give the caramel time to dissolve and meld with the pudding.

Saffron crème caramel

Makes: Enough for 4
Takes: 20 minutes, plus overnight chilling
Bakes: 40 minutes

For the custard
½ a vanilla pod
200ml whole milk
200ml double cream
A small pinch of saffron threads
2 eggs
2 egg yolks
65g caster sugar

For the caramel
175g sugar
2 tablespoons warm water

1. Heat the oven to 120°C fan/140°C/gas 1. Slice the vanilla pod in half, and scrape out the seeds. Place the milk, cream, vanilla seeds, vanilla pod and saffron threads in a medium-sized pan and bring to steaming, then set to one side to infuse.

2. While the cream infuses, make the caramel. Put the sugar into a pan, place over a medium heat, and allow it to cook: do not stir, but once the sugar has melted, you can swirl the pan to keep

the mixture even. Cook until the syrup turns a deep gold, almost mahogany. Carefully pour the water into the caramel – it will spit! Swirl, and briefly return to the heat if necessary to dissolve any lumps. Once smooth, immediately (but carefully!) pour the caramel into four 150ml ramekins. Leave the caramel to set hard (this won't take long).

3. Put the ramekins into a roasting tray, and boil a full kettle. Whisk the whole eggs and yolks with the sugar in a bowl. Sieve the warm milk directly on to the egg and sugar, and whisk gently until combined. Divide the custard between the ramekins.

4. Transfer the roasting tin to the oven, and carefully pour water from the kettle into the tin until it comes halfway up the sides of the ramekins. Bake for 45 minutes, until the custard is just set. Immediately remove the ramekins from the tray and, once cool to the touch, transfer to the fridge overnight.

5. To serve the crème caramels, run a dinner knife round the inside of each ramekin, place a plate over the top, and confidently, quickly invert. Serve straight away.

10

There are a few hills on which the syllabus of Le Cordon Bleu is willing to die, and one of them is doing things by hand. It's similar to the sugar thermometer theory. By carrying out each individual process by hand, they believe, students will come to recognize their subtleties – the point when cream is just about to overwhip; the precise colour of properly creamed butter. The theory gets old quickly. Every station in every kitchen – not just those specifically set up for pastry – boasts an industry-standard KitchenAid that we are prohibited from using during the whole of basic term except in very exceptional circumstances and with express permission. Creams will be whipped by hand, butter creamed by hand, meringues beaten by hand. And, as we would discover today, cakes would be made by hand.

In *Miss Leslie's New Cookery Book* (1857), Miss Leslie, an American cookbook star of the Victorian era (long before a housewife, or anyone, could call upon a Kitchen-Aid), noted that, 'To stir butter and sugar is the hardest part of cake making. Have this done by a manservant.' How I longed for a manservant.

So far, we'd made a pound cake and a handful of madeleines, which was fine as far as it went, but nobody came to pâtisserie school to make a lemon sponge. Today we were making genoise à la confiture de framboise, which sounded significantly fancier. Or at least it did until I put my brain into gear and worked out I was making raspberry jam cake.

It was a Friday afternoon in late November, and once I'd survived this demo and practical, I was jumping on a train with Sam and heading up to visit my sister in Lincolnshire, where she now lived. We were going to meet her new puppy, Freya, and take her to the beach. We were going to get up late, and nap on the sofa together, and then go out for dinner. I was ready for a relaxing weekend after seven weeks of Le Cordon Bleu, and was excited that Maddy was the first person other than Sam who would see what I'd been making at college. I imagined turning up at her door with an exquisite ivory cake, with intricate piped decoration and acting nonchalant. *Yes*, I thought, *this is pleasing.*

This is, in many ways, a simple cake: vanilla sponge, soaked with eau-de-vie, filled with raspberry jam, and covered all over with smooth, linen-coloured buttercream. The buttercream is then overpiped with chocolate to make it stand out from the pale background. A very *fancy* raspberry jam cake, then.

Chef Nick was taking this demo, and I watched him closely, determined not to make any mistakes this time. We started with the raspberry jam, which seemed simple to make, and we were even going to be allowed to use our thermometers, rather than relying on how many layers of skin the jam lifted when touched, or another equally sadistic Cordon Bleu-approved technique. I was a bit nervous about the sponge, I admit. Unlike the lemon cake, this one used a genoise, a whisked sponge, which relied only on mechanical aeration, rather than chemical, i.e. elbow grease as a raising agent, rather than baking powder or similar. In order to get the greatest rise on the sponge, you heat the eggs and sugar over a bain-marie before whisking, but you mustn't heat them too high or they'll lose their rise. The process is knackering, performing the same repetitive movement with the enormous balloon whisk, and made me extremely aware that I had absolutely no upper body strength. Of course – Chef Nick told us, after spending twenty minutes showing us how to whisk the eggs properly – ordinarily you wouldn't even need to heat the eggs, as the horsepower of a mechanical mixer will do all the hard work for you. I rolled my eyes, probably less subtly than I thought.

The cake is then covered in French buttercream, which is made from a pâte à bombe and, ironically, required us to use the KitchenAid. Essentially, you add boiling sugar syrup to egg yolks, and whip the bejeezus out of them, before adding butter until it is light and fluffy. It's a bonkers buttercream, richer than Rockefeller, and less subtle than Liberace in its sweetness, but a technically classic one. Chef Nick had shown off several different options in the demo for our piped decoration, piping beautiful swirls with ease; the traditional design the school teaches is two back-to-back swans. I decided to go for a relatively simple fleur-de-lis design, because if Le Cordon Bleu had taught me anything, it was that you can't go wrong if you go classic. I spent the half-hour between the demonstration and the practical class nursing a coffee in the college café, idly doodling my design in the margins of my recipe notebook.

When you mask a cake with icing, there's one easy way to do it: you use a tall, straight-edged dough scraper (a D-shaped piece of plastic) that you grip at the rounded edge, and hold at a very acute angle to the sponge, and spin the cake – quite fast – on a turntable. You end up with a beautiful, marble-smooth, evenly coated cake. Of course, any element of that here would make things far too easy. Dough scrapers (which, I should point out, we had in our knife kits) were out, and narrow palette knives were in. Each swipe of the palette knife left a tidal wave of off-white buttercream that I would then have to smooth down, only for another one to appear when I tried. It felt like a greasy game of whack-a-mole. Turntables were also prohibited at Le Cordon Bleu, which was beginning to feel increasingly Amish in its resistance to all forms of technology. When I was done, it looked like an amateur plastering job done by, well, a lawyer. No matter, I could redeem myself with my decoration.

I consulted my notebook, took a breath, and tried to follow my pattern. I piped the melted chocolate over the top, to make the pattern stand out. I added the raspberries required by the rubric. I set down my piping bag and appraised the cake. Oh. No. My cake decoration didn't look like a fleur-de-lis. I don't know how I'd done it, but I'd piped a pretty anatomically accurate, if slightly lopsided, uterus, complete with raspberry ovaries.

I packed up the cake and began my journey to Lincolnshire. I placed it on the bag rack above our seats on the train, peering up on tiptoe every time the train stopped to see if it looked as ridiculous as I remembered it. 'Stop looking at it, for God's sake!' Sam chided me. Madeleine picked us up from the station car park, and I handed over the cake box to her. I couldn't help myself: 'It looks like a womb! I'm sorry: I've brought you a womb cake.' 'Oh. That's OK. I'm sure it'll be lovely,' Maddy replied, clearly wondering if seven weeks of culinary school had sent me actually mad.

Two weeks after the womb debacle, everything was different. The tone of both demonstrations and practicals had suddenly changed: we had hit our first exam dish. The practical exam required us to reproduce one of three dishes over a period of three hours: for basic term, these would be coffee éclairs, a charlotte de cassis (a blackcurrant sponge cake), and today's lemon meringue tart. Three of our demos and practicals during the term would focus on these dishes, giving us a chance to get the hang of them, and hopefully iron out our mistakes before the exam itself. As we sat nervously clutching handouts on lemon meringue tart, Chef Graeme talked us through the configuration. I felt inexplicably reassured by Chef Graeme's presence in the kitchen or the classroom: a natural teacher, he exuded a calmness that was at odds with the clichéd mania of a professional kitchen. I was glad we had him for this dish.

The Cordon Bleu exam system is bonkers. It is broken up into a variety of exams and assessments: 45 per cent of our mark was progressive assessment (my unadventurous fruit cutting had already put paid to doing well in that), 45 per cent was the final practical exam, leaving a puny 10 per cent for the theory exam. I suddenly grasped that I had thrown myself headlong into a course that prized manual dexterity, technique, careful organization and execution over my preferred reliance on blagging, good luck and memory. (I was a *lawyer*, for God's sake.) We wouldn't find out our exam dish until we walked into the actual exam, and it was a lottery as to which we would get. It would need to be reproduced from memory, without notes. Before we even started the practical exam, we would have to complete the 'bon d'économat'. The bon d'économat was a copy of the recipe with gaps for us to fill in – ingredients, exact quantities, methods, techniques – as well as requiring diagrams of the cross-sections and top-down views of the exam dish.

Each recipe encompassed at least three individual components. For the tarte au citron, Chef Graeme demonstrated every step. First, a shortcrust pastry shell (pâte brisée, not too sweet, to account for all the sugar elsewhere in the dish), blind-baked until golden brown. Next, a lemon curd filling, and finally an Italian meringue topping. The Italian meringue was piped using a V-shaped St Honoré piping nozzle, to create a seamless herringbone pattern. The meringue was blowtorched, then topped with some julienned candied lemon zest. The finished product was a thing of beauty.

I wasn't too worried about the pastry or the lemon curd (I'd already worked out that if the curd went lumpy, I could surreptitiously push it through a sieve and all would be well). But the Italian meringue was a different story. I was not so subtly terrified of Italian meringue. It had, along with the very similar pâte à bombe, been, to date, the only exception to the school's no-KitchenAid rule, as it's extremely tricky to make without one. Here's what you do: you make a sugar syrup which you cook to 118°C (soft ball texture). Just before it arrives at this temperature (and know that it will sit at 114°C forever and then *swoop* up those final four degrees in a heartbeat), you whisk egg whites to stiff peaks in the KitchenAid. Then, with the mixer still going, you pour your boiling sugar syrup into the egg whites. You hope that your pouring angle is correct, such that the boiling syrup doesn't hit the whisk as it goes in. If it does, the molten syrup will shoot out like Spiderman's web. If you manage to avoid this pitfall, the whisk will fold the syrup through the whites without incident. Soon, the mixture will balloon like marshmallow, becoming fluffy and glossy. Italian meringue is something you need to practise over and over, preferably wearing heat-resistant clothing. Unfortunately, I had instead dodged making it every time it had come up, fobbing that element off on whoever I was partnered with while I concentrated on, for example, cutting fruit unadventurously. But with exam dishes, that didn't fly: we had to make every element ourselves just as we would in the exam. This time, there was nowhere to hide.

So I began my attempt at recreating the tart. I made, rolled out and baked my pastry, then turned my attention to the lemon curd, cooking it slowly and carefully, praying that I wouldn't end up with lumps. I didn't even need to sieve it; I was on fire! I meticulously shaved my lemon, then sliced it into little strips. I cooked it once, twice, three times in hot water, and then once more in a syrup solution. And then, I could put it off no longer: I had to make Italian meringue. I weighed out my egg whites, I cooked the sugar syrup, feeling thankful for my thermometer. The syrup reached 115°C, and I began whisking my egg whites at top whack. They foamed and thickened. One hand on my pan of syrup, and one on my KitchenAid controls, I adjusted my thermometer and saw that we were at Defcon 5. I slowed my mixer down, lifted my small pan of boiling sugar, tipped it, closed my eyes, and waited for the fall-out. I didn't hear the cartoon *pings* of sugar splattering across the room, or, more realistically, the yelps of my fellow classmates. Nor did I feel the telltale sting or smell of burning flesh. I opened one eye. Oh! The mixture had stayed in the bowl. Well, that was a good start. Perhaps I wasn't as bad at this as I thought. I scraped the whole thing into a piping bag, wondering how the teaching chefs managed to do so without getting it all over their hands and the outside of the piping bag and the bench and, somehow, my knife kit, which was tucked away two shelves beneath me. I began piping.

Funny. The consistency didn't seem quite right to me, more like shaving foam than meringue, but as established, I wasn't very well acquainted with Italian meringue, so perhaps this was how it was meant to be: sort of . . . mousse-y and spume-y. I continued, because what else was I meant to do? I looked around the room: Georgie was to my left, and James to my right. Their piping was crisp and defined, zigzagging neatly across the tart. Daisy, across the bench from me, had already finished her tart, and was carefully placing little strips of lemon zest on to a patterned meringue so perfect it looked woven. Meanwhile, mine was coming out sort of wibbly, like it was out of focus.

I suddenly felt very, very alone. OK, no need to panic, I thought. Nothing that a bit of blowtorching couldn't fix. I waved the blowtorch across the meringue. Oops, bit fierce. The tips of the piping caught and blackened. I eased off a little. The meringue continued to darken, and sort of sizzle. It was blotchy. It didn't look like any of the other meringues I could see in the room. Chef Graeme cleared his throat behind me; I jumped and almost turned the blowtorch on him by accident. 'Chef!' I squawked. 'Bonsoir!' It was 11 a.m. And Chef Graeme was English. And I didn't speak French.

'I don't think your sugar syrup was hot enough,' he said gently. 'Was your thermometer touching the bottom of the pan instead of the syrup? It won't have cooked completely.' Fuck. I thought back to what they said in our first ever demo: equipment is fallible. Or vulnerable to inept user error. And I was one inept user. This would never have happened if I was squeezing molten sugar between blistered fingertips. I must have looked sufficiently upset that he felt that he had to comfort me. 'Don't worry! It's just one element. And it's just a pie!' He was right, it was just a pie. I felt a little bolstered. And then he leaned over and peered more closely. 'Your candied lemon cutting is inconsistent.' Chastened, I resolved to buy a ruler for my knife kit.

Luckily, one week later, I had the opportunity to

redeem myself. We were making a gateau St Honoré: a sort-of-cake, sort-of-tart consisting of a shortcrust base topped with little choux pastry balls dunked in hard caramel. The tart is then filled with crème pâtissière loosened with whipped cream (then called crème légère), piped in the same herringbone pattern that I'd so spectacularly failed to reproduce on my lemon meringue pie. Of course, everything went well until I began piping. Each squeeze from the piping bag was coming out like little custard slugs, soft and undefined: how had this gone wrong *again*? I figured it was my technique, so I kept going, just more carefully this time, trying to be more precise. Georgie peered over my shoulder. 'Why's your piping doing that?' 'I don't know,' I replied. 'I don't get it. I'm doing it the way we were shown!' 'Weird.' I stole a glance at Georgie's tart, and swallowed a sigh: perfect, perky criss-cross peaks of cream.

Chef Jérôme was taking this practical, and he moved round the room slowly examining each tart in turn. I was fairly sure Chef Jérôme already thought I was an idiot, thanks to a combination of general culinary clumsiness on my part, and a lot of raised eyebrow on his, so I wasn't delighted he was about to be introduced to my custard slugs. Finally, he reached me. 'What happened to your piping?' he asked, bewildered. 'I, um, I don't think my nozzle works,' I replied. 'Your *nozzle* doesn't *work*?' he repeated, giving, frankly, too much weight to each word. 'I know!' I replied. 'Chef, I'm as surprised as you are.' 'Give me your piping bag,' he said. Chef Jérôme took the piping bag from my hands, looked me in the eye, and turned it 180 degrees, so that the deep 'V' of the nozzle was facing skywards, rather than downwards towards my tart. He paused, dramatically, and piped out perfect herringbone. I had been holding the bag upside down the whole time. He handed the piping bag back to me, suppressing a smirk.

I should have been writing up my notes to make the following practical easier for me, but instead I was drinking bad coffee and staring into space. My teaching group sat in various states of slump in the Cordon Bleu café, killing time in the gap between our demo and practical. I was thinking about why I was here, why I was doing this whole thing. I hadn't exactly enjoyed much success so far, and doubts were beginning to creep in. My peers were a disparate bunch, who'd come to Le Cordon Bleu for all sorts of reasons.

A couple of the very young members of the class were attending in place of university. They were living in halls, and enjoying house parties and a pace of social life that made me simultaneously nostalgic for my early twenties and the smell of stale beer and cigarettes, and very glad that they were over. Alex had never baked before, but thought she might enjoy it. At the other end of the spectrum was Margaret studying just the basic term, so she could provide her husband and young children with more elaborate home baking.

James had been a wedding cake maker before he came to Le Cordon Bleu, but wanted to expand his repertoire into pâtisserie more generally. Daisy had spent time in professional kitchens and was here to hone her talents, and maybe strike out on her own with a food business. Georgie was twenty, and hungry for the sharp end of restaurant work; she didn't balk at the prospect of unsociable hours and chefs on power trips. She made me feel extremely guilty about my wasted degree and postgraduate qualifications, as she rushed off to pull twelve-hour restaurant shifts after class, and I sloped home to eat a sandwich and read a book.

But the person whose motives were most unclear was – surprise! – myself. Why was I doing this? Why would someone want to spend nine months of their life and a not inconsiderable amount of money on a full-time pâtisserie course? If my goal was professional acumen, it could be gained in a working kitchen where they would actually pay you for the privilege, never mind charge you thousands of pounds. But I'd known from the get-go that I didn't want to work in a professional kitchen: my bad joints would never stand it, and the thought of being shouted at by some blotchy nineteen-year-old on a power trip was, strangely, not appealing.

Why had I jacked in a perfectly good career, a career that people longed to do, and for which I'd spent my entire life preparing? OK, perhaps I was never going to be a justice of the Supreme Court, but I was competent. I was doing perfectly well, thank you very much, until I swept everything off my desk in a fit of pique.

If I could work out why I had felt this compulsion to study glorified cake baking, perhaps I would find some profound insight into myself. Or at least a justification for this abrupt change of plan.

Perhaps I was just feeling a little disillusioned by cakes. The genoise à la confiture de framboise, and a lemon loaf cake that was so boring I haven't even told you about it, had left me frustrated. As nice as Madeleine had been about the raspberry jam/womb cake, it looked like a child had made it. The lemon loaf cake looked like . . . a lemon loaf cake. I'd been trying not to think about it, but deep down I worried I was wasting my time on a quarter-life crisis version of finishing school.

Black Forest gâteau would be our third cake in as many practicals and I wasn't looking forward to it. I sat down heavily in the demo room and sighed as I opened up my notebook and turned to today's ingredient list. Black Forest gâteau was exactly the problem, I fumed: stupid old-fashioned cakes straight from the 1970s, which no one wants to eat any more. I'd got myself on to a course where I was going to spend nine months learning to make complicated, underwhelming cakes that belonged in a museum.

The first thing to turn my head was the cherries. Chef Nick brought them out in a tall, slim Kilner jar. I'd never seen cherries like this before: griottes, dark red morellos, bathed in an equally garnet-coloured liqueur. The smell when the jar was opened was intoxicating. The second thing was the chocolate. This would be the first time we'd used chocolate – although we weren't tempering it ourselves (we couldn't be trusted yet with such technicalities) – and even in my funk I couldn't suppress a small thrill at the prospect. We were each given a sheet of acetate, and melted chocolate was ladled on to it by the chef for us to spread to the very edges and then cut into small squares. The sheets had been printed with coloured cocoa butter which would transfer on to the chocolate as it set; mine was covered in shimmering gold swirls. As the chocolate was setting, we made the individual components for the cake: trays of chocolate sponge from which we stamped circles, and then painted them with the boozy juice from the cherries. Next we layered the soaked sponge with the cherries themselves and big dollops of whipped cream. The top of the cake was a festival of yet more cream. We dragged plastic combs across it to create waves, and then piped swirls of softly whipped cream on to the cake, with a single griotte on each of the swirls. I peeled my chocolate from its acetate, and placed my chocolate tiles around the edge, impossibly shiny, and glinting with gold. They were beautiful, kind of glamorous. Looking at the finished, assembled cake, my tiles were wonky and my rosettes were imperfect. And the whole thing looked kitsch as hell. But to my surprise, I loved it. I couldn't stop looking at it. It was cool and retro and fancy, in its own ridiculous way. I wanted to show it off, and say hey! I made this! Me! Maybe this old-fashioned course wasn't so bad after all.

A peculiarity of the pâtisserie course, along with its predilection for doing things by hand, was that we did not taste our dishes. Nor did the chefs. The recipes are so precise that even the salt is weighed to the gram. This wasn't like the cuisine kitchen, where the exact level of seasoning, or the composition of a sauce is dependent on the make-up of the meat, or the temperature at which you've cooked it, or the quality or concentration of your stock. Here, there was simply no need for the input of your tastes. The recipes did the work for you. And the chefs could tell at a glance – by the colour and texture of your sponge, the way your custard sat – whether you'd added the right amount of salt, or aerated your cream properly.

Let me be honest: it wasn't just my palate that was offended here. In truth, it was my greed. When we rushed at the end of each demonstration to try the chef's creations before we headed off to practical, it was less for the educational benefits and more that we were a bunch of overgrown kids who a) were hungry, thanks to weirdly timetabled back-to-back classes, and b) had signed up for a pâtisserie course. Our priority was custard, and chocolate, and crisp, buttery pastry. Custard first, the love of technique and learning second. OK, perhaps I am speaking more for myself than for my fellow students.

From the gluttony perspective, this problem was mostly surmountable: the majority of the dishes we made, we took home, packaged in flimsy, cardboard cake boxes. It was, to my mind, one of the principal advantages of studying pâtisserie over cuisine. Rather than scooping tepid chicken chasseur, or some perfectly turned turnips, into a Tupperware, we got to take a proud, beautiful (in theory) cake home to our loved ones. My freezer was full of brioche; my worktop always bore some kind of pastry. But plated desserts were a different kettle of fish. So to speak. You can't easily take a hot pudding home – or at least, it's likely to be fairly unappetizing at the other end of the journey. We still got away with tasting things in class all the time, and most of the teaching chefs turned a blind eye. But for one of the chefs, this was a particular bugbear. 'Why are you tasting? You're not in a cuisine kitchen!' Chef Dominique yelled across the room at Alex, as he spied her sneakily dipping a spoon into her perfect soufflé after it had been marked. I jumped, vicariously guilty.

In the 1954 film *Sabrina*, starring Audrey Hepburn, Sabrina is in love with a man above her station. In an effort to remove herself from the situation, she decides to attend an unnamed Parisian cookery school, clearly supposed to be Le Cordon Bleu. There she learns 'the correct way' to boil water (no, no idea) and how to crack an egg without 'tormenting' it (she can't get this right either). But Sabrina can't keep her head in the game: she forgets to turn on the oven when asked to make a soufflé, so it never rises. Her teaching chef – a little more forgiving than mine – blames her love life: '*A woman happy in love, she burns the soufflé. A woman unhappy in love, she forgets to turn on the oven.*'

It's not clear what kind of love life a woman needs to make a perfect, towering, shivering soufflé, but whatever it is, I had it in today's practical. 'Look at my soufflé!' I wanted to cry to all those around me, but they were busy with their own puddings, and I felt now probably wasn't the time. I saw in that moment a tiny glimmer of what I could be as a cook. And I suddenly remembered how it made me feel when I made something well: elated, proud . . . happy. That was how I felt right now. I felt happy.

Only a monster could have resisted the quivering

pistachio soufflés we had made, with a perfect square of dark chocolate melting on top, and a neat pile of boozy morello cherries. I took my soufflés to the sink in the corner of the kitchen, ready to wash them up, pretending to myself as well as Chef Dominique that I wasn't trying to find a quiet spot to eat them. I set them down on the bench and, as my left hand reached to turn the tap, my right took the spoon. Before I could draw a breath I had eaten the first soufflé. All of it. It was hot – so hot! – and fragrant and lighter than air. I thought I'd eaten decent soufflés before; I thought I'd made them – I thought I'd made and served decent *pistachio* soufflés. But this was different: this was intense and complicated, sweet and almost floral, and tasted as green as it looked. Without even checking over my shoulder for an angry, looming chef, I inhaled the second one.

*

For a long time, I didn't really understand the appeal of soufflés. I now know that was because I'd never had a good one. After that first sink-side misdemeanour at Le Cordon Bleu, I began seeking them out, from curiosity more than anything: a perfect fuchsia pink raspberry one on a cold night in Rye, tall and proud; a pale, pale green Bramley apple one in Kent on my thirtieth birthday. And here's what I discovered: soufflés are magical. As a pastry chef, it's often frustrating how short the shelf life is of products; how quickly they go from perfect to pathetic, soggy or stale or deflated. Soufflés embrace that truth, leaning in to their ephemerality. For them, a short shelf life is a feature, rather than a bug. The life of a soufflé is fleeting, and all the more glorious for it. Perhaps there was a slightly twee life lesson to be learnt from this: about embracing momentary pleasure without embarrassment; that life itself is fleeting. I don't know, maybe it was just about taking a moment for the joy of a perfect pudding.

This one is a riff on the American classic PB&J, fancied up a bit. PB&J is a classic pairing for a reason: the sharp sweetness of the raspberry sits perfectly with the rich, slightly salty peanut butter. And so it is in this pudding: the raspberry purée breathes life into the soufflé; using crunchy peanut butter gives little bits of interest against the soft soufflé and softer custard. And it is beautiful: on the outside pale bubblegum, and on the inside, vivid flamingo.

Like so many things, soufflés are easier to tackle once they are demystified. Fortunately, Harold McGee has done just that. In his book *On Food and Cooking: The Science and Lore of the Kitchen*, McGee explains that a soufflé will, in fact, almost always rise. All you need to do is to get air into the mix, which will expand when it's heated. But actually, much of the rise on a soufflé doesn't even come from the air you've whisked into it, but simply from the evaporating water in the mix forcing its way into air bubbles, and pushing the soufflé up. This is to say, the oven will do most of the rising work for you; any extra aeration you manage to whisk in is a bonus. So, don't be intimidated.

Raspberry soufflés with peanut butter crème anglaise

Makes: 4 soufflés
Takes: 20 minutes
Bakes: 12 minutes

For the soufflés
Butter, for greasing
4 large egg whites
100g caster sugar
Icing sugar, for dusting

For the custard
1 vanilla pod
250ml double cream
250ml milk
4 egg yolks
100g caster sugar
4 tablespoons crunchy peanut butter

For the raspberry purée
300g raspberries
2 tablespoons caster sugar
1 tablespoon lemon juice
20g cornflour

1. Melt the butter, and brush half of it into each of four 150ml ramekins, using upward strokes. Chill the ramekins for 10 minutes, just until the butter has set, then add a second layer of brushed,

melted butter. Place a tablespoon of caster sugar in each ramekin and jiggle and twist and shake them, covering the inside with the sugar, and knocking out any excess. Return to the refrigerator.

2. Meanwhile, make the peanut butter custard. Slice the vanilla pod in two, and scrape out the seeds with the back of the knife. Place the cream and milk in a saucepan with the vanilla seeds and pod over a medium heat. Whisk the egg yolks with the sugar in a bowl. When the milk and cream are steaming, fish out the vanilla pod and discard, then pour a third of the hot milk on to the eggs and sugar in the bowl, whisking gently. Return the whole mixture to the pan and cook gently, stirring until the mixture thickens. Dip a spoon into the custard and run your finger down the back of it: if the line remains clean, and the mixture doesn't rush to fill the gap, it is ready. Stir in the peanut butter and leave to cool, with clingfilm touching the custard to stop a skin forming.

3. Blitz the raspberries with the sugar in a small food processor until they form a purée, then pass through a sieve, to remove the seeds. Stir in the lemon juice. Bring the purée to a rapid boil in a small pan, until it has reduced by one third. Stir a little cold water into the cornflour to make a paste, and add this to the purée; then cook,

stirring throughout, until the purée boils vigorously. Set to one side.

4. Preheat the oven to 180°C fan/200°C/gas 6, and place a baking sheet in the oven to heat up.

5. In a clean bowl, whisk the egg whites until they form stiff peaks: when you lift your whisk the mixture should hold itself up, without flopping over. Add the remaining 50g of caster sugar one tablespoon at a time, whisking the mixture until stiff and glossy before adding the next spoonful.

6. Take a tablespoon of the egg whites and stir it into the raspberry mixture until completely mixed in. Using a large metal spoon, gently fold in the rest of the egg whites. Do this by turning the spoon on its side and cutting it through the middle of the mixture, then fold the bottom of the mixture up and over the top. Give the bowl a quarter turn and repeat, until the mixture is a homogenous colour – avoid overmixing!

7. Divide the mixture between the four chilled ramekins. Using a palette knife, smooth off the top of each soufflé. Take a finger and run it just inside the rim of each ramekin, to create a little moat.

8. Bake for 10–12 minutes, until the soufflés have risen and burnished; dust with icing sugar. Stir

the peanut butter custard thoroughly before serving, to distribute the crunchy bits. Serve in little jugs alongside the soufflés, and encourage your guests to break a hole in the centre of their soufflé and pour the custard inside.

From the moment we'd decided to throw an engagement party, I'd been single-minded. Parties meant party food, and party food meant my chance to impress. I started off simply with chipolatas and cookies, but as the guest list grew, so did my culinary plans. I would make macarons, dozens of them, in a variety of pastel colours; truffles filled with boozy ganaches; Parmesan and black pepper shortbreads; hoisin pork belly; tiny pies filled with oxtail; tiny pies filled with mushrooms . . . It went on and on.

On the morning of the party, as our families descended on our house from various parts of the north, and Sam served them tea and cuddled our brand-new niece, I was busy erecting a kransekake, a Norwegian wedding cake, made up of a tower of almond dough rings, white icing zipping along them.

There had been murmurs from certain quarters of the family that perhaps I was making a slight rod for my own back, that *maybe* people were coming to see me, and would be quite happy with a glass of fizz and a shop-bought sausage roll. But I was having none of it. I decided that, if I wasn't going to cater my own wedding, this was the next best thing.

It was chaos. We live in a little two-up, two-down in

east London, and had invited a stupid number of people on the basis that Christmas party season would cut down the numbers. It didn't. People kept turning up – twenty, forty, eighty – sardining themselves into a space that could comfortably occupy perhaps fifteen. No one could move except Maddy's dog and Sam's five-year-old nephew, Sebastian, who ran between people's legs as though they were weaving through a forest.

I was stuck in the kitchen; I hadn't seen Sam since the party began, which was quite a feat given that we only had two-and-a-half rooms to play with. Trays of food were passed like parcels from person to person. All I could do was fill them with sausage rolls and biscuits and pies as they came to me, then send them on their way. I started to think I might have taken on a little too much. It is a cliché of weddings that you don't really get any time to relax, to enjoy. Well, at least this was a good rehearsal.

No one could hear the doorbell. We only knew some-one else had arrived when the dog erupted into frantic barks, as she did over and over.

'Could everyone step back?' I shouted for what felt like the hundredth time, as though I were a police officer controlling a crowd. A little semicircle of clear space formed around me. I opened the oven and whipped my sixth tray of sausages out, narrowly missing the backs of three people's legs, muttering slightly passive-aggressive apologies.

The doorbell rang again. I glanced at the oven clock: 10 p.m. It was too late for any more guests, surely. But it kept ringing. I got cross, wondering why Sam wasn't answering; why I was having to do everything for this party. I shouldered my way through the masses and to the front door.

'Hi,' Sam said when I opened it. 'I took some bottles out, and . . .'

'This is the first time I've seen you all night,' I said. 'I'm really sorry I got all obsessive about the food.'

Sam put his arms round me, and I thought he was going to gently chastise me for biting off more than I could chew. We stood by the bins, arms wrapped around each other in the freezing cold, as noise from the party burbled through the open door. 'You're doing great, Liv,' he said. 'We're doing great.'

'You will not get your cake back when we are finished with it because it will be murdered, like a frog in a dis-section glass,' Chef Nicolas told us ominously. In yet another lecture about our exams, Chef Nicolas was tell-ing us in his own unique way that when it came to the practical, we wouldn't be seeing our dish once we had handed it over to the supervising chef. But what really put the fear of God into me was this: no re-dos. If you made a mistake with one of the elements, you couldn't bin it and start again. If you added salt to your pastry instead of sugar, you had to serve a salted pastry. If your lemon curd was too thin, you couldn't take a breath and have another crack. If your custard was lumpy, you used lumpy custard; if your sheet of cake was so crispy it shat-tered into crumbs, deal with it; if you dropped your pastry on the way back from the oven, tough luck. No throwing away, no re-runs, no second chances. Cautionary tales were told of students who, in the heat of the moment, had forgotten this rule, ditched their products, and then received zero marks for the element they'd binned.

All any of us could talk about was which dish we might be required to make in the actual exam. By now we had tried our hands at the other two exam dishes: coffee éclairs and charlotte aux cassis. The coffee éclairs were made up of a choux pastry base, filled with a coffee-flavoured crème pâtissière, topped with coffee-flavoured fondant, and then a piped chocolate design, basically poshed up versions of the ones you get in the supermarket. The charlotte aux cassis was a vanilla genoise sponge, cut into long strips, spread with a blackcurrant mousse and then layered so that the outside effect was sponge and jam pinstripe. The cake was topped with more blackcurrant mousse, and on top of that, a blackcurrant glaze. It tasted, overwhelmingly, of Ribena.

The charlotte had gone pretty well for me in the practical: Chef Julie – head of pâtisserie, the only woman on the teaching staff, and my ultimate culinary role model, unflappable, and carrying her incredible skill lightly – had been positive about it. I reckoned with a little practice, I could nail it.

Daisy, Alex and I sat in the café in between practicals. 'As long as we don't get éclairs, I don't care,' Daisy declared staunchly. The problem with éclairs was that the riskiest bit was the choux pastry itself. Unlike most of our recipes, there wasn't a definitive quantity of egg to add, but rather, a range, which was dependent on the humidity, the flour, the eggs themselves, and how fast you cooked out the water. Too little and the choux would be stiff and wouldn't expand properly in the oven. Too much and the mixture would be so loose you couldn't even pipe it. It is both a precise and an imprecise art, in this the most structured and categorical of culinary arts. The closest you get to a 'rule' is that when you shake the mixture from your spatula, it should form a deep V. That is not enough of a rule for my liking. If you overbake your shortcrust for the lemon meringue tart, or under-bake your sponge for the charlotte de cassis, it will affect your marks, of course, but it won't stop you having a good old crack at the whole shebang, and making sure you have something to present at the end. If your choux fails – as it did for a host of us in our first éclair practical – you have nothing to pipe your coffee-flavoured crème pâtissière into, nothing to glaze with fondant, nothing to pipe chocolate work on to. You are trying to build a house on sinking foundations, and you are, to all intents and purposes, fucked. 'Anything but éclairs,' we all muttered in dark agreement.

At home, all I did was practise. I made pastry cases before breakfast; Sam got very sick of putting lemon curd on his morning toast; I julienned lemon after lemon, candying the zest until the house smelt like Christmas. I resigned myself to giving the Italian meringue a miss – without a stand mixer, I didn't fancy my chances. Le Cordon Bleu had all sorts of cheap and cheerful hacks for practising techniques cheaply at home: instant mashed potato piped is the same consistency as buttercream, shaving foam apes whipped cream, and toothpaste could be used as a sub for royal icing. One Tuesday morning, I had a crack at the charlotte aux cassis, attempting to bake enough genoise on my undulating, rusting, lipped baking trays, rolling it up with slightly gritty strawberry mousse I'd made from fruit I'd found in the freezer aisle. But, of course, it was the éclairs that gave me the most heartache.

I made tray upon tray of choux sausages, trying to perfect that nonchalant flick that the teaching chefs demonstrated. I ordered fondant from the internet and practised heating it to the right texture. I spent hours practising my chocolate decoration with tiny baking-paper piping bags of chocolate and threw away hundreds of imperfect choux shells. Each new batch coming out of the oven ballooned in a different way to its predecessor, like the limbs of gargoyles. The chefs made it look effortless – in fact, my main takeaway from the demo had been the fun of Chef Nicolas making non-syllabus-required choux swans, and then making them kiss – but I couldn't even pipe twelve of them without covering myself in raw choux. Why was this so hard?

I was one of the lucky ones. I lived in a small terraced house in east London, which had a functional if not spacious kitchen. My oven ran hot, my fridge ran warm, but at least I had space and time to practise. James, who was clearly the most talented of my little friendship group, was staying in rented student accommodation with nothing more than a hotplate and a mini-fridge. Cordon

Bleu students are not allowed to use the kitchens outside of their practicals; there are simply too many other classes going on. So basically he had to wing it.

I was also genning up on my theory. I filled whole notebooks writing and rewriting recipes and ratios, praying that they would stick. I wandered around the house reciting ingredient quantities for crème pâtissière or methods for puff pastry.

Now that the novelty of being at culinary school was beginning to wear off, I could take in more of the detail of how the place worked. I'd started to become bothered by the amount of waste that went on during classes. Admittedly, I now lived with a man who was vigilant to the point of obsession about food waste. (Sam would use a tub of butter weeks after I'd given up on it, and once made us eat a whole pot of totally burnt vegetable soup instead of just ordering pizza because he couldn't bear the thought of throwing it away.)

But still, Le Cordon Bleu's food waste was ridiculous. Every time we made meringues, hundreds of egg yolks went into the bin; when we made custards, the same happened with the whites. Yards of sponge were trimmed off the edges of cakes every day. Pistachios were thrown away like it was nothing. Do you know how expensive pistachios are? And these were the Chanel of pistachios: emerald green, skinned, smooth, toasted, unlike anything I've ever found in the shops. And we threw them on to our cakes with wild abandon, sweeping away any that didn't stick. I didn't tell Sam.

Standing outside the classroom one day, the class before us had overrun; it was a group of superior students, each packing up their own intricate-looking cake. One by one, they finished their chats, and left. We watched as the penultimate student finished up, and packed away his knife kit, picked up his cake and, pausing, just before he opened the door, calmly chucked the whole thing in the bin. A cake that must have taken six hours to make. Gone. In one fell swoop. Literally. I was so shocked I couldn't speak.

I did try to make small amends in my own cooking, though. After scraping the seeds from a vanilla pod, I'd rinse it and dry it, then take it home surreptitiously in my knife kit to make vanilla sugar. (Sometimes, I'd forget about it, and my fragrant knife kit would spit out the leathery black husks when I was trying to find a piping nozzle or a teaspoon.) I took home offcuts of any pastry we didn't use, baking them into cinnamon palmiers or shortbread biscuits. I'd probably taken it too far the day I brought home an enormous Tupperware of banana mousse. Sam and I ate and ate without making any appreciable dent. A week later, I finally brought myself to throw it away.

Our little house was perennially overwhelmed with baked goods. At any given moment, our freezer contained at least five types of bread, and two full-sized cakes. There were tins and Tupperwares of slowly staling biscuits on every available surface. And since many of my fellow-students lived in tiny student digs, and knew no one in London, they gave me their cakes to distribute, too.

I became a cake-centric Robin Hood, foisting millefeuille and pastries on friends and family; on our neighbours, and on Sam's colleagues. Once, I gave a box of pastel pink and green macarons to a homeless man on High Holborn, and felt like an idiot when I panicked at the last minute and asked him, 'You're not allergic to nuts, are you?' The experience made me feel like a total dick. I had spent the previous several hours making the most frivolous of cakes while this man shivered on the street.

Shortly before exams, Dad came to stay at our house for a couple of days. He brought with him several large cardboard boxes. Dad had met someone – Gill – and fallen in love. She was clearly good for him: tempering his slight tendency towards the manic, stopping him from taking himself too seriously, and most importantly, she found his jokes genuinely funny. It was obvious to anyone how much happiness they'd brought into each other's lives.

He was moving out of mine and Maddy's childhood home, the only home I'd ever known, and the place where my mum had died. During the packing process he had unearthed things that we'd overlooked when we'd cleared out Mum's things. And here they all were. The morning after he arrived, I started sorting through them, piling the contents on our dining room table. Most of it was easy enough. My childhood books went straight into the loft; thirteen years of school reports, textbooks and certificates went straight into the bin. The Swarovski crystal animals I'd collected when I was little went on eBay, where they failed to raise the fortune I was anticipating.

Some of the stuff I didn't even recognize. Do you keep jewellery your dead mother never wore? Why would you? Does it tell you something about them, about their tastes? Well, maybe, I guess. But then why did she never wear it? But, whatever, I'd see if a charity shop would take it.

There were photos I'd never seen. Hundreds of them. Photos of Mum with me when I was very little, petering out as she and I got older and she began to avoid the camera. I'd always known how camera-shy she was, how much she hated having her photo taken, how, when pressed, she would sigh, remove her glasses, and pose reluctantly. I'd assumed this had always been the case. But here she was in a swimming costume on holiday, chasing after me; looking relaxed in the garden with both sets of grandparents, in Dublin with all her friends (a surprise fortieth birthday trip), hosting children's parties and cooking Christmas dinner. She was so glamorous and so beautiful and looked so happy. This wasn't how I remembered her. I felt unmoored.

Then I found the prescription sunglasses. Seven pairs. At least a decade and a half's worth of summer holidays, of car journeys, of sitting in that same garden. Dad had brought them all with him. I stared at them, speechless. Mum had worn glasses since she was little, but I barely needed reading glasses. I had no use for seven pairs of very 90s-ish sunglasses, in a prescription that wasn't right for my eyes. Why would he lumber me with them? 'Why did you bring these, Dad?' I asked him, barely able to keep the disbelief out of my voice. 'I didn't want to throw them away without your say-so,' he replied simply.

The sunglasses sat on our dining table for two weeks before Sam lost his patience. 'Liv. When are you going to sort these things out? They've been here for ever.'

I shouted at Sam. Screamed, I think. I stormed upstairs, and threw myself on to the bed, like a grounded teenager, which was pretty much how I felt. Wronged. Seething with injustice. It was all so fucking unfair. I was furious. With Dad for bringing them. With Mum for keeping them. With Sam for existing, and having the temerity to question me. Sam, bewildered, came upstairs and tried to console me, as I lay face down on the bed, sobbing. Once the very immediate shock of the death had been over, I cried so rarely. Those whole-body racking sobs, guttural and animal-like, the only real tears that come close to expressing the pain and externalizing the grief? Those I didn't indulge in. And yet here I was, racked by sobs. Wrecked. 'It's because they're mine now,' I said, between sobs. 'It's because they're mine to throw away. Because she's dead.'

Exam week finally came. First up was theory. The corridor outside the exam room was brimming with anxious-looking students. I tried to calm myself down: I felt surprisingly jittery, bearing in mind that it was worth such a small proportion of our overall score, and was, let's not forget, multiple choice. Next to me, someone was manically and loudly reciting the different sugar stages. I clenched my jaw. This was, in my book, Very Bad Exam Etiquette. But before I had the chance to launch into a treatise on why this was the case, the doors to the exam room opened and we filed in.

I answered questions about how gluten forms in bread; about the biological make-up of an egg, and the three different types of raising agents. I guessed at the minimum percentage of fat in 'dry' butter (the traditional French butter used for puff pastry – it has a higher fat percentage than the stuff we buy in the shops), and what a 'boucher' was. I identified photographs of rambutans and cardamom pods. An hour later, I shuffled out, to a chorus of people quizzing each other, and second-guessing themselves. 'Did you know the definition of a gelato?' 'What the hell is a Napoleon?' 'I can't believe I forgot to revise milk!'

But the real challenge was always going to be the practical exam, which came a couple of days later. We queued outside the kitchen, just as we had for our eighteen basic practicals, all leading up to this moment. My nerves jangled. *It's just cake*, I told myself. *It's just cake, it's just cake. Or éclairs. Oh God, let it not be éclairs.* My group's conversation was stuck in the same groove as it had been for the last two weeks: what would the exam dish be? One of the kitchen porters walked past us rolling a trollied set of stacked trays, which Chef Graham began disseminating around the room, one per station. We peered through the window. There was a grater on each of our prep trays! The only exam recipe that required a grater was the lemon meringue tart, the easiest dish of all. Everyone visibly relaxed.

The door opened and we were ushered in, taking our stations in alphabetical order. Sheets of paper were in front of us, face down. We turned them over, and the air left the room as we all gasped in unison. We'd been had. Fondant. Coffee. Chocolate. We were making bloody éclairs.

Chef Graham laughed as Alex, one of my classmates, pointed out the grater on our prep trays, barely suppressing her tone of betrayal. 'Sorry, guys, every tray for every exam gets a complete set of utensils. No clues there!' I filled out the bon d'économat feverishly, nervous energy coursing through me, making me itch to get going.

For the first forty minutes of the practical, I felt singular focus. I diligently sorted my station, prepped my trays. I melted butter into water, beat in flour, then slowly, incrementally, added the eggs, checking after every drop for the crucial V shape that the mixture should form around my spatula. Meanwhile, fifteen other students watched fifteen other spatulas around me. I pulled mine up through the mixture and then flicked it hard down into the bowl: a V of batter hung from it. Bingo.

I started piping. Piping was not my strong point, I knew that. Often, in pâtisserie kitchens, éclairs will be piped with a star-shaped nozzle, the striations helping the éclairs to rise more evenly as they bake. Naturally, we were forbidden to use star-shaped nozzles today. I examined the twelve bulbous slugs before me, each with an end like a drunk's nose. What a stupid rule.

My gaze drifted to the girl at the station opposite mine, Marie. It was Marie whose cut fruit had been dismissed as 'disappointing' in our very first practical. She, like the rest of us, was about to pipe her éclairs. But her mixture was running out of her piping bag. I watched her try over and over again to pipe, the liquid batter dribbling out on to her tray, pooling in sad puddles. Her forbearance was extraordinary. By this point, I too would've been a sorry little puddle, crouched on the floor, weeping. But she persisted, loading her tray into the oven with barely a sigh.

My coffee crème pâtissière went without a hitch. For this task, I was facing the wall, and I was glad not to have to see how everyone else – especially Marie – was doing. It was just me and my custard. I knew where I was with custard. Good old custard.

After twenty-five minutes, I pulled my tray of choux buns out of the oven. They were wonky – very wonky – but they'd risen. It was going to be OK. Things were looking less rosy for Marie, who was staring down a dozen éclairs so flat they were practically 2D. I filled my éclairs, then turned to my least favourite part of the process. Fondant glaze icing is a pain in the arse. It needs to be soaked, drained and melted, before slowly adding water to get it to the right consistency. But too much heat and it loses its sheen, too much water and it's impossible to handle. There's a real knack to it, as there is with most things in pâtisserie, and it was another I was yet to acquire. I didn't know quite what I was looking for in either consistency or temperature, so I relied on a combination of luck and a lot of hard staring that I hoped would reveal the fondant's secrets, as though it were tea leaves in the bottom of a teacup. Once again, Marie caught my eye. Her fondant was like water. I quickly understood what had happened: she'd heated her block of fondant along with all the water, instead of adding just a little syrup incrementally. Her fondant was, essentially, sweet water. At this point, I would have turned around, walked out of the door, probably the school, and never looked back. But Marie was made of sterner stuff. She began glazing her flat pastry with the sugary water, before piping chocolate on top. I felt physically sick at her predicament.

Twenty minutes later, after a flurry of glazing and piping, I stood back to admire my work. My pastry was skew-whiff. My fondant was on the matte side of shiny. My decoration was, at best, squiggly. I left feeling neither despondent nor buoyant, but with the sharp understanding that it could have been significantly worse.

At the conclusion of each term, after exams are over, there is one additional demo and practical for students to complete. These demos and practicals are supposed to be – comparatively, at least – fun. This last topic of the term was going to be our first attempt at tempering chocolate.

I thought, perhaps, chocolate was going to be My Thing. This wasn't so much based on experience as a process of elimination. It hadn't been choux pastry, it wasn't looking hopeful that it would be bread, and as I'd never really turned my hand to chocolate before, I could only assume I'd have a natural bent for it.

Our first crack at chocolate would be fairly straightforward: we would make boozy ganache centres, and then dunk them in tempered chocolate. We made the

ganache and put it into the fridge to force it to crystal-
lize; when it had set, we took small spoonfuls and rolled
them between gloved palms to form little orbs. Except
that last part didn't work for me. You know the phrase
'cold hands, warm heart'? Well, I have very warm hands.
Make of that what you will. Not sweaty, you understand.
Just warm. Consistently so. Which is extremely useful
on bitingly cold country walks, or if I'm trying to, I don't
know, melt ice cubes between them. It is less useful in
the context of chocolate. Instead of becoming perfect
spheres, the ganache flattened into soft, sad discs against
my palms. Again and again I squished and pressed, my
latex gloves covered in smeared, melted chocolate. Eventually, I admitted defeat, quietly passed my softened
ganache to James, and let him take over. I decided I'd
stick to chocolate puddings for now.

Chocolate making felt like a bit of a stop gap while we
waited for our exam results, and our minds had collectively been elsewhere as we tempered for the first time.
We got our results about a week after the exam, in person. I'd received a lot of exam results in my time, but I'd
always enjoyed the privilege of doing so by reading them
from a sheet of paper. This time, I had to receive them
individually in person from a teaching chef. There's
nothing like human contact to ramp up the nerves. We
queued outside the classroom where I'd learnt about
milk and eggs, nuts and seeds, where I'd filled in worksheet after worksheet identifying pictures of fruits.
Students came and went, none betraying their success or
otherwise. No tears, no whoops, just a lot of poker faces.

Finally, it was my turn. 'Congratulations!' said Chef Nicolas, happily getting straight to the point. 'You passed!' My wonky choux hadn't let me down; my coffee crème pat was found to be smooth and well-flavoured, and I'd known enough about butter percentages to see me through to the next stage. I'd survived basic term.

Last Christmas, I'd languished in London waiting for my trial to end, while Sam went north. This year I was going up north to spend Christmas with his family. This would be the first time I'd spent the Christmas period anywhere other than at home with my family, and I was nervous. It's surprisingly discombobulating giving yourself up to the rhythms of someone else's festive traditions. Board games featured heavily at Sam's, which, despite my Scrooge-ish protests, at least meant that my mind was occupied for much of the time. We went on bracing walks through fields and along hills, far away from the crush of London. Still relatively newly engaged, I ran the relative gauntlet, meeting the entirety of Sam's extended family in one day, fielding questions on venues and dresses, flowers and cake. This time next year, we would be married.

Christmas is such a personal thing. Your idea of Christmas non-negotiables probably bears no relation to mine. For me, Christmas must include going through the *Radio Times* with a highlighter, and squirrelling away my preferred Quality Street (the pink-wrapped fudges), and turning the Christmas lunch leftovers into toasties in a Breville sandwich-maker.

For Sam's family, it was photocopies of the same cryptic crossword for everyone, so we could all solve them together (even though his dad solved 95 per cent of them). It was fruit cake (of course it was), served with cheese, as northern tradition dictates. It was an evening Baileys, and a lot of bread sauce. Sam loves bread sauce beyond all reason. His family own a specific bread sauce pot, used only for that purpose – a small lidded tureen with a face, which apparently is supposed to resemble an animate loaf of bread; I had assumed it was a gargoyle. I have different feelings. (Jennie, Maurice, if you are reading this: please look away now.) I don't get bread sauce: a sauce that is infused with various strong flavours – cloves, onion, nutmeg – but remains resolutely bland. Its texture is inexplicable; thick, lumpy, and unappetizing, like having porridge as a condiment for your meal.

So imagine my horror when, on Christmas morning, I was entrusted to make the bread sauce. I couldn't remember the last time I'd eaten bread sauce, and I'd certainly never tried to make it. Culinary school didn't help – bread sauce doesn't have a lot in common with a sponge or a meringue. For the first time, I wished I'd plumped for cuisine. But I devoted the same amount of care to that little pan of soggy bread as I had to any simmering custard, and a greater quantity of nerves. I decanted it into the strange little gargoyle bowl, and waited for the verdict. Would it make the grade? Would this put the kibosh on our forthcoming nuptials? How stupid would they think I was if I couldn't even nail a bread sauce after three months studying cookery?

When we sat down for lunch, I put some on my plate as a show of confidence, but ignored it, obviously, because bread sauce is horrid. 'Good bread sauce!' Sam said in an encouraging if slightly performative way. Sam's mum and brother murmured assent. This wasn't enough for me: Sam's dad is the ultimate bread sauce arbiter. A pause. 'It's good!' I exhaled for the first time since I'd arrived in Cheshire.

By Boxing Day, I was back up in Tyneside, for a standing appointment in our village pub with a small group of friends. Several hours and too many pints in, a man I vaguely recognized was chatting to one of my friends. He turned to me: 'I know you! We used to go to Sunday school together!' he said. 'You're Ruth Potts's daughter!' I looked at him levelly, or as levelly as I could after the amount of lager I'd drunk. 'I used to be,' I told him bluntly. 'She died.' He looked shocked. He began backtracking, apologizing. God knows why, I was the one who'd just been unforgivably rude to him. But I didn't care, I was too busy revelling in the viciousness. When she'd first died, my bluntness was just that, an inability to articulate it any other way. But this? This was just me baring my teeth, snarling, lashing out. Grief had made me cruel. The next morning I was overcome with shame. Why would I do that? What did I think I was going to achieve? It felt like it might dilute or franchise my own pain. Of course, it never did. It only served to make it more immediate. Saying it so baldly, to someone who after all this time still didn't know, was like hearing it for the first time again. But I didn't care. I didn't know how to care.

The anger was still there, it turned out, as raw as ever. I'd become so used to living with it that I didn't see it for what it was; it was simply part of my makeup now. When I say I didn't know how to care, I mean it: I didn't have it in my emotional skill-set. Cautiously, I had, on occasion, been trying to work out how I actually felt about Mum's death. But it hadn't gone well. When I drilled down beyond my superficial coping, all I found was sheer panic. I slammed the door on that horror show as fast as I could.

*

I long ago shelved my aspirations to be a chocolate intuit, and am, instead, quite happy to confine my chocolate to puddings. And chocolate fondants are the king of chocolate puddings. I don't make chocolate fondants like Le Cordon Bleu do. Their fondants are beautiful, and 'correctly' (read: classically) made. Mixture is placed into the moulds and then baked for a precise period of time, until the outside is set and the inside is molten, spilling out when cut into. But, in unsurprising news, domestic ovens aren't as reliable as big professional baking ovens. We've all seen sad pucks of chocolate cake served up on *Masterchef,* while the contestant swears the dish has never gone wrong for them before.

This, on the other hand, is a foolproof method for that sweet spot of perfectly formed chocolate pudding and oozing, gooey centre, no matter how your oven functions. Yes, it's a cheat. No, I'm never going back.

Here's what I do: I freeze teaspoons of whatever I want the centre of the fondant to be, and drop it into the rest of the batter just before baking. You can do this with teaspoons of the fondant mixture itself if you want to keep it simple, but I prefer to bring in something different, for a little colour and flavour contrast: it's great with Nutella, or peanut butter, or salted caramel, but my favourite is to use caramelized biscuit spread. I particularly love the contrast between the dark, bittersweet sponge, and the unabashedly sweet, caramelly centre. These little puddings can be made in advance and refrigerated for up to 2 days before being baked. Just take the filling from the freezer and submerge it in the mixture moments before cooking, and add 5 minutes to the oven time.

Generally, I loathe foods being called 'sexy'. It's weird. Food isn't sexy. It can be delicious or comforting or exhilarating or disappointing or even unnerving. But not sexy. But the thing is, these puddings kind of are. They're rich and sweet and oozy, and they're absolutely perfect for a romantic dinner. You can multiply the recipe for as many portions as you wish, and it will work well, but to my mind, it was made for two.

Speculoos melting chocolate fondant

Makes: 2 fondants
Takes: 25 minutes, plus freezing
Bakes: 15 minutes

2 teaspoons Lotus Biscoff spread
6og butter, plus extra for greasing
Cocoa powder, for dusting
6og dark chocolate, chopped
6og caster sugar
1 egg
1 egg yolk
2 tablespoons self-raising flour

1. Scoop the Biscoff on to a small baking tray and place in the freezer for at least an hour. Butter two dariole moulds or individual pudding moulds, and place them in the fridge for 10 minutes. Butter the moulds again and pour in some cocoa powder. Manipulate the moulds until the entire inside is coated in a fine film of cocoa powder; tap out any excess. Place the moulds in the fridge until you're ready to use them.

2. Preheat the oven to 180°C fan/200°C/gas 6. Set up a bain-marie by placing a small pan of water over a medium heat until it is simmering, then balancing a heatproof bowl on top of the pan; the simmering water should not touch the base of the bowl. Put the chocolate into the heatproof bowl, and heat until melted. Stir briefly with a spatula, then set aside to cool slightly.

3. Cream together the butter and sugar in a mixing bowl until pale and fluffy. Add the egg and

the egg yolk and mix until combined. Add the chocolate and the flour and fold into the mixture gently.

4. Divide the mixture between the chilled moulds. At this stage there should be about 1cm free space at the top of each mould.

5. Remove the Biscoff from the freezer and drop a teaspoon into each mould. Smooth the batter over the top so it is covered; you want it to sit in the middle of the pudding, ideally.

6. I bake these for 20 minutes exactly, but it will depend a little on your oven. The pudding should be risen, and slightly puffed: the sponge will just spring back when pressed gently with a finger. Don't worry if the top is a little cracked.

7. Leave to cool for a couple of minutes (no longer!). Run a knife very gently around the edge of the mould: if you angle the knife slightly so that the blade faces the metal mould, you're less likely to tear the pudding. Place a plate on top of the pudding, and confidently invert. You'll need to use a tea towel for this, as the moulds will be too hot to hold. Gently wiggle the mould until the pudding slips free. Serve warm, with really thick double cream.

I returned for intermediate term with a spring in my step. There's nothing like two weeks surrounded by those who both love you and have low standards for baked goods to make you feel good about your baking.

Chef Nick greeted us with a wry grin. 'Congratulations. You've all made it through to the next round.' There were significantly fewer of us now – not because so many had failed, but more because they had never intended to go further, or had changed their minds. Susie had gone back to America to see out the rest of her training in restaurants; Margaret had only ever wanted the basics. Jo's childcare arrangements had fallen through, so she had to pause her training. Marie was missing: she had failed basic term after her éclair disaster, and had opted not to resit the whole term again, the only way of progressing further.

Chef Nick distributed our new term binders, which were at least twice as thick as the ones they replaced. Much of the coming term would be devoted to the intricate business of cake decorating – in particular, sugarcraft and chocolate. The intermediate exam was going to be a cake: either the opera, the fraisier, or the Sabrina. Lesson after lesson focused on different sponges and constructions, each trickier than the last. We made opera cake: layers of almond sponge, soaked in coffee syrup, sandwiched with ganache and coffee buttercream, and covered in a chocolate glaze. The Alhambra – which I persistently misspelt as Alahambra, as if it was some sort of magic trick, or the password to open a genie's cake – was a little like opera cake, but with hazelnuts rather than almonds. Its name was also piped in chocolate, and a fat, clotted-cream-coloured rose made from marzipan sitting atop. The following week we made poires au caramel réligieuses – another chocolate-filled, chocolate-covered cake, but this time with added pears. The day after, we switched to the fraisier: two layers of genoise sponge, sandwiched with vanilla mousseline, and with halved strawberries standing like sentries around the edge, their flat tummies facing outwards. I quickly got cake fatigue.

The Sabrina cake was a younger model than the others. It had supposedly been made by one of the Cordon Bleu chefs to celebrate Audrey Hepburn's role in *Sabrina*, the same film in which a heartbroken young woman uses the implausible excuse of being in love for her sunken soufflé. It had a shortcrust base; on top of this were long strips of genoise sponge spread with strawberry mousse, winding round and round, until it created a spiral of cake. This was covered with more strawberry mousse, decorated with chocolate-covered marzipan and pistachios, and topped with yet more mousse, with tempered chocolate squiggled on top. When it was cut into, the sandwiching and rolling of the cake created a stupid, vertical pattern inside, blonde, pink, blonde, pink. It was not a subtle cake.

When done properly, the piped names on these cakes can look kind of cool in a retro way. But – despite practising three times a week in classes, and at home on sheets of acetate – I could not get the knack. My piping looked like a child's first attempt at cursive. I spent demos repeating the same words over and over again in my notebook, with curlicues and flourishes – *opera opera opera, fraisier fraisier fraisier* – like a lovestruck teenager writing out her crush's name. But the moment I had a little paper piping bag in my hands, I lost all motor control, with chocolate splurging from the top of the bag all over my hands. That said, when I had my first go at a marzipan rose for the fraisier and Alhambra, I absolutely nailed it, carrying it home in cupped hands for Sam, before clocking that I was holding a piece of marzipan that I had spent twenty minutes manipulating with my sweaty little paws, and had, ever since, been drying out. It was now roughly the texture of plasterboard. It's hard to think of something less appetizing.

Intermediate term hadn't begun with fanfares and glitter for me: I'd produced a triangular cake made from sheets of sponge so brittle it was like trying to construct a giant Toblerone with Melba toast. My marks had reflected my poor baking, and I was still avoiding the poor girl who'd been my bench partner and had had to share my crap sponges.

Thankfully, there was a brief respite from cakes after that. Our focus turned to pastry – specifically, a kind of puff pastry pie called a pithivier. A pithivier consists of two discs of pastry enclosing a filling, which produces a distinctive domed shape. My description makes it sound lumpy and frumpy, but it's quite the opposite.

Traditionally, pithiviers are decorated with beautiful patterns of swooping, spiralling knife marks and indentations. They can be filled with anything, from beef to apple. In our case, we would be using pastry made in an earlier practical to make the pies, then piping frangipane into their centres.

I set about preparing the various elements necessary for construction: rolling out the pastry, chilling it, cutting it; creaming the butter, sugar and almonds for the frangipane. All of these bits went well, but then they usually did. It was the assembly that always got me.

I have always been a rusher. At school, I was repeatedly told off in French lessons for jumping in with the wrong answer, desperate to give *some* response to the question, before anyone else (I know. I was unbearable). And it didn't really change at university or law school. I was impatient to my very core; things that took time were a *waste* of time. I talk over people, trying to finish their sentences. I don't mean to; it's a horrible habit which I try to catch before it happens, but I just *can't wait*. I try to tell myself that it's just enthusiasm, that it's endearing, but it's not. Sam finds it wildly irritating. I would leave essays until the last minute, telling myself I was good under pressure, but actually just unable to contemplate spending more than a day on any given project. More than that, if I didn't immediately get the hang of something, I wasn't interested. I would give things up if I showed no immediate aptitude. For the three years I was forced to take piano lessons at school, I would do anything to avoid playing, happy to talk to my piano teacher about soap operas I'd never watched, rather than try out my ropey arpeggios. I have rejected most sports due to ineptitude. You can't pay me to play Scrabble, and I recoil from cryptic crosswords. Rationally, I know that these are all things that come with practice, but I've never been very good at practice. I just don't have the temperament.

From the beginning, baking was the exception. I think, if I wasn't so mired in grief, I maybe wouldn't have stuck with it in the same way. But I was, so I did. Subsequent forays into calligraphy, embroidery, several languages, and pottery have all fallen by the wayside. But baking stuck. As I baked, and made mistake after mistake, I slowly learned that mistakes didn't have to be fatal. If I buggered something up, it wasn't the end of the world: you could often salvage something, or remake it – and even if you couldn't, it was only a cake. This contrasted deeply with life at the Bar, where the stakes couldn't have been higher: a mistake could cost someone else their liberty.

So, as I continued to bumble my way through my course, I was starting to feel OK about it. In the pastry kitchen, there's no substitute for time and patience. You need patience for individual tasks – you can't hurry gelatine into setting, or ganache into cooling. You can't half-arse tweezing gold leaf on to quartered blueberries – but you also need patience to play the longer game. You *will* screw up the first thousand or so macarons you pipe. But that's OK. The fiftieth will be better than the first; the five-hundredth will be much better still. Learning how to bake properly was forcing me to be patient. I was changing.

I took my time with the pithivier: easing the top layer of puff over the mound of frangipane, smoothing it out, until it was plump and wrinkle-free. Using the metal lid of a Cointreau bottle, cut in half – this was, unbelievably, the high-tech implement provided – I cut away the excess pastry into the shape of petals around the edge. I egg-washed the pastry, then scored curving lines from the centre to the edges with the back of my paring knife, creating a neat spiral. And then I scored lines in between those lines, swooping downward, and then more lines in between those. It looked great, actually. It looked professional! But, contra the saying, I knew the proof of the pudding was actually in the baking. To bake evenly, puff pastry needs to have even layers of butter rolled and folded through it. If I'd got it wrong, the pie would deform as it rose; the filling would burst out through one of the score lines, like something from *Alien*.

Forty minutes later, I pulled the pithivier from the oven, and caught my breath. When we put dishes into the oven, we would scribble our name in Sharpie on a piece of greaseproof paper, and attach it to the tray with a small magnet. I had to double- and triple-check that the name on the tray was, in fact, mine. The pithivier was beautiful. It was perfect. The top shone golden brown, puffing around the score lines, translating the 2D pattern I'd scored into a third glorious dimension. I felt extremely proud. But then, I'd also been proud of my grape crowns; it didn't matter what I thought.

Chef Nick appeared by my side, marking sheet in hand. He appraised my pithivier silently. 'Very good,' he said, almost managing to keep the note of surprise out of his voice. 'Really?!' I squawked. He nodded. 'Yes. Nice knife work, good rise on the puff. It's good. It's very good!' I peeked illicitly at the score sheet he was scribbling on, and saw a five. I got a five! A *FIVE*! For pastry! For puff pastry that I had made from scratch! Two days ago, that had been flour and butter sitting in front of me, and with my own not-terribly-fair hands, I had transformed it into something worthy of top marks. Daisy asked if I wanted a photo with my pastry child. I sheepishly said yes. In it, I am flushed, and a bit sweaty, with tendrils of hair that have worked their way free of my hat plastered to my face. I look properly, radiantly happy. And I was.

Le Cordon Bleu's ever-changing teaching schedule continued to afford me time for thinking. Too much time. Whenever I wasn't cooking, my mind filled with the thoughts I was trying to avoid. In particular, I kept thinking about the last time Mum and I had spoken. I'd become obsessed with whether my recollection of her death was accurate, whether there was something that I'd missed in our last conversation that I should have spotted. I couldn't have known what the yawn meant; but perhaps there was other stuff I'd missed? My memory of the moments that surrounded Mum's death was unreliable: some days it was piecemeal, scattered glimpses, and I wanted to gather them together and protect them, try to preserve them. Other days the whole thing was one hazy dream, like a drunken memory; it felt spongy, pliable, like I could put my hands round it and squeeze it. I was scared to fiddle with my recollection too much, to think too hard about it in case I made an impression in it, my fingerprint, knocked it out of shape. I was too scared to compare notes with Maddy and Dad, terrified that their recollections would shine light on mine in ways that would only formalize my guilt. When we spoke, I swerved away from Mum as a topic. But I couldn't leave it be. I worried away at it, like a receipt in a pocket, fingered until it is cotton-like, and the text has worn away. I kept on combing my memory for meaning, as if I could make sense of it, if I just looked hard enough.

This type of thinking was slipping more and more into the hours of my day – and my nights. I continued to swallow down any urge to cry in a way that was obviously grieving. I cried at weddings, almost immediately, and with abandon, deeming them a socially acceptable place to let out my pent-up emotion. I cried at films, even dreadful saccharine ones. I cried at television and books. But otherwise, I was dry-eyed – at least when I was awake. Now, in my dreams, I cried constantly. Huge, great, racking sobs. I would wake up gasping, convinced that the dreams were true.

I am – I hope – generally quite a warm person, someone able to show concern for others' pain, or celebrate their triumphs. But since Mum's death, I had become hardened and brittle. And when that care was turned round on to me, when I couldn't stick to my carefully rehearsed script, I couldn't cope. The reaction to kindness was as visceral as any emotion I had experienced since Mum's death. I deflected kind words, clamming up, becoming at best facetious, and at worst, cold, clipped. I was incapable of receiving comfort in any form, lest it pull me under, into the emotions that threatened to drown me. Someone touching me – as a gesture of kindness – sent me off into spirals of panic. My skin crawled, and like a ticker-tape the words ran through me: *don't touch me don't touch don't touch me.* I struggled to contain the panic within me.

I had tried so hard, I thought, to let grief run its course. Yet here it was, every day, and every night. It informed everything I did. You can't trick grief into not existing. Fake it till you make it. It doesn't work. No one had tried harder than me to outsmart grief. I didn't want to be Grief Girl any more. My mother dying wasn't just something that had happened to me, but something I had absorbed into my bones. It had become a foundation of my identity. Its grip on me was as strong as ever, stronger even, as if it had calcified parts of me. The fact of Mum's death was a set of crib notes for who I was. I was worn out, worn through. I wanted to be the person I'd been before she died, but I wasn't sure if she was still there. Mum's death was the only story I had to tell.

I had expected to take grief out of the box I'd locked it in and find that it had diminished, starved, wasted away. But it was thriving. I was beginning to think I was wrong to have written off therapy after one unhelpful experience. If I knew nothing else, I knew that I had to do something.

I picked up the phone.

*

At Le Cordon Bleu, we made sweet pithiviers, but in my opinion, savoury is where it's at. I've filled them with beetroot, shallots and goat's cheese, and wild mushrooms cooked slowly with cream and thyme, but oxtail stew is one of my favourites. Oxtail works really well here because the gelatine in the bones means that the stew will cool and set into a dome, which creates a beautiful shape for the finished pithivier. I use Marmite because it gives a savoury depth that I love, and using it as a glaze on the pastry gives it the most incredibly glossy, mahogany finish.

Marmite has always tasted of comfort to me. When I went to university it was a literal taste of home, a foodstuff that united the whole family in our love for it. The smell of Marmite has followed me: when I was very little, on those trips to visit my Auntie Jan in north London, home of my samosa awakening, we would go armed for the train journey with Marmite spread thickly on to sliced white bread, sandwiched, and cut into perfect triangles. It was how I made my first friends in college: eating Marmite toast, sitting on ratty old sofas, or cross-legged on floors. To me, it smells of love and friendship and nerves and anticipation. And, to be frank, if you're going to make a pithivier, there needs to be at least two of those four elements present, because it's something of a labour of love. But it's worth it.

Oxtail and Marmite pithivier

Makes: Enough for 6
Takes: 3 hours
Bakes: 45 minutes

For the filling
500g beef cheek, or stewing beef, cut into chunks
1 oxtail (get your butcher to chop this for you)
2 tablespoons plain flour
Salt and pepper
2 tablespoons oil
1 bottle of dark ale
1 carrot, diced
2 sticks of celery, diced
1 onion, diced
1 tablespoon Marmite
500ml beef stock

For the pastry
1 egg yolk
1 teaspoon Marmite
500g all-butter puff pastry

1. First, make your oxtail stew. Preheat the oven to
    150°C fan/170°C/gas 3. Roll the beef and oxtail
    in seasoned flour. Heat the oil in a casserole dish,
    and brown the beef and oxtail in batches,
    cooking each batch for 5–10 minutes until the
    meat takes on colour. Return all the meat to the

casserole dish, add the ale, and deglaze by scraping any sticky bits off the pan's bottom. Add the vegetables to the dish along with the Marmite and stock. Bring to the boil, cover, and place in the oven for 3 hours. Allow to cool for 15 minutes before removing the oxtail bones. Taste, and season with salt and pepper.

2. In the meantime, line two bowls (approximately 12cm across) with two layers of clingfilm each. Spoon the mixture into the bowls and pack tightly. Refrigerate until completely cold; the casserole will have set into the shape of the bowl.

3. Heat the oven to 180°C fan/200°C/gas 6. Divide the puff pastry in two, then divide each half again into two pieces, one twice the size of the other. On a floured surface, roll each of the smaller pieces of pastry into 15cm circles. Place these discs on a lined baking tray. Remove the filling from the bowls and clingfilm and set one in the centre of each of your discs of pastry. Roll out the larger portions of pastry into two 20cm circles.

4. Put a teaspoon of Marmite into a bowl, add a tiny splash of boiling water, and stir to loosen. Stir in an egg yolk. Dab the border of the smaller pastry circle with the Marmite mix, then drape the larger circle of pastry over it. Press down at

the edges with the tines of a fork and then, using the back of a small knife, indent the border at regular intervals, so it looks like petals. Brush the Marmite and egg yolk mixture over the top of the pastry. Run the back of the knife from the centre of each domed pastry to the forked edge, in a swooping curve. Repeat this mark until you have covered the entire dome.

5. Bake for 15 minutes, then drop the oven temperature to 170°C fan/190°C/gas 5 and bake for another 30 minutes, until puffed and golden. The filling will be extremely hot, so allow to cool for 10 minutes before serving.

13

'By the end of this term, you will have learned to shape and bend chocolate to your will,' Chef Nicolas told us. In just a couple of weeks, we would, he assured us, be able to temper chocolate by eye. This seemed highly improbable, as the last time I'd had a go at tempering, it had taken me three attempts even using a thermometer. But I liked the idea. It fitted in nicely with the image I couldn't shake (despite earlier struggles) of becoming a chocolate whizz, able simply to intuit when the chocolate reached its setting point.

Where the ingredients lists for our recipes had been getting longer and longer, requiring sponges and fillings, syrups and decorations, now we were faced with just one ingredient: chocolate. The huge sacks of chocolate pellets that the classroom assistants were lugging around, distributing to students, made a mockery of the piddling amounts we'd played with in the previous term.

When you temper chocolate, what you are doing is controlling its heat, melting and cooling and then reheating it, taking it to precise temperatures. As this happens, the fat molecules in the chocolate realign. Chocolate tempering is a precise art, and dark, milk and white chocolate all have different required temperatures for the three tempering stages. The basic theory is simple. Let's take dark chocolate as an example: melt the chocolate, drop the temperature to 27°C, stirring all the time, and then raise it to 32°C. That's it. Your chocolate is now tempered. Tempering ensures that the cocoa solids, the fats, set in the most aligned structure. This means that the chocolate will set firm at room temperature, but will melt at body temperature. It will look handsome, glossy, and make a sharp *snap* when broken. Chocolate is a temperamental beast, so to speak, and can quickly lose its temper if it isn't cooled properly, or if it's then warmed to too high a temperature. If this happens, the chocolate simply *won't* set properly. It'll be dull, and crumbly, and will melt too easily. Have you ever melted chocolate, then left it to set, only for it to become tacky and lose its definition once out of the fridge? Or opened up a bar of chocolate and found a white film on the surface? That's because it's fallen out of temper.

There are several different ways of tempering chocolate. You can heat and cool it over a bain-marie. This is precise but fiddly – and there's always the possibility of spilling some water and the whole thing seizing. Or you can use the seeding method, where, after melting the chocolate, you add unmelted chocolate to bring the temperature down. Or you can 'table' the chocolate, which is the cool, cheffy way of doing it. If you're cool and cheffy, you swoop the melted chocolate across a slab of marble with a palette knife, scraping and sweeping, until it reaches the right texture. This is what I wanted to do. This is who I want to be. I am an insufferable show-off, and chocolate was my chance to show off. I want to have a slab of marble in my kitchen, have a bunch of friends over, like Nigella does on her TV show, and when they arrive I'll be casually and maybe slightly suggestively spreading chocolate across my marble slab. Naturally, Le Cordon Bleu taught us the fiddly way.

In previous terms, intermediate students had always made a 2D image out of chocolate, piping outlines and filling them in to create a picture. But the powers that be had decided that this didn't test students sufficiently. I don't know, I sort of felt that asking us to create a free-standing picture in multiple chocolates and colours with intricate piping might be fairly challenging – but apparently not. Instead, we would make a chocolate box, out of chocolate. It would have cutesy little feet and a removable lid, a patterned body, and decoration on top, all made from chocolate. You may ask: why? And I would reply: that is a reasonable question, and one to which I still don't have an answer, even after creating it.

The next day, in pursuit of this, I found myself standing over a double boiler, sweat dripping down my cleavage beneath my chef's jacket, melted chocolate all the way up my sleeves. The double boiler method creates a certain level of jeopardy: the introduction of even the smallest amount of water into melted chocolate will cause it to seize. Dunking a load of melted chocolate repeatedly into alternating bowls of hot and ice water under timed conditions should have some kind of PG 'Mild Peril' rating. I was almost as sweaty as my chocolate, which, like me, was barely holding its temper. I was staring intently at the thermometer, waiting for it to drop to 27°C. Chef

Julie came up behind me. 'Look for the air bubbles,' she said quietly. I jumped. I hadn't heard her approach. Chef Julie picked up my spatula and lifted some of the chocolate up, letting it trail back into the bowl in a thick ribbon. 'You see those air bubbles?' she said. 'How they burst as the chocolate falls?' I nodded. 'When the chocolate is cool enough, the chocolate will be able to hold the weight of the air bubbles, and they won't pop. Look for the bubbles,' she repeated, and then vanished as unexpectedly as she'd arrived, like some kind of chocolate fairy godmother. I stirred the chocolate, scraping it against the sides of the round-bottomed metal bowl with my over-sized spatula. I lifted it up, let it fall, watched the bubbles burst. I dipped the base into my bowl of ice water and repeated the action: stir, scrape, lift. The bubbles held, the chocolate noticeably thicker, ribboning down into the bowl. I drizzled a little across my paring knife, and left it for a moment, trying not to fiddle. A watched pot, and all that. I returned to the knife: the chocolate had set hard. And, just like that, I'd tempered chocolate by eye.

As I settled down for our first boulangerie demonstration of intermediate term, I was still bruised from my bread-based embarrassment in basic term, and was feeling even less confident when I realized that the stakes had been raised: we were now officially in viennoiserie territory. The days of soda bread were long gone. Viennoiserie is, essentially, breakfast pastries: yeasted doughs that are enriched by beating huge amounts of butter into them, or sandwiching butter between layers, or sometimes both. Basically, a lot of butter. Think croissants and pains au chocolat, brioches and Danishes. Adding eggs and butter and sugar to a bread dough retards the proving process, and ultimately leads to golden brown pastries, sweet and rich. In croissants and Danishes you can see the honeycomb structure where the sheets of dough have been painstakingly folded with butter, flaking and crisp; in brioche and bun dough, you'll find a fluffy, tender crumb that is butterscotch yellow.

To make the brioche according to the Cordon Bleu method, you combine the ingredients by hand, and then put them into a stand mixer with a dough hook and mix on top speed for ten minutes. The KitchenAids that the school have are industrial, professional standard, but once they're going on top whack, they judder around the work bench like a pair of joke-shop wind-up teeth. The only way to control this is with the very high-tech method of holding tightly on to them as they attempt to bounce off the bench. While you do this, you add an implausible amount of butter incrementally, slowly creating that rich, golden dough that is so distinctive of brioche.

True to form, I didn't have all my other bits and bobs ready before I began preparing the dough. I set it going in the mixer and returned to the central work station to weigh out my butter. The fancy French butter we used at Le Cordon Bleu came in huge, flat slabs, a kilogram apiece. There was something intensely pleasing about seeing butter laid out like that. I grabbed my paring knife and dragged it through the huge tablet. I registered what I'd done before I felt the pain or spotted the blood: I'd cut through the butter, clean and fast, and continued through the top of my thumb. I clamped my thumb in the nearest piece of blue kitchen paper, less in a form of rudimentary first aid compression, and more out of sheer shock.

I looked around. No one seemed to have noticed that I had possibly lost a digit while carrying out the most banal of kitchen tasks. I gingerly removed the blue paper, which was now saturated with a combination of sweat from my right hand, and blood from my left. The top of my thumb remained attached to the rest of it, but only in the most tangential way. My stomach dropped and I decided that my original idea of just pressing one bit of my thumb to the other was preferable to further inspection. It was at this point that I became aware of not one but two brioche-filled KitchenAids behind me about to jump off their benches. Chef Dominique was nowhere to be seen. Nor was Alex, my bench partner, with whom I was supposed to be sharing the workload. I had no idea where she'd gone, but she definitely wasn't there when things got bloody. I began to wonder whether it was possible to bleed to death from what was, let's be realistic, a small slice through my thumb. I figured that while my chances of death might ordinarily have been unlikely, they were increased now by a task equivalent to wrestling two pneumatic drills into submission. Somehow, I managed to get the KitchenAids into a sort of one-armed headlock, while holding my thumb as far away as possible from my chef's whites. Of course, as soon as I turned out the doughs, Alex reappeared nonchalantly, and seemed not to notice my incapacitation. I slunk up to Chef Dominique (who had also miraculously returned) and showed him my thumb; he gave me a small blue plaster, which seemed at odds with the scream for urgent medical attention and commendation for bravery that I was expecting.

Plastered up, I got back to the task at hand, as it were. We were making three different types of brioche using the same dough: one dotted with chocolate, one plaited, and one which was called a brioche à tête, also known as a 'Parisienne'. It was made up of two balls of dough, the larger one baked in a fluted tin, and the smaller one pressed into it, so that they bake up, perched perkily one on top of the other, like a plump body with a head – a tête – on top, a bit like a snowman. You make two pieces of dough: one that looks like a ring doughnut or bagel, and one like a sort of tapered sausage. You place the sausage in the doughnut, and Bob's your uncle. Unfortunately, if you don't adequately press the smaller piece of dough into the bigger, it will not sit neatly on baking. Instead, the head will lurch forwards, like when you squeeze a stress ball and the rubber distends. As I took my brioche from the oven, it was clear that my dough had indeed lurched, spectacularly so. To be frank, my brioche à tête looked exactly like a flaccid penis. Chef Dominique, now present and looming, took one look at my phallic brioche, made a noise in his throat which only the French can really carry off, a sort of scornful laugh-bark, and moved on to the next student.

*

It goes without saying, I guess, that cooking is a physical act. That's what I'd loved so much about it when I first began. I loved using my hands. I'd never really had cause to use them before save for pulling wheelie suitcases and lugging big textbooks. It was cathartic. It also made me feel powerful, changing and creating. I loved all of it: stirring risottos until the starch releases and the grains soften. Chopping celery and carrot and onion into neat piles. Kneading bread, developing and stretching the gluten strands from nothing more than flour and water, sticky and unworkable, to something pliable and soft. It took me several months to understand what cookery books meant when they described 'creaming' butter and sugar together, but when I got the hang of it and was able to change the texture and colour of two ingredients, from something sloppy and bright, to something fluffy and pale, just with a wooden spoon and a bit of elbow grease, I felt flushed with success. It was soothing and rewarding in equal parts.

But I knew cooking in a professional kitchen was different. It's heavy work. It's standing for eighteen-hour days. It's lugging sacks of flour and potatoes. It's endless, repetitive motion. It's butchery. It's hot. It's *so* hot. Burns are par for the course. Your feet ache, your hips ache, your back aches, your knees ache. When you get home, you can't sleep because you're still running on the adrenaline of the service. And a few short hours later, you're back, doing it all again. The whole industry is powered by stress. Let's be honest, it's not a healthy way to live. And it comes as little surprise then that so many line cooks rely on uppers to get them through the working day, and alcohol when they can't wind down at the end of it.

Lots of chefs end up with injuries that pull them out of the kitchen permanently. It's hard to overestimate the value of a healthy back in a professional kitchen. Many of the teaching staff at Le Cordon Bleu regaled us with anecdotes about their years spent in basement kitchens, hunched over stoves. Stories that began with routine heavy lifting, with kitchens that didn't have proper safety measures in place, ended with chefs falling unconscious on the floor, with blinding pain and ruptured spinal discs. They all swore by Pilates.

Even before I'd heard these stories, I was nervous about my physical capabilities. When someone you love dies it can feel like every nerve is singing. Your heart literally hurts. There is strong evidence for a link between grief and a physiological response: when you are bereaved, your risk of heart disease goes up six-fold. It's no surprise: your nervous system is put under a huge amount of stress when you undergo a serious bereavement. Like fear, grief is a stress reaction, and therefore, with it, cortisol levels increase, causing disrupted sleep and weakened immune responses. And when I failed to deal with my own grief, it made perfect sense that this physical response would take root, deep inside me. Maybe I'd brought it on myself, I thought; my façade of resilience had cracked, and my body had shown how unresilient it in fact was. Bodies can change forever thanks to grief. And thanks to grief, mine had. Thanks, grief.

The narcolepsy that accompanied the first days after Mum's death had never really gone away. I was still physically and mentally exhausted all the time. Physically, I was crumbling. Sometimes my left leg refused to lift properly. I sounded like a sheet of trampled bubble wrap when I first stood up in the morning. I would wake several times a night with numb hands and feet, lightning bolts of pain in my elbows and hips, my joints fizzing. It was like I was made of electricity, and was short-circuiting. There were days when it hurt too much to wear a bra, or my engagement ring, or to shave under my arms. I was peculiarly sensitive just above my inner knees, and below my clavicle; knocking these areas even lightly felt like the equivalent of stubbing your toe or bashing your funny-bone. My knees creaked and ached: I couldn't really bend down, and I couldn't kneel or sit on my haunches. My hips sent frightening pains up my back.

Halfway through intermediate term, I found myself sitting in a consultant's office, at Guy's Hospital, with a diagnosis: fibromyalgia. 'But a previous consultant I saw discounted fibromyalgia!' I said, confident that this would dissuade her. 'It says so in this letter!' 'I know,' she replied gently, more patiently than a woman who had two dozen patients in a waiting room down the corridor should be able to be. 'But the diagnostic criteria rely on the tenderness of certain set points on the body, and that changes day on day. If you aren't having a bad day, they might not respond, and then the diagnosis could be missed.'

I had known fibromyalgia was a possibility, but I was hoping the first, uninterested, perfunctory consultant had been right. That it was something else. Anything else. Just not fibromyalgia: the made-up illness of malingerers and hypochondriacs. Please not that.

Fibromyalgia is a chronic pain condition, which presents as muscular and tissue tenderness, worst in eighteen points on the body, nine pairs of pain buttons that are found in the same location in all fibromyalgia sufferers. One of the distinguishing features is near-constant physical and mental exhaustion, sometimes creating confusion, an inability to think clearly. A sensation of waking up unrefreshed, more tired than when you went to sleep ten hours ago, is common. This feels a very sanitized description of how I felt each morning: I felt like a wrung-out dishcloth, and my body crackled with pain. I felt swollen and raw. The exhaustion on waking and the vivid, technicolor nightmares were both thanks to the pain that prevented the body reaching the stage of deep sleep, where the body is actually able to rest and repair. It's often described as like having a body with a broken smoke alarm: the body reacting to even benign stimuli with pain.

There is no cure. There is no real palliative treatment. There is counselling and physiotherapy available, if you're lucky, both aimed towards keeping the patient mobile. It can help to be aware of triggers – stress, exhaustion, grief, illness, extremes of weather, travel, surgery, childbirth, change in circumstances, anything that might tip you off an even keel. 'What you really need to avoid,' the consultant was saying to me, 'is any kind of boom and bust lifestyle; being gentle with your body, kind to yourself, no hard physical work, predictable routines, and time for resting, that's the key.' I swallowed. 'I've just left my job to go to culinary school.' She raised her eyebrows.

Even before my diagnosis, I knew I was never going to become a line cook in some Michelin-starred restaurant. It was never the plan, but as I saw friends applying for stages (restaurant work experience, pronounced French-style *stah-juz*) at the Ledbury and the Dorchester I mourned the loss nonetheless. I couldn't stand for more than three hours without my hips starting to whine, and my back threatening to spasm. The prospect of eighteen-hour days, heavy lifting, and repetitive movement was laughable.

In a strange way, though, it was a relief. It was as if everything I'd been refusing to feel, all my pain for Mum, had been externalized into something physical. The dull ache in my heart and my head had just spread outwards until my fingers cracked and my knees creaked. It made sense that everything hurt because, well, everything hurt. It was melodramatic, but it was a melodrama I held close. I thought I wanted to know what was wrong with me so that I could fix it, but perhaps I didn't.

It seemed only days ago that I had been waiting to head into my basic exam. How on earth could intermediate exams have come round so quickly, before I could catch my breath, let alone get my head around how to pipe actual writing in chocolate? But here I was, standing outside the door to the same teaching kitchen, waiting to find out what my genoise-based fate was. All the exam dishes are tricky bastards in their own way but it was the Sabrina that nobody wanted. It required so many different elements:

shortcrust and sponge, a mousse that was prone to splitting, icing the cake in the maddening palette-knife-wobbly-hand way, and worst of all, tempered chocolate. I wanted the fraisier – it was by far the easiest of the three cakes, with fewer components, and would give me a chance to show off my marzipan rose skills – but I'd settle for the opera.

Of course we got the Sabrina. How was this fair, after I'd had to endure the bloody éclairs too in basic term? The two worst dishes and I'd got them both. I railed against the injustice until I remembered that I wasn't in the Old Bailey any more, I was taking a cake exam. There's one thing you can say for criminal law: it doesn't half give you perspective. And after my outrage, the exam was surprisingly anticlimactic, or at least distinctly less dramatic for those around me than that of basic term. There was one hairy point where, while smoothing the strawberry mousse on to the cake, balancing it on my right hand, I lost control, and wobbled like something from a farce, regaining my grip on the cake milliseconds before it plunged to the floor. Just my luck that Chef Nicolas would be standing less than a foot away at the time, his eyes widening in horror, and then creasing into laughter.

The final practical that followed our exams was cake decorating. A break from the overwhelmingly French syllabus, proper, old-school *English* cake decorating: sugar flowers. Chef Jérôme, giving the demo, didn't disguise his distaste for the topic: 'We don't do this in France,' he said, shrugging his shoulders gallically. There was almost no running commentary, and most of the class talked openly, voices at full volume, for the entire three-hour demonstration. But I sat in the front row, rapt. Sugar flowers used to be the go-to decoration for English celebration cakes. They were practical: they posed no risk of contamination from the foliage, and lasted as long as the cakes themselves, which were then invariably fruit cake – months or even years. Now we tend to celebrate with sponge cakes, and decorate them with buttercream and fresh flowers, and eat the whole thing in a day or two. So no one bothers to make elaborate sugar flowers any more.

But I thought they were beautiful. I watched in awe as Chef Jérôme brought peonies, and lilies, carnations and cherry blossom to life. I couldn't believe it was possible to make these flowers from mere sugar and food colouring. They were nothing like the clumsy marzipan roses we'd made for our fraisiers earlier in the term, or the pulled sugar roses that I'd seen superior students making (which were beautiful, but glossy and glassy, neon and baroque). These were impossibly delicate, and completely realistic. Even close up, you could easily mistake them for real flowers.

We'd made the fruit cake in an earlier practical, ready to be iced and decorated. In this practical, all three hours were to be dedicated to decoration. We were given a small amount of sugarpaste, a host of tools that looked more like they belonged in a dentist's surgery, and then let loose. I rolled tiny pieces of the palest pink sugarpaste with an equally small rolling pin, which wouldn't have been out of place in a doll's house. I rolled a ball of sugarpaste, and then tapered one end until it was pear-shaped. I stamped circles, and then, using a plastic scalpel with a small ball at the end, I rubbed the edges until they thinned and moved from discs of icing to something lifelike. I dried them out on egg cartons so that they curved slightly, each one different to the last. Using a paintbrush, I dabbed just a little bit of coloured dust into the centre of each petal, and the smallest amount of green on its very edge. And then, one by one, I glued them on to the pear-shaped rosebud, the smallest petals first, lying tightly alongside one another, working up to the biggest, which flopped open blousily. I looked up a moment later and the three hours had swept by, and in front of me was a perfect, blushing rose. It was the most delicate thing I'd ever done, and I couldn't believe it was mine.

I kept the rose long after we ate the cake. It sat on my desk. Occasionally I'd show it to people: *Look, I made this!* They would gasp at this funny, slightly chipped little rose, without stem or sepals, that ended in a sort of bum-shaped crease. It was totally unlike any rose that has ever existed in the natural world. But if you ignored all that, and looked at it from just the right angle, in just the right light, it was perfect. One day, I put a fat cookery book down on my desk, and heard a sharp crunch. I lifted the book. It was covered in shards of pale pink and white sugarpaste. But I wasn't too upset. The rose had served its purpose.

'But, why?' Sam's dad, a university lecturer in food science, asked me plaintively over breakfast. 'What's the point?' I'd been explaining the syllabus for my final term – superior term – and, to be honest, I could see where he was coming from. The last term at Le Cordon Bleu is about honing skills taught in previous terms, getting you to the stage where you could walk into any high-end pastry kitchen and, if not hold your own, at least not humiliate yourself on day one. But it's also about decoration. I don't mean the tuile biscuit finishing touches of previous terms, or little chocolate feathers perching on top of tarts. Superior term laughs in the face of choux buns made into little swans. Now, we were reckoning with grander – and more ridiculous – creations. Towering edifices of pure chocolate. Sculptures and dioramas made entirely of sugar. Poured sugar. Pulled sugar. Blown sugar. Sugar heated until molten, then shaped into flowers, fruit, birds and bees. Works of art, really, albeit very silly ones.

I've never been a particularly artistic or creative person. It's always riled Sam up when I say it, not because he is leaping to my defence and proclaiming my inherent artistic talent, but rather because he thinks that the idea of 'creative people' is nonsense. 'People who work in business, account managers, financial directors, have to think incredibly creatively!' he rails. 'Why do we fetishize creativity?' Sam's job is one that anyone would call creative – he works as a copywriter and a novelist – which I suppose gives him more licence than most to pontificate on the topic, but there's creative and then there's creative, right? There's a bit of a difference between thinking laterally in a business setting and being able to blow a sugar apple. So when I say I've never been a particularly artistic or creative person, what I mean is that, if my learning curve over the last two terms had been steep, the one that lay before me looked positively perpendicular.

Superior term started in the same way as the two before it: with a fat folder plonked on my desk. This term, we would try our hands at no fewer than seven different modules: modern classics, plated desserts, afternoon tea, sugarwork, modern tart, chocolate, and entremets.

I skipped quickly over the pages concerning all but the entremet module, for this would be our final exam piece. Although each preceding term is required to undertake the subsequent term, there is no build-up of marks, and no laurels on which to rest. Passing superior term – and therefore passing the Diplôme de Pâtisserie overall – depends on not screwing up your superior exam. The entremet pages were so detailed and severe, they looked like a war cabinet briefing.

I should, at this point, explain what an entremet actually is, as I'd never bloody heard of one before I discovered that my entire pâtisserie qualification relied on one. An entremet is a layered and glazed cake, built around a mousse, and which shows off different textures and flavours. In medieval times, the word entremet referred to a small dish served between courses, but in modern pâtisserie it bears no real relation to that. Chef Julie explained the rubric to us. For our final exam, we would be required to produce one 20cm entremet, plus two identical mini-entremets plated as they would be in a restaurant, with extra decoration and (of course) crème anglaise. In order to satisfy the Cordon Bleu exam requirements, each entremet and miniature pudding must have: a sponge layer, a mousse, a crisp layer, a set custard insert, a glaze, free-standing tempered chocolate decoration, hand-piped chocolate decoration, and tuile biscuit decoration. How we went about each of those elements was up to us.

We wouldn't have to make these decisions at the last moment. Ahead of our exam, we had to submit labelled photographs and diagrams of our planned entremets. Our marks would depend not just on the finished product, but on how closely that product corresponded to what we'd actually planned to make. No freestyling allowed. We were also obliged to use a different flavour for each component, with no repeats – so if we chose a strawberry mousse, for example, we couldn't also have a strawberry glaze. I was actually rather pleased by this stipulation. Up to this point, the Cordon Bleu syllabus had left little room for individual expression. I liked playing with flavours; it was part of the joy of cooking.

I flicked again through our file while Julie talked. I knew there were actual modern flavours and interesting combinations being used this term in all the other modules. I'd spied raspberry and lavender éclairs, yuzu tarts, tiny cakes glazed with blonde chocolate, petits fours filled with calamansi gel and Szechuan pepper crémeux. I didn't even know what calamansi was! I'd spent the last two weeks of holiday convincing myself that, seeing as it clearly wasn't chocolate, boulangerie, plating up, or sugarwork, flavour must be my thing. I probably had a really refined palate. Maybe I was a super-taster. This was why I'd got into the whole thing in the first place, I reminded myself: to make things that tasted good.

But then we were handed a list of ingredients and quantities. We couldn't just do what we wanted here: we were only allowed to use ingredients on this list, and not in excess of the amounts prescribed. It felt like *Ready Steady Cook* crossed with *The Crystal Maze*. Gelatine was restricted; eggs were limited; vanilla was in short supply. Lots of the flavours that we'd used time and again during the course weren't on the list. No coffee! No passion-fruit! No citrus at all! Oh, and we had to use a minimum of fifteen – fifteen! – different ingredients. This was an elaborate game of flavour Tetris.

But before we had a chance to get our heads around the exam system, we were thrown into our first demo and practical. It quickly became clear that superior term was going to take us several gears higher than inter-mediate. I scanned our first recipe, which ran to six A4 pages. Our first module was 'modern classics' and to kick it off, we were returning to a dish from basic term that still haunted many of us: éclairs. Naturally, the rec-ipe had grown much more complicated in the intervening three months. We would be filling our éclairs with a diz-zying array of things: Earl Grey crème pâtissière, wild strawberry and basil gel, chocolate and praline cream, yuzu custard. And then, to almost literally gild the lily, we would decorate them with everything from edible viola flowers to tempered green chocolate; gold leaf to shards of lemon meringue.

We each had different versions to cook. Mine were to be filled with passionfruit curd and milk chocolate Chantilly, topped with a passionfruit-flavoured glazed plaque made of marzipan, then decorated with white chocolate and raspberry crunch, and fresh raspberries. When finished, my éclairs stood in a row, gleaming golden, waiting to be assessed by Chef Olivier. I did a bit of assessing of my own: the pastries in front of me bore no resemblance to those I'd produced in basic term. The éclairs I'd made back then had been delicious, and far and away beyond what I'd ever succeeded making on my own at home before. Although I moaned about their lumpiness, I was rightly proud of them. They were a fine piece of baking. But these were something else. These were proper *pâtisserie*. They were miniature works of art. They were beautiful not in a quirky or kitsch way, not simply because I'd made them and loved them. They were objectively beautiful. Me and my choux had come a long way together.

If I was looking for measurable improvement, I wasn't going to be disappointed by the plated desserts module. Here, we were revisiting three dishes we'd encountered before: lemon meringue tart, Black Forest gâteau, and tarte Tatin. You'd think by this stage experience would have taught me that any feelings of optimism would quickly be undone, probably in a slightly humiliating way in the following practical, but no! I was feeling positive! Sure, I hadn't got the meringue right the first time round but I had an extra term and a half's experience under my belt now – and I'd just seen how much my choux had improved in that time. And the decoration on my basic term Black Forest gâteau may have been a little haphazard, but it was perfectly serviceable. And, yes, OK, I might not have made a tarte Tatin, but I'd watched one; how hard could caramelized fruit in pastry be?

Even looking at the subheadings for the elements we would be expected to produce, I could see we weren't in Kansas any more. These were classic puddings only in name. These were classic puddings reloaded. Even, whisper it, *deconstructed*. The lemon tart was made up of a wholewheat biscuit base, a cardamom tuile filled with a lemongrass mousse, topped with Italian meringue, and set among discs of gel and lemon supreme and thyme. The Black Forest gâteau required chocolate soil (did you know that if you pour boiling sugar on to solid chocolate and whisk, it turns into soil? There aren't a lot of situations in which this will be useful in life, but then you could say the same about algebra), and the tarte Tatin a foam. Oh, and a blown sugar apple.

'The plated desserts module is a copy and paste exercise. No freedom or creativity. We don't care. You can do that in three months when you leave us alone. Master, analyse, copy, copy, copy. Then, in a few years' time you can create your own style,' intoned Chef Javier. Chef Javier was the only American chef on the pâtisserie staff; in demos he worked fast and talked faster. In practicals, he was terrifyingly precise, able to spot an out-of-place dot of gel at twelve paces. He would chew you out if he thought you weren't paying attention or didn't care, but was the first to help if he could see you were genuinely trying your best. I wanted his praise more than anyone else's.

We had been encouraged to take photographs of the finished plates to ensure that our end product was a perfect facsimile. And I thought I'd done pretty well with this modern BFG: we'd been working in pairs, and along with Michael, my bench partner, I'd constructed the main body of the pudding, a brownie base, with chocolate mousse, griotte cherries, and a tempered chocolate disc. I'd made cherry-flavoured tuiles and kirsch gel, and my chocolate soil was perfect; I'd dotted halved raspberries across my plate, carefully consulting the photo I was copying, and dusted extra squares of brownie with gold lustre, and had a crack at a rocher of orange-scented whipped cream. Rochers are one-handed ovoid scoops of cream or ice cream (if you use two spoons, they form three-sided American football-shaped scoops, and are called 'quenelles'). They are extremely prevalent in the plating of fancy puddings, are fiendishly hard, and are scooped in a wholly counter-intuitive way. Anyway, my finished dish certainly looked pretty damn close to the picture on my phone as far as I was concerned.

Chef Olivier worked his way round the room, grading our attempts. He was in no mood for pleasantries. 'This isn't a rocher,' he told one pair. 'It's a quenelle.' He moved on to his next victim. 'You have the wrong number of gel dots,' he told Alex, in the tone of voice I might use to respond to someone calling to sell me PPI. Alex looked desolate. Then it was my turn. He leaned towards my pudding, with a critical sneer on his face. 'Your edible flowers are angled wrongly,' he told me. 'And!' He paused dramatically, and I held my breath. 'Your *raspberries* are *upside down*!'

When he reached Bella and Becky, the two students opposite me, he stopped dead and looked at them, with wide, sarcastic eyes. 'Tell me what you've done wrong', he said, plaintively. He waited. There was an unspoken rule that when someone else's work was being marked, you affected indifference, a lack of attention. The reality of this was ridiculous: often you would be centimetres from the plate that was being judged. Now, the rest of us collectively stopped breathing and – despite each of us suddenly becoming very interested in our own plates, or packing up our knife kits, or the whisks we were towelling dry – were on tenterhooks. Bella and Becky looked at each other nonplussed. Chef Olivier stared them down and repeated the question: 'Tell me what is wrong with this plate.' I cringed. Apart from anything else, I had no idea what *was* wrong with their plates, or at least not to the extent that it would incur this level of culinary wrath. Eventually he put them (and me) out of their misery, and I twigged he had meant his question literally. Each word was like a blow: 'You. Used. The. Wrong. Plates. I cannot mark this!' There was a small part of me that was mentally standing in the doorway of the kitchen, cackling at the farce in front of me: two grown women being told off for using a large white plate with a shallow rim, rather than a large white plate with no rim. But the rest of me was experiencing physical, visceral relief that, by accident, rather than design, I had plucked the right plate from the crockery shelf. Superior term suddenly felt very, very stressful.

'This one,' Chef Javier said, pointing at a scar on his forearm. 'This one was from isomalt. Four years ago. I was at a sugar art competition and dropped the isomalt on my arm. That stuff *burns*.' As he took us through the steps of the dish we were expected to recreate, Chef Javier had also been walking us through the various scars he had acquired during his years of cheffing. But it was the isomalt scar that I focused on, in the knowledge that a couple of hours later, I'd be handling the stuff myself.

Isomalt is a sugar substitute. When you walk into Le Cordon Bleu, there are glass display cases showing off the chefs' sugarwork: structures in acid pink or cobalt blue, with gleaming ribbons and hummingbirds, bees and butterflies. These have probably sat here in these same display cases for months, without any appreciable deterioration. For this, they have isomalt to thank. Isomalt is used for pulling sugar because it's more resistant to humidity, so doesn't go sticky and disintegrate as quickly as sugar would. It also doesn't brown like sugar does when cooked. It doesn't taste great; it doesn't really taste of anything – but then, who wants to eat a piece of sugar that has sat around in a display case for four months gathering dust? It also needs to be cooked to a higher temperature, meaning its burns are even more vicious.

We were encountering sugarwork – the craft of creating works of art from molten sugar – in small increments, learning how to pull, to blow, to pour, before we were let loose on the sugar-focused module. You can, depending on your skill, turn molten sugar into just about anything: simple little coils wrapped around kitchen steels, multi-coloured striped ribbons, bent into bows, lifelike fruit and flowers, animals. It is, quite simply, magical. Beautiful, delicate, almost like glass.

Here's how you prepare sugar for sugarwork. You heat sugar and water to 127°C before adding a few drops of tartaric acid, and then cooking the mixture to exactly 162°C. This is significantly hotter (about 41°C hotter) than the sugar we had first cooked and fingered in basic term. At this temperature, sugar transforms into a thick, viscous liquid, with a distinctive smell – it's still one-dimensionally sweet, not like the bitter smoky notes of caramel, but almost like fresh candyfloss. Once it's cooked, you add drops of colouring, then pour it out on to a silicone mat beneath a heat lamp, flicking and folding the mass until it transforms from runny and sticky, to a slow-lava flow. Using the lamp gives you enough time to manipulate the sugar without it cooling and solidifying, but forget about your sugar and leave it for too long under the heat, and it will melt and splurge.

You can wear cotton gloves to protect you from the heat – you know, the ones you get from Boots that you pop on overnight once you've moisturized your hands, which make you look like Mickey Mouse – and latex gloves on top of those to stop the cotton sticking to the molten sugar. But the protection is limited. Your fingertips burn, of course. But your knuckles hurt too, and the backs of your hands, exposed to the bulb radiating heat. They hurt a lot.

I watched Chef Javier conjure an apple from the molten sugar. He stuck a small blob of the bright green molten sugar to the nozzle of a small hand pump. He squeezed the pump, and the small blob expanded with the air inside it. At first it looked like nothing more was happening. But slowly, slowly, it formed an even, green orb. He used a small fan to cool areas of the sugar, and control the evenness of the expansion. You could have heard a pin drop in the lecture room as, using a gloved finger, he created a divot in the top, forcing the surrounding area to bulge out, like a real life apple. With the quietest *crack!* he removed the apple from the nozzle, and filled it with apple-flavoured foam from a siphon.

Gently, he teased little green leaves from some of the spare molten sugar, and a perfect black stalk, and then stuck those on to the finished apple. The apple was placed over folded slivers of actual apple, which sat on top of a disc of caramelized puff pastry. It was exquisite. Silly, perhaps, but exquisite.

Of course, that's not how it worked when I tried. It's surprisingly hard to stick a bit of sugar on to a pump and create an airtight seal, but really, that was the least of my worries. You see, when you fill molten sugar with air, it can be tricky to keep a uniform thickness, and frankly, the miniature fans that should help you control the heat are as much use as a molten sugar fireguard. One ill-advised pump of air, and the little sugar bulbs explode. The sound of smashing glass echoed around the room every few moments, accompanied by profanities. My work bench was covered in shards of sharp green sugar.

Opposite me, Sophie worked quietly. While the rest of us were shattering our lopsided apples left, right and centre, she was diligently producing apple after apple. 'Have you worked with sugar before?' Chef Javier asked her, clearly impressed. 'No!' she replied. 'This is my first time.' I scowled. I just couldn't get my apple to work. My hands throbbed. Everyone apart from Sophie was using one of the spares, or an apple they'd created with considerable hands-on help from Chef Javier. Reluctantly, I took one from the pile, adding my stem and leaf with the help of a blowtorch, and feeling, not unlike one of my own collapsed attempts, utterly deflated. When I left college that evening, the security sensor wouldn't recognize my fingerprints.

But blown sugar apples were just the start: the sugar-work module's literal high point was the croquembouche. We made it over two practicals. A croquembouche is what the French present in place of wedding cakes. It's made up of dozens of choux pastry buns, filled with Chantilly or custard, stuck together with caramel, and piled up into a cone. However ridiculous, the result is spectacular, and any French pâtissier worth their salt (or their sugar) can knock one up. At Le Cordon Bleu, croquembouche was really a vehicle for various types of sugar decoration: we would place ours on a nougatine stand; then, once assembled, we would decorate it with an elaborate pulled sugar rose and a ribbon, like it was a show dog at Crufts.

The ribbon and rose are 'pulled' from the sugar. Pulling sugar is a little different to blowing it. The sugar needs to be aerated, so once it is cool enough to handle, you can get your (gloved) hands involved, kneading and pulling, stretching and folding the sugar. As you pull the sugar, air is incorporated and the clear sugar turns opaque, and begins to look like thick strands of taffy. For the rose, each petal is pulled individually under the heat lamp, the border then thinned out with your fingers to make a delicate, lifelike edge, before heating the base of the petal on a methylated flame, and affixing to the rosebud. I built the rose up slowly, adding one interlocking petal after the next, carefully teasing them so that the uppermost edge of the petals curled outwards. It was just like working with marzipan or sugarpaste, only the backs of my hands hurt, I couldn't feel my fingertips, and every movement felt perilous.

To make a croquembouche, you first make the choux buns, then dip each bun into molten caramel and stick it to its neighbour, as though you are a builder in a fairytale. This is a dicey process, because the caramel will only stick if it's at caramel temperature: 148°C. As soon as it starts to drop and go tacky, it loses its sticking power, so you need to keep it hot hot hot. As I made mine, I assiduously avoided dunking my hands by holding the buns with my fingertips. Unfortunately, this weakened my grip, and before long I dropped a bun into the pan of caramel. The caramel splashed up on to the back of my hand, forming four perfect dots that turned garnet. At first I didn't feel it, such is the nature of burns, and then, suddenly, I really, really did.

The final product looked surprisingly small and squat

for something that had taken six hours to produce. I fixed the ribbon at an accidentally jaunty angle – which made it look like it was blowing in a particularly fierce wind – and stuck the rose on top. It looked hilariously old-fashioned, particularly compared to the modern dishes and bakes we were now producing, but sort of charming in its own way.

Since the purpose of this exercise was to practise sugar techniques, we didn't bother filling the buns with crème pâtissière or Chantilly, which would have made the 'bouche into an edible (if decadent) cake. We were just putting up the façade – the final product was simply a load of dry, slightly softening choux pastry, and a whole bunch of caramel and sugar. Apart from the fact that it was about a foot tall, and not the kind of thing you'd want to try to take home in rush hour, it was never going to be a good eating experience. One by one, we took it in turn to smash up our creations, throwing them melodramatically into the bin, videoing each other, laughing. I thought of how shocked I felt at seeing superior students binning their work, back when I was in first term. This time what shocked me was how good it felt. It felt like saying: we learned something for the sake of learning it, and now we were done with it. It felt cathartic.

'So, tell me about yourself. Tell me why you're here,' the therapist asked me.

Where to start? I gave this man who I'd met only a few moments before my usual whistle-stop biography, just like I'd given when I reluctantly embarked on CBT. That's where I'd normally stop. But something was different. Something in me had shifted over the last eight or so months. I wanted to change. I wanted to live my life. So, for the first time, I kept going.

I described the chaos that raged inside me, the panic that coursed through me, stirring my stomach and compressing my lungs. I told him about Grief Top Trumps. I'd never told anyone apart from Sam how I wanted to snatch grief away from others, that they didn't deserve to grieve, that I wanted to hug it tight, keep it all for myself. The nightmares, too, where Mum was alive, and hated me. I told him about those. I'd never articulated these things before, not really. They felt dirty and heavy, but as I started to express those things that had been weighing me down for so long, I felt just the tiniest bit lighter.

'The thing is,' I explained, 'I get that in the grand scheme of things I'm extremely lucky; that Mum's death could have been far more traumatic, that I could have lacked a support network. But I can't make my body understand that.' I told him that I felt like my life was ruled by missing my mum. 'It feels so unfair,' I told him. 'Even though, rationally, I know that's nonsense. People die all the time. I don't understand how all these people around me just *cope*.'

Every time I mentioned something I struggled with, I qualified it. 'Yes, but of course it could have been worse . . .' 'Yes, but everyone must feel that way . . .' Yes but, yes but, yes but.

John looked at me levelly. 'You know, you're allowed to feel pain, Livvy. You don't have to caveat it.' I looked back at him. Up until that point, I genuinely hadn't con-sidered that as a possibility. I had equated surviving with suppressing the pain that sat there inside me, thinking that the more I ignored it, the stronger I was. That's why I didn't cry. That's why I'd got so proficient at talking a good grief story without ever actually engaging with how I felt. I had expended so much energy, so much *time* trying not to feel the pain that welled up inside me. And maybe I didn't need to.

Chef Nicolas greeted our teaching group warmly: 'Good morning, girls!' We laughed, but it wasn't wholly inaccurate. There were only six men on our course. Overwhelmingly, pastry is dominated by women – perhaps because this is one of the few parts of the cookery world where women feel like they get a fair shake. Baking – with the possible exception of bread baking – has always been seen as dainty and domestic. Women's work. But there's nothing particu-larly feminine about hauling hundredweight (50kg) bags of flour around, or sweating over boiling caramel, or pouring molten sugar from a jam pan that weighs as much as a small adult human.

In professional kitchens, men still dominate by a large margin, but pastry is often the exception. Household feed-ing, on the other hand, has long been regarded as women's work, of course. A woman's place is in the kitchen, unless it's one where she could reasonably expect to be paid. Gen-der blindness doesn't work here. It's disingenuous. At the time of writing, 82.27 per cent of chefs in the UK are men. This is higher than the 76.1 per cent from 2017.

So let's look at the reasons given for this predicament. First up: women are frail and vulnerable in a way men are not. How could they possibly cope with standing for eighteen hours, lifting heavy items in a high-pressure environment? Yet we have no problem with nurses, a traditionally female profession, coping with these conditions.

Second, women are ruled by their wombs. Those pesky uteruses, getting in the way of potatoes and pizza dough. Women child-bear in every career going, and while we still have a long way to go with making maternity leave and return to work more viable across the board, they manage it. Plenty of male chefs have children, and make it work around the antisocial hours and physical requirements. If the answer to that is that we expect women to be the primary caregivers, then that's a more widespread problem. Cooking isn't special, untouchable, and we shouldn't pretend otherwise.

The other reason given is that women don't *want* to be in these kitchens. It's self-selecting. With this one, I'd agree: it *is* self-selecting. But it's not that women don't want to be in professional kitchens, it's that they often don't want to be in *these* professional kitchens. The cliché of the highly-strung, food-throwing, emotionally abusive head chef is not far from the truth. Georgie came back from a stage where she described the head chef at a Michelin-starred restaurant finding fault with their preparation for evening service. In a rage, he threw away their day's work. Georgie didn't mind this; she felt that this was the way professional kitchens were run, and women needed to be able to tolerate that if they wanted to be a part of it. I was appalled.

The professional kitchen environment is notoriously an aggressive one. That's supposed to be part of its appeal. It has historically thrived on heat, adrenaline and testosterone. It's not women but kitchen culture that needs to change. The coke-snorting, walk-in-freezer-shagging needs to be firmly confined to the past. Acting like a playboy in any other professional backdrop would be actionable. I don't believe that women should have to try to 'match' men by tolerating these working environments. I kind of think, if you wouldn't do it in an office, or a school, or in front of your partner or mother, you shouldn't be doing it in the workplace at all. Call me a killjoy, but I don't want to be screamed at, I don't want to engage in horseplay, I don't want to be hazed – all in an attempt to prove that I can cook a piece of fish as well as a man can.

I thought of the times I'd enjoyed cooking most. Kate and I had begun spending more and more time hanging out in our kitchens: baking together, devising recipes, coming up with dream menus. It didn't matter where the conversation began, it ended with cookery. When we cooked together, it just made sense. We knew each other's rhythms instinctively, like we were executing a practised dance, both intimately familiar with the steps. Why couldn't I find a kitchen environment more like this?

*

Caramel is such a simple thing to make, and such a frequent feature of the pastry kitchen, that it's easy to overlook how enchanting it is. For me, it's the simplest example of what cooking's about: transformation of an ingredient through heat. Place sugar, and nothing else, in a large pan over a medium heat and wait. Don't add water, don't stir it, just wait. It might clump. But then, slowly, it will melt, and then turn from translucent to pale amber to mahogany. The taste of that caramel bears almost no resemblance to the raw sugar from mere moments ago: it's no longer simply sweet and insipid, but now dark and smoky, with notes of vanilla and cinnamon. It's still sweet, sure, but also it's complicated: it's bitter and buttery, maybe a little sour or savoury. It suddenly has a smell that is distracting and instantly identifiable, just on the right side of burnt. It's smooth and liquid, but leave it to cool and it will set hard as glass, and you can smash it, or grind it down, or just gaze at it. And all you've done is heat it. This, extrapolated, is a large part of the joy of cooking. The careful application of heat to something raw to make it more interesting, more appetizing, to make it better.

Getting caramel to the right point is part of the skill, pulling it from the heat just as it begins to smoke; take it too far and, like me, you might come dangerously close to having the whole of Le Cordon Bleu evacuated. But taking it too far is supposedly what created one of the most famous puddings in history. The tarte Tatin origin story is one of the more ridiculous, and therefore one of my favourites: it is said to have been created in 1898 at the Hôtel Tatin in Lamotte-Beuvron, which was run by two sisters, Stéphanie and Caroline Tatin. One day, Stéphanie was swamped in the kitchen, and forgot about the apples she'd left gently cooking in sugar and butter. She was alerted to her error by that unmistakable smell of burning sugar: track-stopping when you want it, and heart-stopping when you don't. She tried to rescue it by shoving a puff pastry lid on the apples, bunging it in the oven, and offering up a prayer to patron saint of pâtissiers, St Honoré. While this is the kind of stunt I might pull three-quarters of the way through a dinner party I'm hosting and one and a half bottles of wine deep, and end up with some kind of soggy mess that I half-heartedly apologize for, Stéphanie turned her apple pie out on to a plate, and the hotel guests went mad for it. And the rest, as they say, is history.

I'm not going to suggest you make your own puff pastry here (or blow a sugar pear to sit on top). There's a time for making your own puff, and that is when puff will be the star of the show. If you're making palmiers, or millefeuille, by all means spend two days making your own puff. But here, the melting, tooth-janglingly sweet fruit takes centre stage. And unlike shortcrust, the puff you can buy in the supermarket is pretty good. Make sure you go for the all-butter variety (if this book teaches you nothing else, it should teach you this: always, always go for the all-butter variety), and get it in a block, rather than ready-rolled.

I pre-roll and freeze my disc of puff pastry while I'm getting on with the other steps in this recipe. This method ensures that you achieve both fundamentals of a tarte Tatin: crisp pastry, and soft fruit. This pudding is beautiful, with the tessellated pears and the chestnut-coloured caramel, and it's one of the most delicious things you can make. Pears are a great alternative to the traditional apple in this pudding, and pair beautifully with the flavours of chai, using the spices traditionally found in the masala chai spice mix.

Chai pear tarte Tatin

Makes: one 20cm tart that will feed 6–8
Takes: 15 minutes, plus an hour's cooling
Bakes: 70 minutes

300g puff pastry
100g sugar
1 vanilla pod
1 star anise
1 cinnamon stick
6 green cardamom pods
50ml water
6 large pears, peeled and halved, stalks and pips removed
5 coins of stem ginger
60g butter, cubed
25g butter, melted

1. First, freeze your puff pastry! Roll the pastry to the thickness of a pound coin on a lightly floured surface. Cut it into a circle, the size of a dinner plate, place on a baking sheet, prick all

over with a fork, and freeze while you continue with the rest of the recipe.

2. Now, make a spiced caramel. Place the sugar, all the spices, and the water in a 20cm pan that can be used both on the hob and in the oven (no plastic handles!). Cook the sugar over a medium-high heat until it dissolves, and slowly darkens: resist the urge to stir. Take the liquid caramel to a dark amber; remove from the heat just as it begins to smoke, and stir in the butter. Pull out the whole spices.

3. Heat the oven to 160°C fan/180°C/gas 4. Place the pears in the caramel with the flat side facing up, arranging them snugly top to tail, so there are as few gaps as possible. Lop off the top of one of the pear halves, and place the fat bottom half right in the centre (you can eat the top half now – cook's perks!). Mix the 25g of melted butter with a pinch of ground cinnamon, and brush it over the fruit. Bake for 30 minutes, then remove from the oven.

4. Take the pastry disc out of the freezer and place it on top of the pan of fruit. It will defrost and wilt very quickly, allowing you to tuck the edges inside the edges of the pan. Prick five holes in the pastry, then return it to the oven for 40 minutes, until the pastry is golden.

5. Leave to cool for an hour before running a knife around the edge of the dish, then placing a dinner plate over the dish and inverting confidently. The tarte should drop on to the plate, glossy and plump. Cut into slices and serve with a really great vanilla or nutmeg ice cream.

14

Sam and I sat cross-legged on the living room floor surrounded by a rainbow of paper. The problem with ditching your career for something you don't have a proven aptitude for is that it gives you false expectations of your own competence. Not falling flat on my face with pâtisserie had made me feel invincible. I genuinely believed I could turn my hand to anything. And that's how I ended up making over a thousand origami cranes for my wedding.

Having a thousand origami cranes for your wedding is a Japanese tradition. It's called *senbazaru*. Cranes are thought to mate for life, and in Japanese culture, they represent long life, happiness and good luck. The cranes can be presented by the father of the bride, or the parents of one of the couple, or made by the couple themselves as a demonstration of commitment and a task that teaches patience and communication.

We had a large yurt to decorate, and a passing comment from a photographer had ignited the flame. Sam, always game, had agreed. I'd never tried origami before, but how hard could it be? Quite hard, it turns out. I ordered some paper squares, pulled up a YouTube video, and set about the task. The first one took me twenty minutes, was a little shabby thanks to a few false starts and some re-folding, and still didn't look exactly like the perky paper bird at the end of the video. I did the maths. If I didn't get my speed up, I was going to need to spend fourteen full twenty-four-hour days without breaks, to make enough cranes.

We'd recruited family to help us, but Sam and I had taken on the vast majority, and most of our evenings consisted of a couple of hours of papercraft. This evening, I was deep in thought about the wedding. I suppose, given the last few years of loss, I shouldn't have been surprised that I was feeling a little wobbly about getting married. There was a real disconnect: I had absolutely no doubts that Sam was the man I wanted to marry. But there was this niggle. Well, more than a niggle: I was absolutely terrified of committing to him. To anyone or anything. The thing I'd loved most in the world had been taken away from me without notice, warning or permission. Why would I willingly put myself through that again? Why would I put myself in harm's way? What if something went wrong? How would I survive? I'd coped with declarations of love, cohabiting, buying a house, engagement. More than coped: embraced, wanted. But there was something about the wedding itself that wigged me out.

I hadn't brought it up with Sam yet, because it was so stupid, and it didn't in any way affect how much I wanted to get married to him. But as we sat on the floor, I couldn't stop myself asking. 'You're not . . . nervous about getting married, are you?' He answered without looking up from his folding. 'Nope.' That was it. I think he thought he was being reassuring. Chastened, I returned to my cranes.

If I'm honest, I'd taken them on for mostly aesthetic reasons: I liked the idea of multicoloured paper birds fluttering across the roof of the yurt, swooping and undulating on maypole-style ribbons. But there's no way of gaming the system. If you're going to make a thousand cranes, you have to devote the time to it. You'll get faster, of course, but, however speedy you are, it's a lot of folding. As I folded my forty-seventh crane of the evening, probably the three-hundredth I'd made so far, I got it. This was what mattered, this was the big commitment. The wedding was just a party really. The commitment was the daily stuff: the being present in the relationship even when stuff was tough. Even when the other person irritated the hell out of you. It was the slow, tricky bits of a relationship that spelt out true commitment. It wasn't walking down the aisle, or a string of sentimental speeches; it was the hours and hours spent sitting at home, making cranes together. And I realized that there was no one I'd rather make hundreds of stupid paper cranes with; no one I'd rather chastise for not following steps properly; no one I'd rather congratulate when he got the hang of it.

This was the man I loved. I loved the songs he made up and sang when he thought no one was listening. I loved how he loved all animals, even wasps (I *hate* wasps). How he loved pyjamas, and crochet, and supermarket cafés. That he loved even the things I hate about myself: the stupid crease that I get on the snub of my nose when I rub it, the Orion's belt of tiny moles on my neck, that I fall asleep the moment my head hits the pillow. I loved his club sandwiches over and above any dish I'd ever eaten, no matter how fancy or well-executed. I loved how hard he worked, how much he wanted to be a better person. How he made me want to be better. I loved that, for all his cautiousness, he had absolute faith in my abilities. I loved that his anxiety matched mine, but that we dealt with it in a see-saw fashion, making sure that when one struggled, the other bolstered. I loved that we were a team. I loved him, and life is too short to hold your heart in reserve.

The all-important final exam was only a few weeks away. But first, we had to tackle what the teaching chefs assured us was the high point of the course: afternoon tea. By this point, each practical was a marathon, rather than a sprint. Even the 'simpler' superior practicals were six hours, but for the afternoon tea, we would do a total of fifteen hours of preparation, before serving up our wares to friends, family, and distinguished guests of the school. It was celebratory, a showcase of what we'd learnt over the previous nine months. But of course, it was also assessed, and would count towards our final mark – the equivalent of four ordinary practicals.

We were put into teams. Mine was allocated carrot cake, with piped orange cream cheese icing and candied orange zest; lemon possets with tiny macarons and candied lemon zest and sugar decoration; marcelins, which are individual pastry tart cases, filled with marzipan, macerated peel, raspberry jam and a kirsch-almond-egg white mixture; princes noirs, and a whole host of scones.

A prince noir is a sort of very elaborate Black Forest gâteau, comprised of a chocolate-almond sponge soaked in boozy cherry syrup, crisp praline feuilletine, and milk and white chocolate mousses piped on in tight strips, which gives the effect of a curving, undulating top. The whole thing is spray-gunned with milk chocolate, then cut into small rectangles and topped with bright green pistachios, kirsch-soaked cherries, and little twists of tempered dark chocolate.

No two teams had the same tasks. There was everything from chocolate and salted caramel choux buns, to tarte aux fruits, ginger praline millefeuille, and strawberry and champagne mousses. There were a whole host of cakes and petits fours which I'd never even heard of: the glazed orange mousses sandwiched between dehydrated orange slices called clairfontaines. Something enigmatically called a 'galaxie', which used a flourless chocolate cake base soaked with framboise, topped with raspberry chocolate mousse, raspberry glaze, three different types of decoration and 'optional' gold leaf. There was the even more baffling 'citrus garden', which hid a grapefruit jelly inside a citrus mousse, sitting upon a base of coconut lime dacquoise (a coconutty meringue, a little like a macaron), piped with Italian meringue, and decorated with toasted coconut and candied lime zest.

Even the seemingly straightforward items were anything but: almost every one required individual pieces of sugar or chocolate work, which would need to be painstakingly prepared. A bunch of éclairs needed bubblegum meringue and raspberry gel, and the coffee and walnut cake required a blonde chocolate (a bit like posh Cara-mac) glaze. Even the chocolate fudge cake needed a two-toned dark and white chocolate cigarette.

One of the mantras of the professional kitchen – and when I say mantra, I mean something you will regularly hear people say without irony in a professional kitchen – is *Teamwork makes the dream work.* As well as being trite, and not quite scanning, this mantra was anathema to me. It set my teeth on edge. I'd done a degree that required you to squirrel yourself away with just your books for company. I'd been self-employed for almost my whole working life, and in a profession which, for the most part, directly pits you against your contemporaries. In the earlier terms, although we'd been working in pairs, you were still presenting your own dishes, still con-structing your own stuff, responsible for what you were being graded on. But now things were different. Every-thing was collaborative. I didn't like being dependent on other people, nor deferring to them. Teamwork was unfamiliar to me, and made me feel stupid. When forced, my general attitude towards it is to define my role clearly early on, stick doggedly to it, avoid other members of the team as much as possible, then ask to be judged only on my bit (unless my fellow team members have really excelled themselves, in which case I will graciously accept a bit of reflected glory).

We began our prep. Savannah, the slowest member of the team, was tasked with the simplest dish: the carrot cake. Penny took on the marcelin and the scones, I the princes noirs and posset. To tell the truth, I was pretty pissed off I'd ended up in a team with Savannah: she didn't seem to care, and worked so languidly it made me want to shake her. We had so much to do. That was the whole *point* of this exercise – to see how we coped with big workloads, with enormous numbers of products. Three hours into our first six-hour day, she was still grating carrots. I hadn't arrived with a huge amount of patience, and it was rapidly diminishing. Meanwhile, Penny had blind-baked dozens of tart shells, made marzipan and a frangipane topping; I had made my little nubbly macaroons, my possets, prepped my orange for dehydrating, and made the feuilletine base and first layer of milk chocolate mousse for my princes noirs. I went home and bitched to Sam about the ineptitude of other people.

On day two, Savannah arrived twenty-five minutes late, and seemed to have little idea what she was supposed to be doing, despite the three-hour planning session. I bit my tongue and got on with my tasks. I couldn't be penalized for someone else's poor work, I reasoned. Plus, all she had to do was candy some orange peel and make some cream cheese icing to pipe on to the carrot cakes. She couldn't get it *that* wrong.

Meanwhile, I spray-gunned chocolate on to my prince noir, covering the undulating strips of mousse with edible velvet. Carefully, I cut the cake into perfect rectangles, using my ruler to measure to the millimetre. I tempered dark chocolate, spread it on to sheets of acetate, dragged a plastic comb through the melted chocolate, then positioned it carefully on curved baking trays, normally used for shaping baguettes. When they had dried, they peeled away from the acetate in glossy spirals that could be placed on top of the individual slices of the cake. At the same time, Penny was piping white chocolate mousse, assembling her marcelins, and making dozens of scones. I checked in on what Savannah was up to. She was two hours into day two, and all she had done so far was candy a few strips of orange, a task that should have taken her a fifth of the time. I put my head down and got on with my own work.

I flew through the remaining four hours in blind panic, trying to catch up the time we had lost through Savannah, frantically stirring, cutting, piping, assembling, like a beetle on its back. Where had all the time gone? Was this how the afternoon tea always went? Or were we just really, really shit?

As we neared the final portion of the practical I was reaching the end of my tether. We had had to work so fast to make up for Savannah's incompetence and snail-speed that I felt like we hadn't done justice to any of our bakes. I'd lost perspective a bit: objectively, the princes noirs were pride-inducing, one of the most elegant things I'd made, and my chocolate work was glossy and sharp, but I was so disappointed by how much we'd rushed, that there were elements I'd had to miss off. I'd stopped talking to Savannah by this point; there'd been no blow-up between us, I'd just lost any last remnant of patience. How she'd managed to pass the first two terms was beyond me.

Each superior student is allowed to invite one, and only one, guest to the afternoon tea. I had been sad in the weeks leading up to the afternoon tea project that I couldn't invite my mum as my guest, like most of my classmates were. The afternoon tea is the one opportunity the pâtisserie students have to showcase what they've achieved over nearly nine months. As I walked around clutching teapots, and trying not to spill milk over guests, I avoided Sam's eye. Our finished cakes looked lovely, now that they were out on their stands, but I felt so *stupid*. Suddenly, I was heart-tearingly, skin-blisteringly glad that my mother wasn't here to see me unable to turn out a handful of cakes without losing my rag and letting my work suffer.

The marking took place in our teams after the guests had left. Now that it was all over and the prospect of a stiff drink wasn't too far away, I was feeling slightly more positive, especially with an example of each of our products in front of us which, somehow, had ended up looking quite handsome. We sat down as a three in front of Chef Julie, and I waited to be congratulated on pulling more than my weight, on my feverish work over the last few days. I was sure that it couldn't have escaped her notice that our team had been unbalanced and that I had done the tasks assigned to me, and turned out decent dishes. Chef Julie congratulated us on our cakes, and then turned her attention to our teamwork. She explained how demoralizing it can be to be the only person on a long task, how isolating that can feel. She looked pointedly from me and Penny to Savannah. The subtext was clear: *you hung her out to dry.* She gently suggested that good teamwork is more about the spirit of the word than mere divvying up of tasks, that delegation only works if you check in, if you support each other. I felt like a prize tit. In many ways, afternoon tea taught me what I'd already known: that I simply wasn't built for teamwork.

After much deliberation, and a little bit of trial and error, I had decided on my entremet design and flavours. The base would be a salted milk chocolate praline feuilletine, crisp and compulsive, like a truly grown-up chocolate cornflake cake. On top of that would be a white chocolate and cardamom mousse, with a mango custard layer set inside it. Wrapped around it would be a hazelnut joconde sponge, a light, flexible sponge made with ground hazelnuts, where normally it has almonds, and over the top, a strawberry glaze. I would decorate all of this with apricot-flavoured tuile biscuits, dark chocolate shaped into feathers and twirled into ribbons, just like I'd made for the afternoon tea's princes noirs. Hoping for a steady hand, I planned to pipe in chocolate the same double helixes that had served me so well way back in basic term; those would hold mango and strawberry purée, and the bizarrely compulsory crème anglaise.

The sponge layer, we knew, must be patterned. This is achieved by another little bit of kitchen magic: you mix together icing sugar, flour and butter to create what's called a pâte à décor, then spread it or pipe it on to a baking tray, and freeze it. Once frozen, the cake batter can be spread over the top with a palette knife and baked; the pâte à décor will retain its shape, while baking into the sponge. It can be swooshed, or piped, or spread over a template: the pattern possibilities are limited only by your imagination and the steadiness of your hand, and it looks pretty whizzy when it works. I'd started off with an inexplicable plan for a steampunk-themed entremet, despite having no interest in steampunk, and had planned to pattern my sponge with different-sized cogs, but when the template arrived, it was hopeless, far too small. Daisy, braver than I, made her own stencil, a beautiful design of carousel horses, dancing their way around the edge of the round entremet. James was making an exquisite bird pattern which he would echo in his tuile shaping. Others in my class went as simple as possible: running combed plastic through the pâte à décor to create stripes or waves. Post-steampunk, I went for the middle ground, with a fleur-de-lis template, repeating around my cake.

I practised the entremet at home but I hit a brick wall when it came to my mango insert. For the first time, we were being judged on our flavour combinations, so I couldn't just sub in a different fruit like I had done in previous terms, caring only about the technique and texture. The problem was, it's pretty hard to find mango purée in the shops. I looked online and balked at the price of the industrial stuff that we used at college. I traipsed the aisles of my supermarket hoping that the answer would appear. And then inspiration struck: baby food. If I went for the good stuff, in the little brightly coloured pouches, it would be pure fruit purée. Buoyed up by own brilliance, I gleefully grabbed a pouch and headed to the checkout. Luckily, just before I poured it into the white chocolate mousse base, and folded it through whipped cream, I glanced at the packet. It turns out that mango baby food and chicken casserole baby food pouches are almost identical colours. I'm sure a shivering, perfectly set gelatine chicken casserole would have been a dinner party hit in the 1970s, but I was glad to avoid finding out the hard way.

It wasn't just my entremet that was demanding cake-based decisions. The one question everyone asked me about the wedding was: are you going to make your own cake? My answer was always accompanied by an eye-roll. 'Of course not! I'm not a masochist!' But when it came to deciding who *would* make it, and what it might look like, I was stumped. I knew that the cake was important to me; far more important than it would be to most, and that I was therefore devoting perhaps a disproportionate amount of thinking time to it. But if you're going to give up a perfectly good career for cake, you'd better make sure you have a good one at your wedding. James, I knew, made the most incredible wedding cakes. Each was an intricate, baroque sugarcraft sculpture, as if carved from marble. But it turned out that James couldn't make mine. He was living in student accommodation, after all, and worse still, he was due to undertake an internship at a Michelin-starred restaurant when I was getting married, and so would be working every hour that God sent. I'd been half-heartedly googling other wedding cake designers, but none looked quite right. It didn't help that I still hadn't worked out what I actually wanted.

Sam, susceptible to basically any visual stimulus, and

incredibly impulsive when it came to wedding planning (he took me *quite* by surprise when we met the florist to discuss the pared-back and, frankly, cheap style we were going for, and he suddenly blurted out that he wanted a ten-foot flower arch covered in roses), was not helping. Every time I came home from school with a new bake, he used that as a not-terribly-realistic springboard for a new cake suggestion. At one point, he straight-facedly suggested four stacked entremets. The day I failed to make the blown sugar apple was particularly galling. 'I'm sorry, let me get this right. You want me to find a cake maker who will produce twenty-four blown sugar orbs on what I'm assuming is some kind of Christmas tree-themed wedding cake?' 'Yeah, exactly!' Sam said, missing my point, my face, my tone.

I was pissed off. It was important that we got the wedding cake right, and I didn't think Sam was adequately engaging with my dilemma. I knew I was obsessing, but *I'd quit a career for cake.* I cared about the flowers and the music, sure, but cake was my thing. I just wanted it to be special.

One night, after wasting more hours looking fruitlessly for my perfect cake online, and more idiotic suggestions from Sam, my caprice got the better of me. 'Do you know what?' I said to Sam. 'I'll bloody do it myself.' 'Liv,' Sam said, in that controlled tone of voice that means he is indulging me, but thinks I am an idiot. (I know this tone of voice all too well.) 'You've said from day one you wouldn't do your own wedding cake. You didn't want the faff. And you're right! You don't want to be messing around with a cake on the morning of our wedding.' 'I know,' I said. 'But I've got this idea. Hear me out.'

*

If our afternoon tea module was distilled into its most essential parts it would be this: something bite-size and crisp, filled with something creamy and unusually flavoured. I'm almost certainly never going to make a citrus garden again, or decorate Battenberg with sugar lace butterflies. But these choux buns are an afternoon tea treat for the real world, and I make them regularly when I want to impress and delight.

The Earl Grey custard is the star of this dish. Its base is a simple vanilla crème pâtissière, but before you start, you infuse the milk with Earl Grey until it's sepia. The custard retains the bitter, complex flavour incredibly well – a perfect counterpoint to the sweetness of the vanilla, and the richness of the cream.

The second thing that sets these buns aside is the craquelin. Craquelin is a little disc of sugary dough that sits on top of the choux pastry and cracks as it cooks, giving the buns a beautiful cratered and rutted appearance, like the surface of the moon. It helps the choux rise evenly, and covers any imperfections: it's one of my favourite cheats in the pastry world. It's also made with light brown sugar, so adds an extra note of caramel complexity.

Earl Grey choux buns

Makes: 18 buns
Takes: 30 minutes, plus cooling
Bakes: 30 minutes

For the custard
250ml milk
3 Earl Grey tea bags
1 teaspoon vanilla extract
2 egg yolks
60g light brown sugar
30g cornflour
200g double cream

For the craquelin
70g plain flour
35g light brown sugar
65g butter

For the choux
120ml milk
50g butter
1 tablespoon sugar
½ teaspoon salt
75g strong white bread flour
3 eggs, beaten

1. Place the milk in a medium-sized pan with the
   tea bags. Bring up to simmering, then remove
   from the heat and leave to one side for half an

hour. Then squeeze the tea bags and discard, and stir the milk. Pop it back on the stove, add the vanilla, and heat the milk until it is steaming again.

2. Whisk together the egg yolks and light brown sugar until the mixture is noticeably paler than when you began, then whisk in the cornflour.

3. Pour a third of the steaming milk mixture on to the egg yolks, whisking gently the whole time. Stir until the mixture is smooth. Pour the milky-egg mixture back into the pan and bring slowly up to the boil, whisking the whole time, making sure you're reaching the edges of the pan. Once you see big gloopy bubbles appearing at different areas of the pan, your custard is ready. Decant it immediately on to a clean tray or plate, and cover with clingfilm; the clingfilm should touch the hot mixture. Leave to cool completely in the fridge.

4. Rub the ingredients for the craquelin topping together until they resemble breadcrumbs, then squish together into a dough. Roll out between two sheets of baking paper to 1mm thick, and freeze.

5. For the choux, combine the milk, butter, sugar and salt in a pan, and bring to a quick boil over a medium heat.

6. Beat the flour into the choux using a spatula, and continue to cook while beating until you can hear sizzling and the mixture comes away from the sides of the pan. Turn out on to a large dinner plate, cover with clingfilm and leave to cool for around 10 minutes, until the dough is warm, rather than hot.

7. Place the mixture in a bowl and add the beaten eggs in small increments, beating each addition thoroughly into the mixture. You will probably only need 2 of the eggs, so go slowly. When you think the choux is ready, pick up a dollop on your spatula and shake it off: if what remains on the spatula drops down in a deep 'V' shape, you have added enough egg; if not, add a little more and test again.

8. Heat the oven to 170°C fan/190°C/gas 5. Spoon the choux into a piping bag fitted with a medium-sized piping nozzle and pipe small blobs – about the size of a ping-pong ball – on to an oven tray lined with greaseproof paper.

9. Remove the craquelin from the freezer and stamp out small circles, about the same circumference as the choux, and place one on top of each blob.

10. Bake for 20 minutes, then drop the oven temperature to 150°C fan/170°C/gas 3. Bake

for another 5 minutes, then open the oven to release any built-up steam, and bake for a final 5 minutes. The choux is ready when it releases from the tray, and moves around easily. Pierce the base of each bun with a slim skewer. Set to one side on a cooling rack.

11. Scrape the custard into a stand mixer or food processor; it will be solid and wobbly, but don't be disconcerted. Whisk the custard vigorously or blitz it in the food processor until smooth and lump-free.

12. Whisk the cream to medium-peak: when you lift the whisk out, the cream should support its own weight, but the very end of it will flop over. Add a third of the whipped cream to the custard, and beat it in vigorously until the mixture is combined. Take the second third of the whipped cream and fold it in gently, using a large metal spoon: do this by turning the spoon on its side, and cutting it through the middle of the mixture, then fold the bottom of the mixture up and over the top. Give the bowl a quarter turn and repeat, until the mixture is a homogenous colour – avoid overmixing! Repeat with the final third. Place the lightened custard into a piping bag with a 0.5cm piping nozzle.

13. Using a skewer or small knife, create an opening in the bottom of each choux bun. Pipe in the custard gently, until the bun is full. Neaten the buns by wiping away the excess custard from the hole.

15

Every day brought with it more details, chores and decisions that needed to be made for our upcoming wedding. And with every decision I became more acutely aware of the hole Mum's absence left in my life.

She would have been a nightmare, but that didn't make it any easier to bear. Every point in the planning process would have been trickier with Mum by my side; she had just as many opinions on the propriety of weddings as she did on funerals. She would have wanted things just so. She wouldn't have approved of my wedding invitations (*They should be from me and your father! You can't invite people to your own wedding!*), and she especially wouldn't have approved of when we chose to send them (*No more than six weeks before!*). She would have longed for the wedding to be up north – specifically, at our village church, where I would have been able to walk from my home to the ceremony on the big day. But without her, a northern wedding felt wrong. We didn't live there any more. It wasn't my home.

I had a peculiar internal dialogue of trying to work out what she would have wanted, and then arguing the toss with her about any decisions I had made that may not have met with her approval. This quickly crept into actual conversations. Sitting next to Sam surrounded by names,

317

we tried to decide on a table plan: 'I don't want a top table,' I told him. 'I know, Liv,' he replied, 'we've talked about this. I agree with you.' 'It's just that I want to mix up friends and family. Plus there'd be too many people who'd need to go on the top table!' 'Yes, I know, I think that's sensible.' A slightly tired note had entered Sam's tone. 'Look, I know top tables are traditional, but it's just *not the solution here,*' I explained, plaintively. 'Liv. I get it. We are not in disagreement here. You don't need to persuade me.' I paused. 'I know,' I said. 'I know.' It was like I needed to give voice to her opinions, even when they clearly were at odds with mine and Sam's. We went through the same farce with every decision: flowers, invites, readings, vows, menus, veils. It went on and on.

In a rare moment when I wasn't entremet planning, I went dress shopping. Alone. I didn't feel terribly sad at the prospect; I honestly saw it as squeezing a chore in between a morning demo and an early evening lecture. Maddy lived so far away that it seemed silly to drag her down to London, and I'd been around a couple of shops with Ruth. I had a very specific brief for the dress, and I was, I told myself, being an efficient and competent woman. I sat at the front of the shop, waiting for an assistant, as countless mothers and daughters bustled in past me. I tried on dress after dress, everything from meringues to clinging Grecian togas. Alongside me, my fellow brides-to-be did the same. But with each dress they tried, there was a mother to dissolve into tears at the sight of her daughter. Shining, beaming. My resilience faltered. I felt very, very lonely.

I'd never done anything like this before, but I'd read books, I'd seen films: if there isn't your mum there, eyes welling up, whispering, 'That's the one,' how on earth do you know?

Panicked, I called Charis. Charis lived in Sweden and, as well as being one of my oldest friends, happened to be a disgustingly talented fashion designer. 'I don't know what to do,' I told her. 'Nothing looks right. Nothing feels right. I've tried everything.' 'Don't worry, we'll fix it. We're going to make you a dress.' Immediately, I felt relief wash over me.

I'd been sure that I didn't want bridesmaids (and I rather suspected my mother would have found the idea of grown-up bridesmaids vulgar). I'd always planned to have Maddy as maid of honour – in fact, I'd already asked her – along with my goddaughter as flower girl and my soon-to-be nephew as page boy. As was my wont, I had been pretty vocal about the fact that I didn't want bridesmaids. But suddenly, abruptly, more than anything in the world I wanted the women in my life standing alongside me on my wedding day.

When someone you love dies, they don't just take their thoughts and memories with them. They take yours. They, whether or not you or they are conscious of it, act as a kind of witness to your life. Without that witness – that person who can say, *Yes, that happened, just as you remember it,* or, *Remember when . . . ?,* or even, *That's not how it was! –* your identity falters. Without Mum, parts of my identity felt gossamer thin, unverifiable, consigned to the realm of unreliable memories. Along with Maddy, my four oldest friends – Ruth, Suzy, Charis and Steph – had been the witnesses to my life. They held parts of my identity in their own lives. I needed them with me. Also, I loved them, and I knew they loved me, and I was ready to make an active choice to be surrounded by love on my wedding day. In one hour, and several phone calls, I went from zero bridesmaids to five.

It would be stupid to pretend that my wedding day wouldn't be tainted by Mum's absence. That I could overlook that absence and its effect in the way that I had tried so hard to do in every other aspect of my life. By now, I knew that I'd dealt with my grief badly by denying its existence, or its effect on me. The truth was, I was still a complete mess.

I'd been going to therapy now for a few weeks. Slowly, with patient probing and direction, I was learning how to sit with the pain I had ignored for so long. John and I picked away at the narrative I had carved and smoothed out. We broke away from my hypothesizing, my justifying, my caveating. Fortunately for me, my therapist was not interested in nice turns of phrase, or narrative structure. I tried to be more open with Dad and Maddy, forcing myself to talk to them about how I was processing the grief, rather than just trying to make them laugh, so they'd forget about their own.

'What is it that makes you sad when you think of her?' John asked me quietly. My mind went blank. I'd got so good at not allowing myself to engage with those thoughts, and letting the pain sit untouched, that I genuinely didn't know how to begin thinking about what specifically made me feel so overwhelmingly sad. When I didn't respond, John just waited. I thought of sitting on the sofa next to her, I thought of our daily phone calls, I thought of her perfect ham and tomato sandwiches. I thought of her always, without fail, being on my team. I thought of everything she had missed and everything I wanted to tell her. I couldn't speak. Eventually I managed to get the words out. 'I just miss her,' I said. And I cried, properly, without immediately trying to stop, without feeling embarrassed, for the first time in front of another person. It sounded so obvious once I'd said it.

I turned up to our very final practical ready to resent it. This was the 'modern tart'; a whole module squeezed into a single six-hour practical. For this dish, each student would produce a different tart made up of a variety of elements, those elements dictated by the number they drew on entering the kitchen. I was having none of it: we were about to sit exams that required focusing on about a dozen different recipes – why on earth would I want to waste some of my precious revision time to make something completely unconnected to our final dish? We had been told to view it as an opportunity to practise techniques that were relevant to the exam, but I wasn't interested. I was, at best, truculent.

I was tired, too. The afternoon tea had unsettled me. I didn't really know that baking could make me sad, that it could make me feel incompetent or incomplete; it had always been my antidote to that. I knew I had the exam to go, and to a certain extent, was ready simply to endure it. Grit my teeth, get through it, and hope to God I passed. I was here to satisfy my attendance requirement, and then move on. This was a six-hour practical – small fry after afternoon tea. I just had to get through it, and then I was done.

I plucked a number from Chef Olivier's hat as I walked into the classroom: station two. I looked up the tart elements I'd been given on the chef's spreadsheet: a pâte sablée (shortcrust pastry) base, with a pineapple and vanilla jam layer, a white chocolate and banana crisp, a lemon success, a mango and lime mousse, and a white chocolate glaze. OK, that sounded all right. I didn't actually know what a 'success' was, ironically, but the beauty of superior term, unlike the previous two, meant that I had recipes for all of these items. All I had to do was follow them.

The 'modern' element of this modern tart appeared to amount to making a shortcrust pastry case about five centimetres bigger than the cake that sat inside it. This would create a moat around the tart filling that would be filled with the poached pineapple, and then topped with fresh fruit. (You could make the whole thing – pastry and interior – square, but frankly that was a bit *too* modern for my liking.)

I made my pastry case without incident, and the so-called lemon success turned out to be very similar to a macaron recipe, piped or spread on to a baking tray. My insert – the banana crunch – was made by tempering white chocolate and cocoa butter, stirring in blitzed freeze-dried banana pieces, rolling between two pieces of baking paper, then chilling until hard. To cut the correct shape from it, I warmed a metal ring gently on the stove and placed it on the chocolate crunch until a clean disc of banana chocolate came away from the cut-offs.

It took me forever to prepare my pineapple: trimming it, removing its eyes, and then slowly, slowly, finely dicing the entire thing, reducing the fruit to the size of Tic Tacs. Other people had been allocated Bramley apples, pears, and raspberries – things that simmered down with minimal effort, and didn't try to attack you as you cut them up. I felt envious. If I'd been keener on this practical, perhaps I would have seen it as a labour of love. But I wasn't, so I didn't. I tossed the pineapple into the pan, split a vanilla pod, pulling the seeds out with the back of my knife and scraping them into the fruit pan. I added a splash of water and a few tablespoons of sugar, turned the heat to low, and thought no more about it. I had bigger fish to fry (or mousses to whisk).

Twenty minutes later, I was distracted by the smell coming from my hob. But not in the way I was becoming reluctantly used to: the simultaneously nutty and acrid smell that points to burnt chocolate, the panic-making whiff of smoke from a bubbling caramel. The pineapple smelt *amazing*. I'd never smelt anything like it, complicated and aromatic. It was like the platonic ideal of pineapple. I looked around, feeling almost suspicious; did everyone here know how amazing this combination was? How was it possible that the application of heat and a bit of vanilla could produce something so magical? How could it be so much greater than the sum of its parts? I'd spent nine months intensively learning about pastries and puddings, and something as simple as pineapple and vanilla could knock me sideways! It could make me happy.

I returned to my other tasks feeling buoyed. I demoulded my mousse and placed it atop the lemon success and banana crunch. I made a glaze using milk, gelatine, glucose and white chocolate, then added yellow food colouring until it was the shade of daffodils, and poured it over my tart interior. I lifted it into the pastry case and spooned my precious pineapple jam around it, topping it with fresh fruit. I took a piece of isomalt sugar from the silicone mat, twisted it around my steel and pulled it free, creating a little spiral, and made another that looped around a metal ring. Pulled sugar didn't faze me any more. I propped the spiral across a piece of fresh pineapple, and balanced the loop around a small cluster of raspberries. And with that, I was done. This was the last time I'd be in this kitchen before my final exam. I'd entered the room six hours earlier hacked off, but I was leaving feeling pretty damn good – about my tart, about my course, and about myself.

Thinking about the tart on the Tube on my way home, the penny had finally dropped. The sablés and genoise, the mousses and glazes were not ends in themselves, but were there to drill us in components for more complicated, impressive and delicious dishes. I'd been undergoing the pâtisserie version of *The Karate Kid*: training, building muscle memory through what felt like pointless tasks. It had taken me a while to understand that we were not

324

being taught a string of recipes, however much it felt that way as I ploughed through practical after practical. We were being taught techniques – a thousand different ways to manipulate the ingredients we were given into almost anything. We were now at a stage where we could follow the briefest of instructions for the most complicated of elements, and then we could combine them into impressive, professional puddings. We could smell when caramel was cooked, hear when cakes were baked, feel when bread was proved, and see when chocolate was tempered. We could create our own recipes for these elements, we could design our own dishes. We were ready.

There was almost no one in the locker room as I dressed for my final exam. For the last time, I put on my chequered trousers, wound my neckerchief, buttoned up my chef's jacket, tied on my apron, smoothed my oven cloth and tea towel around my waist, and tucked my ponytail into my hairnet. Where only a few months ago I'd felt like a total idiot in the uniform, and didn't even know how to tie my neckerchief, now I felt that I'd earned the right to wear it with pride, even if the jacket and trousers didn't quite suit me. I picked up my knife kit, my sheaf of papers listing my recipes, my time plan and my diagrams and, making my way up to the exam kitchen alone, began the loneliest ascent of the last year.

Six hours is a very long time. It's a long time to concentrate for. It's a long time to be surrounded by people without speaking to them. It's two-thirds of the *Lord of the Rings* trilogy. It's a long time to plan down to five-minute intervals. At the same time, it's a very, very short period in which to produce one full-size and two individual entremets that require multiple refrigerations. There's no real time for mistakes, even if you were permitted to remake elements. Our exam start times for the superior exam were staggered. The rationale is a good one: every person has to present their three dishes to the judges, and it would be carnage trying to get three large plates of pudding for every student up to the judging room at once. The reality is that the blast chiller, required for just about every element of every dish, is opened continuously, meaning that it never really reaches the temperature it should be at, making every 'set' element more of a risk. You could guard against this by upping your gelatine content – how much you used was up to you – but as every teaching chef had warned us, producing an over-gelatined, rubbery dish was a cardinal sin. An entremet that bounced instead of shivered, one that didn't yield to the spoon, would be looked upon *extremely* poorly.

In truth, a bouncy cake was the least of my worries. For the last three weeks, horror stories about final exams had abounded. Rumours flew between us – about students miscalculating their ingredients and running out of eggs halfway through, or throwing away their sponge by mistake. One of the peculiar requirements of the exams is that the candidate has to personally carry their entremet to the judges. Last year, so the rumour went, one student had tripped on this journey, sending her entremet flying, and had failed the course. It made me feel extremely aware of my small, clumsy feet, and the clowny kitchen clogs I was forced to wear.

I felt the panic rise as I unpacked my knife kit and set up my station. I'd made stacks of notes, each element on a separate page, in its own plastic folder. I'd brought little plastic tubs, each labelled with masking tape showing ingredients and quantities. The idea was that this would make everything idiot-proof, that even if I, the idiot in question, panicked, my recipes and methods would be impossible to get wrong. But what I'd actually done was give myself a whole new way of working for the exam, different from every other time I'd been in this kitchen. I felt lost. I took a breath, tried to ground myself. *Come on, Liv. One foot in front of the other.* I started with the crispy chocolate layer, the simplest of all my elements. I tempered praline and milk chocolate and feuilletine wafers together, and spread them on a tray, before cutting a circle from the mixture and placing it at the base of my metal ring. Standing over the bain-marie filled with chocolate, as I had done dozens of times over the past nine months, stirring the bowl and scraping down the sides, I relaxed just a little. I found myself easing into those kitchen rhythms that had drawn me to baking in the first place. I made a mango custard and entrusted it to the blast chiller. I froze my fleur-de-lis pâte à décor pattern, then made my hazelnut joconde, spreading the mixture on top of the frozen pâte à décor. When it was baked – hot pink fleur-de-lis set against a tawny background – I pulled the unwieldy tray from the oven easily, stretchering my oven cloth between my two hands, calling 'Backs please!' as I wound my way past Alex and Savannah. I cut the sponge to size before lifting it from the tray and winding it round the inside of my metal ring. I had made a white chocolate and cardamom mousse, praying that it would neither over- nor under-set. And now I spooned the mousse inside the joconde border, dropping the mango custard in the middle, and then topping with more mousse and smoothing it off with a palette knife. I put it into the blast chiller and hoped for the best.

We were two hours in when Penny, in the position opposite me, suddenly stopped dead. There was a look of complete horror on her face. I paused on the chocolate I was tempering and tried to work out what was wrong. Oh, no. Oh no oh no oh no. She had just made her mousse for her entremet, and like I had just done, spooned it into her metal mould, with her sponge on the inside, levelled it off, and put it in the blast chiller. Then she had returned to her station, clearing as she went, like a good superior student, intent on not losing marks for hygiene or work method. And now she was standing there holding the five sheets of unused gelatine she had forgotten to melt into the mousse. Without gelatine, the mousse stood absolutely no chance of setting. It was just a mixture of fruit purée and whipped cream and a little bit of custard; there was no way she would manage to unmould the cake without it splurging out.

Chef Matthew, one of the two chefs invigilating our exam and sensing trouble, stepped in to find out what was going on. 'I can't tell you what to do,' he said gently. 'What are your options?' Penny, eyes wide, looking like she might bolt, or heave, or both, clearly racked her brains for the pâtisserie knowledge that at any other point would come easily. Between sobs, she replied: 'I can add the gelatine in, or I can leave it,' she said. 'Right,' said the chef. 'What happens if you leave it?' 'It won't set,' she said, clearly heartbroken. 'And what happens if you add the gelatine?' he prompted. 'I'll need to add it to the mousse, which means heating the mousse, and then all the body from the whipped cream will fall, so it *still* probably won't set firm!' She couldn't start again with new ingredients – no repeats; no take-backsies – so re-adding the cream wasn't an option. 'I can't tell you what to do,' Matthew said again. Penny made her choice, and retrieved her entremet from the blast chiller: she was going to add the gelatine. This is what I'd have done too in the same sorry circumstances, but I felt sick for Penny, as I watched her scooping her beautiful, whipped mousse out of the mould into a pan on the hob, knowing that it likely wouldn't set properly. Nine months of good, hard work, of technique and skill, could be lost in a moment's distraction. It seemed so unfair.

With effort, I returned my focus to my own bench, and my to-do list. I polished serving plates until they shone and then, as we'd been taught, wrapped them in clingfilm to protect them from dust and grease. I made apricot tuiles and crème anglaise and a bright pink strawberry glaze. I tempered my chocolate and made chocolate feathers with it. Done properly they are exquisite: so delicate that they look like they could float. It looked like a Labrador puppy had had a hand (or paw) in mine.

I took my cold entremet from the chiller and licked the sides with a blowtorch, easing it from its mould. It slipped out cleanly, releasing with a slurp, showing my brightly coloured patterned sponge, a strip of ivory mousse, and at the top, the thinnest line of pale pink. I looked at it critically: the jelly glaze simply did not want to set, but at least it wasn't running off the sides. The tuiles were a little sad and floppy; I'd never managed to get the hang of them, no matter how many times we had encountered them in class. In brighter news, my crème anglaise was perfect, and sat neatly in the chocolate pattern I had piped on to the plates.

My hands shook as I placed the chocolate feathers on my entremet, the very final step in my cake-baking marathon, both the six-hour and the nine-month one. I finished this precarious step and moved my still-trembling hands away, seconds before Chef Dominique called time. I carried the entremet carefully to the judging room, heart pounding, trying not to think about my clodhopping kitchen shoes, or the ramifications of tripping. I handed over the entremets, shook hands with the chefs and, for the last time, picked up my knife kit. For better or worse, my time studying pâtisserie at Le Cordon Bleu was over.

*

OK, let me be straight with you: I tried to include the full entremet recipe here. Really, I wrote the whole thing out. Every element of it, right down to the chocolate feathers, and those slightly floppy apricot tuiles. But my publishers were having none of it. It went on for *pages* and, if I can't honestly say that I will ever make the damn thing again, it seems foolish to imagine you will. So instead, I'm going to cut straight to the best bit: that crisp chocolate layer. Even after nine months of sampling every item I made at school, right from the fruit salad through to the afternoon tea, it was the chocolate crunch that Sam couldn't get enough of: he ate piles and piles of the offcuts, then begged me to make more.

Where, in the entremet, it can get a little lost among the mousses and crémeux, and forms a predominantly structural role, on its own it is compulsively delicious. Once set, it can be broken into shards and eaten alone, or put into cellophane bags and tied with ribbon, to make gorgeous gifts. I make my own praline here, and sub in cornflakes in place of the feuilletine wafers we used, as both are hard to source other than in industrial quantities. Yes, it is kind of a grown-up version of cornflake crispy cakes, but let me tell you: it is a seriously good version of cornflake crispy cakes.

Salted milk chocolate praline crunch

Makes: 250g of chocolate bark
Takes: 20 minutes, plus chilling time
Bakes: 20 minutes

60g cornflakes
15g milk powder
15g light brown sugar

40g butter, melted
35g caster sugar
65g whole, unskinned hazelnuts
100g milk chocolate, broken into pieces
5g salt

1. Heat the oven to 140°C fan/160°C/gas 2. Crush the cornflakes in a bowl with your hands to a quarter of their original size. Add the milk powder and light brown sugar, toss, then stir through the melted butter until all the cornflakes are completed coated. Spread on a parchment-lined baking tray and bake for 20 minutes, until lightly toasted. Leave to cool completely.

2. Next, make the praline. Put the caster sugar into a small pan with 1 tablespoon of water, and bring to the boil over a high heat. When small bubbles start to form around the edge of the pan, add the hazelnuts, stirring to coat them completely with the sugar syrup. Reduce the heat to medium and cook until the syrup turns a dark gold, occasionally swirling the pan. Pour the hazelnuts and caramel straight from the pan on to a sheet of baking parchment, and leave to set.

3. Once solid, break the caramelized hazelnuts into pieces and put into a food processor. Pulse the mixture: it will first become crumb-like, and then, slowly, turn into a paste as the oils come out of the nuts.

4. Place a small pan of water on the hob and bring to a simmer. Set a metal or glass bowl over the pan of simmering water and add the milk chocolate and the praline paste, along with the salt. Set up an ice bath, by filling a large bowl or pan with water and lots of ice.

5. When the chocolate has completely melted, remove the bowl from the heat (but leave the pan of water simmering!) and stir with a spatula, scraping the sides, dipping the base of the bowl into the ice bath just for a second, before lifting and stirring again. Keep stirring, dipping, and testing the temperature with an instant-read thermometer until it drops to 27°C. Now, place the bowl back over the pan of hot water for just a moment, and stir the chocolate mixture just until it becomes liquid enough to pour; the chocolate temperature should read 29–30°C.

6. Mix the cornflakes through the melted chocolate, and spread thinly on a silicone mat or a sheet of baking parchment. Place another sheet of parchment on top and use a rolling pin to gently flatten the mixture, creating an even layer between the parchment. Slide the whole thing on to a chopping board and pop into the fridge for 20 minutes. Break the chocolate praline mixture into shards.

16

The inside of Le Cordon Bleu was quiet. Classes had ended, the locker rooms were cleared out. I was standing outside one of the classrooms, waiting to receive my final exam marks, to find out whether I'd passed or failed. There was a queue, a backlog to see Chef Javier. I leaned against the wall, next to those naval photos of the teaching staff that had looked so peculiar nine months ago, and now were just part of the scenery. When Mum died, I didn't know it was coming. I didn't know anything at all. Now, I felt that rare, peculiar mix of excitement and dread that comes when you know a period of your life is about to end, and everything is suddenly about to change.

The student before me slipped out and Chef Javier beckoned me in. It felt strange to be sitting opposite the chef, he in his whites and tall toque, me now in my own clothes. He turned the computer screen towards me: it was covered in photos of my entremet, different angles and zooms. It felt like spotting a photo of yourself when you weren't expecting it, or catching sight of your reflection before you clock that that's what it is. Chef Javier smiled at me: 'Well,' he said, 'you passed!' I had passed with decent marks – better than I had expected. My mousse was light, wibbly, my tuiles a little lacklustre; my plate design good, my chocolate in temper. My crème anglaise was perfect. Chef Javier congratulated me and shook my hand, wished me well in the future. 'Thanks, Chef,' I replied. 'For everything.'

Penny passed, despite not having been able to demould her unset entremets. Savannah failed. One of the guys on the cuisine course failed by half a mark out of eighty. *Half a mark*. We sat drinking cocktails in the sunshine, swapping injustices and surprises from our results, talking about our plans. Georgie had about seven *stages* lined up; she wanted to get as much experience as possible, so she was trying out every high-end kitchen and bakery that would have her. Enthusiasm shone out of her, but also determination. James and Daisy were staying on for the culinary management course, a three-month add-on for people who wanted to run food businesses. Miriam was going back to France, where she hoped to teach cookery classes. And as for me? I wasn't sure.

What had I expected to get out of going to Le Cordon Bleu? When I look back at my decision to go, it sometimes feels like the height of caprice, ditching a perfectly good job for something so self-indulgent. I thought I'd find something I was naturally good at. I thought I'd be a chocolate savant, an entremet wizard, or have a knack for pulling miracles out of sugar. I didn't find any of these things. I found that hard work, mostly, pays off. I found out that there's no substitute for practice. I found out that's it's not shameful to fail, if you're willing to pick yourself back up and try again. I learnt that it was OK to be sad when something went wrong, so long as you show up again the next day and try again. I learnt that there would always be opportunities to redeem myself (and that I needed them).

I found that patience really can be a virtue, much to my irritation. I found that leaving your career, even if you don't quite have a perfect plan in place, won't cause the world to fall apart around you. It might have been a half-baked idea, perhaps, but it was also a good one.

I'd learnt a lot about myself. I'd learnt that I was tougher than I thought; that I cared more than I thought. I'd learnt that determination took you an awful long way. I found that I had greater endurance for pain than I thought. I learnt that I could be brave.

My knife skills were still rubbish: my onion-chopping was, at best, haphazard, and I wouldn't know where to begin with turning a mushroom. I'm not even sure I truly know what a turned mushroom is. Maybe I'll never make a handsome tuile. I cannot work with chocolate – or anything, in fact – without ending up with it all down my chef's jacket. But I can make 120 plated puddings. I can put together a gâteau. I can work in a team. OK, I can't do that. But at least I know that now. I can communicate. I can pick myself up when I bugger something up. I can fix broken custards and split creams. I can practise until I get it right. I can find joy in my work, and in the process.

My hands bear a whole new collection of scars. Four perfect circles where my thumb meets my hand where the caramel splashed me when I was making croquembouche have faded from deep red to pale coral. The slightly blunt end of my thumb where I accidentally attacked it with a knife during that brioche practical. The still raised, pink crescent moon from where I put my hand through the glass bowl of a KitchenAid that fell off my bench at home and smashed when I was making doughnuts. I can trace my learning and my experience on my hands. I may never have the scars that Chef Javier showed us, but I don't really want them; I've made my peace with the fact that I will never be a restaurant chef. Still, the scars I do have are a map of my recent past. Those hands that had started to resemble my mother's told their own story. My hands have never been my best feature, and they certainly didn't get prettier in the last nine months, but for the first time, they say something about me. And I think I like what they say. They say that I'm not afraid of hard work. Maybe that I'm less afraid in general.

Not all my scars show. They say that scars tell stories; so what happens if you can't see the scars? Do the stories go untold? Do they stay silent? What happens if you suppress those stories? I don't need my therapist to tell me that this isn't helpful.

George Engel, an American psychiatrist and founder of the biopsychosocial method, described grief as being psychologically traumatic in the same way that a wound or burn is physiologically traumatic. He argued that it belonged in the pantheon of disease, that grief represents a departure from a state of health and well-being. Just as time is necessary for healing in the physical realm in order to bring the body back to a healthy equilibrium, so too is a period of time needed to return the mourner to emotional and psychological equilibrium. It is therefore madness, literally delusion, to pretend that you are fine without ever having undergone any healing. I would jokingly give myself as an example of bad grieving – *don't do what I did, and you'll be just fine!* But finally, I had faced up to the fact that work needed to be done. I had thought I could do this alone, be self-sufficient, self-reliant. I was wrong.

The gap Mum left in my life doesn't get any smaller. As I get older, it gets bigger. There are more occasions missed. Motherlessness doesn't just connote the loss of a mother, but her continued absence. A lack of mothering as much as a lack of mother. It's why people who lost their mother when they were infants – even before memories were formed – feel that ache, that loss. You can only grieve according to your life experience at the time: an eleven-year-old girl can mourn her mother as she knows her at that time, but she can't grieve for losses she hasn't yet experienced. She can't grieve for the missed graduations, or weddings, or births, or her own sickness. Those will have to come later. I try to work out what it is that is the defining feeling of being motherless, beyond self-pity that sits with me like a hangover: it is that I feel unsoothed. There is no one to soothe me. It was Mum's hands. When I am sad, or sick, I push Sam's hand flat on my forehead, reaching for, trying to find that comfort, trying to soothe myself. It doesn't work. I still want my Mummy.

My mother always told me that it was giving birth to me that had turned her hair white. For my whole life, she had dyed it, progressing from her natural dark brown that matched mine to a pale copper that was closer to Maddy's. She was twenty-nine when she had me. By the time I was twenty-nine, my hair too was streaked with white, white that after eighteen months of resistance, I stopped dyeing and let grow through, soft lines of cool grey breaking up my straight, dark hair. By the time I was twenty-nine, she had been dead for four years. It wasn't me, I wanted to tell her. It wasn't me that sent your hair white. It was you. It was us. It was something we shared. But I couldn't share that fact with her.

Every joy is also now a sadness. Getting tenancy. My graduation from Le Cordon Bleu. Every Christmas, every birthday. My engagement. My wedding. Every amazing meal, perfect anecdote, the *Gilmore Girls* reboot, that I cannot tell her about. Even this book, my book. Her book.

I often wonder what she would be like now. I grieve for her life unlived: the things she didn't get to see, to experience, to know. I grieve for my future without a mother, where any children I have won't know their granny, where my husband never met his mother-in-law. But I grieve for my life unlived too: I grieve for the life I might have had if Mum hadn't died, the ease with which I would have moved from day to day. Of course, that's not how it works. My spectacles are rose-tinted; with Mum or without her, my life was always going to have ups and downs. That's life. But this is fantasy, so permit me my flight of fancy.

Loss is transformative. I would give anything to have

my mother back, but it would be wrong to say that her death has changed me for the worse. I am a better person for her death. And I have a life that, save for her loss, makes me happier. Grief has changed me. For a long time, I let grief define my life, while doing everything in my power not to engage with the reality of it. By trying to ignore it, I allowed the rot to set in, until it became bigger than me.

The shape of my grief has changed over the years. It feels a little like one of those electric buzzer games, where you have to guide a loop of metal along a live circuit without touching it; touch the circuit and the whole thing will buzz and squeal. When Mum first died, the loop was barely bigger than the wire; it was impossible to move it at all without it activating the circuit, sending shocks through me. As time has passed, the loop has increased in size, but it still sits on that circuit. Knocking against it becomes more infrequent; I've become more adept at playing the game. But when I falter, and it touches, the feeling is the same.

A month before my wedding, Jan died. Auntie Jan – my mum's sister.

The day before my thirtieth birthday, she was diagnosed with aggressive stomach cancer. She was sixty-two. Dad phoned me to tell me that she was unwell. He tried to explain to me that the prospects were bad, but I clung to the crumbs of possibility in what he said, things he didn't really mean, about further tests, care plans. And then, a week later he phoned again. 'You should go visit her.' I didn't want to. I tried to put it off. 'Look, we have a wedding in the Highlands this weekend, so I'll try and head up after that,' I told him. 'Don't,' he said. 'Don't wait that long.'

So I took a train to Lincolnshire, and then a taxi from the station to the hospital. 'Going to visit someone?' the cab driver called back cheerily to me when I gave him the destination. 'Yes,' I replied, unable to find something positive to rejoinder. 'Ah well!' he said. 'Hopefully they'll get better soon.' He dropped me off at the north end of the hospital, oblivious that this housed the palliative care centre.

Jan was seeing doctors when I arrived, so I sat in the waiting room, waiting. In almost every way, I didn't want to be here: I didn't want to say goodbye. I didn't know how to do it. There was too much pressure. I was so scared; my hands trembled.

I sat beside her in her hospital room in Lincoln, and held her hand, and talked to her about her sister. When Mum died, there hadn't been space in my head for Jan's grief. It had irritated me that she could suggest that her heart ached for my mother even a tiny proportion of the amount mine did.

When Mum died, Maddy and I, executing our brutal executrix duties, saved a perfume bottle. Not for us, but for Jan. It felt like preserving a memory for her, something that you could leave on a table, or take out of a drawer when you needed it. It was sentimental and sweet, and we did it without too much thought. Later on, she told us she had built a routine around this perfume bottle. Each morning, she would sit at her dressing table and smell Mum's perfume, and permit herself to miss her, to be deeply, all-consumingly sad. And then she would put the lid back on the perfume and go about her day. When she told me this on one of our phone calls, which I think we both secretly hoped would act as a substitute for those calls we had separately had with Mum, I inwardly rolled my eyes. *How sentimental*, I thought. *How unnecessary. Why can't people just get on with their lives?* How could I not have seen that Jan's way of dealing with her sister's death was so much healthier, more direct, kinder to herself, than mine?

A year earlier, Maddy, Jan and I had sat at the big kitchen table of the farmhouse we had congregated in to celebrate Dad's sixtieth birthday, and talked about how Mum used to smell. To my sister, she was Chanel Chance, the perfume she wore as we got older. To me it is Chance mixed with the Clarins facewash she used and the Silk Cut cigarettes she smoked. I remembered further back, too: to the Max Factor face powder she always wore, and Elizabeth Arden's Sunflowers, a scent she sprayed throughout the 90s, that makes me think of family holidays and summer and her dressing table. Jan, however, could reel off all my mother's perfumes, her smells, her signatures and signs, smells that eluded me, that predated me. The perfumes she'd worn when she was a teenager, a young woman, a newlywed. Smells that were my mother before she became my mother. We sat together, shouting over each other, yelling brand names triumphantly, like we were on a strange game show, clutching at things that we could still hold on to, that were tangible. Names of things that, unlike their wearer, still exist. I'm so glad she had that perfume bottle. I wish I had kept one, too.

Jan died less than a fortnight later. We had talked about Mum in that hospital room. At first, we didn't cry, working hard to smile through the brutal reality that was underlying our conversation. And then when we did cry, we couldn't stop. But not in the way I feared; not in a way that felt like I was drowning. I left the hospital feeling, I suppose, like you should feel after you've been able to say goodbye to a loved one; that I hadn't given in to my cowardly instincts not to confront the truth of her death. And I was fiercely jealous that I hadn't been able to have the same with Mum. But then, of all people, I think Jan would have understood that.

At university I'd studied tragedy in literature, and been frustrated by it. As a class, we watched *Brief Encounter*, and discussed it in the context of the tragic form. Normally ill-prepared and ill-informed, any strong opinions I held in supervisions and seminars were generally smoke-screens designed to hide the fact that I'd spent more time carousing and pursuing extra-curricular activities than reading up on my Foucault and Freud. But this was different: here I felt strongly about something – the idea that *Brief Encounter* is tragic was, I expostulated, nonsense. Two married people falling in love and then returning to their respective spouses is not tragedy. There is more tragedy in a single episode of *EastEnders* than in a couple who decide to have an affair, no matter how much they feel it is driven by fate. It's selfish, self-involved. Of course, my self-righteousness came from a fundamental misunderstanding of the tragic form, and a failure to read most of my set reading. But, still, my mother's death, I knew, wasn't a tragedy. It was just one of those things. It was life. Or death. It happened to everyone. However unfair it felt to me, my suffering and her suffering were not *tragic*.

Sam entered my life just as my mother left it, making it feel more like a drawing room farce, or a comedy of manners than a conventional tragedy. And a comedy has to end with a wedding. Such are the rules of drama.

The night before our wedding, we went to a pub near the venue with our family, the bridesmaids and grooms-men. After dinner, my soon-to-be brother-in-law hosted a pub quiz based around my and Sam's hobbies and interests. (Never let it be said that I am anything but an advocate for organized fun.) There were rounds on law and animals – Sam had studied zoology, and just really liked dogs – and places we'd lived. Halfway through, we reached the pâtisserie round. After some questions that made me feel extremely smug, half a dozen Victoria sponges were sud-denly whipped out by Sam's sister and one presented to each team. A surprise bonus round! Each team must deco-rate their cake, and the most impressive cake would score extra points. My chest puffed up and I grew three inches in my seat: that morning I had dropped off my very own wed-ding cake that I'd made over the last three days, and felt invincible. I was trained, I was experienced, I was about to come into my own. Those little tubes of icing that you get from supermarkets were distributed between the teams, and of course, I immediately took control of our team's. I began squeezing out wiggles of icing, but those tubes don't work quite the same way as the little paper piping bags we folded and used at college. I was making a not-inconsiderable mess. I got about halfway through before my teammates, Maddy and Gill, gently prised the little tubes of icing away from me. I half-sulked in the corner, tutting at the simple, neat design that was being executed by the rest of my team. Much to my chagrin, our team won.

Our wedding took place on a cold December day. As I sat at breakfast with two of my bridesmaids, Ruth and Steph, unforecast snow began to fall. From the rafters of the barn, fairy lights twinkled, and an enormous fir tree sparkled with white lights. Outside, a yurt was strung with hundreds of those origami birds that we, with a little help from both sides of the family, had made, dancing across brightly-coloured ribbons, curving down from the top point of the yurt to the very edges, like a circus tent and a maypole had had a baby, just like I had hoped. In the end, we needed 1,700 cranes to fill the space. And we did it with two days to spare. We ate big sharing platters of roast pork and crackling, plum tart and stem ginger ice cream. It was perfect, in every way but one.

Every inch of that day, I wished she was there. I wished she was there when, alone in the bridal suite, I had to get out of the bath to answer the door in my towel to receive my wedding flowers. I wished she was there when I put on my dress and my bridesmaids sat in a row on my sofa and cried. I wished she was there when I walked down the aisle to the overture from the film *Little Women*, the last book she read to me at night, and our shared favourite film.

I don't buy into the whole dead-remaining-with-you malarkey. I'm not religious. As far as I'm concerned, Mum isn't watching over me. She is dead. But though I don't feel her presence in any spiritual way, she was there that day.

She was there in every choice I made for my wedding. She was with me in her opal earrings, the ones she'd worn every day, and that I had set to one side, unable to wear them until it really mattered. She was with me in my brilliant sister, who had silently held my hand today in the wedding car, just like she did in the car on the way to Mum's funeral. She was with me in my friends, whom she loved, who loved her, who mourned her with me, who stood next to me at her funeral, who stocked my fridge and held me. She was with me in Dad's speech, warm and wise, filled with love and laughter. She was there in Maddy's speech too: so clever and funny, eloquent and heart-breaking. Mum would have been *so* proud of her. In that speech, Maddy described Mum as our North Star. Up until that point, I'd always thought of her as our anchor, but Maddy was right: she wasn't. She hadn't been tying us to one place, she'd been directing us. And that's why I felt so lost when she died. But I was beginning to feel like I'd found a new direction.

She was even with us in our last dance. We had, like most normal couples, chosen our first dance, of course, but beyond that had left the DJ with a list of songs we liked and a general instruction to play Christmassy wedding music. So I was surprised when, having kicked my feet up on a chair and helped myself to a cone of chips and a pint of ale, I was summoned to the dance floor. 'It's the last song!' the DJ bellowed from the mezzanine above the dance floor. 'Join the happy couple as we see them off.'

Everyone flocked to the dance floor and jostled us into the centre, forming an enormous circle around us, like an extremely formal hokey-cokey. 'Am I missing something?' I hissed at Sam. 'Is the last dance a thing?' I didn't remember seeing it at any of the weddings we'd been to, but then I was probably three sheets to the wind by the time it came round. 'I don't think so,' Sam said, giving me wild, what-the-fuck eyes. 'I guess we just . . . go with it? Let's look like we love each other.' The music began. 'Oh no. No, God, no, not this song.' We stared at each other, unable to move. 'Well, I suppose he doesn't know,' Sam said with a shrug. The DJ was playing 'Angels' by Robbie Williams. As Robbie roared about death and angels, I leant into Sam's shoulder and dissolved into helpless laughter. I could not believe that of all the songs in the entire world, he'd plumped for that one.

Mum was dead, to begin with. Where does my story begin, and where does it end? Grief is messy. It doesn't have a neat ending. The very nature of grief means that even when you are able to face the pain, you are not diminishing it, just learning how to live with it, rather than fighting its very existence. For twenty-five years, my Mum was my great love story. Now I have a new one. Is this my happy ending? I hope so. Though it is, of course, bittersweet.

Standing next to a friend at a wedding that I'd attended in my now-common capacity as both friend and go-to cake maker, we watched the couple cut into the cake I'd made. 'Doesn't it make you sad when you've made a beautiful wedding cake, and then it just gets chopped up and destroyed?' he asked. 'No!' I cried, appalled. 'That's the best bit!' I understand the need in big hotels, or bakeries, to show off the skill and style of the chef or kitchen in a way that will sustain long-term, and therefore is never intended to be eaten – towering isomalt sugar structures, or chocolate showpieces made from a pretty unappetizing cocoa-powder-vinegar mixture, even wedding cakes that are actually just iced on to styrofoam bases – but it's not for me. Even after nine months of sugar blowing and measuring millimetres, what I loved above all else was seeing people joyfully eat the things I had made with my own hands.

Getting married seems to me a mad, hopeful thing. A commitment that we make in the face of statistical evidence to the contrary. And despite being cynical in most of the rest of my life, I think there are few things more moving than seeing two people stand up in front of their friends and say, yes, we're going to do our best here. Two people who, until two, maybe three years ago, have lived their lives quite contentedly without having met each other. Two people choosing readings and songs and dances and – God, if they want to – *chair covers*, that say something about them as a couple, that celebrate friendship and partnership and family. That, I think, is pretty wonderful. That they and their friends put into actual words their feelings, their *love*. It is the absolute opposite of every way I have approached grieving. It is openly sentimental, steeped in emotion, and represents the boundaries of people's lives blurring.

And so I decided to do it. To follow my own wedding with a career in weddings. Making cakes for them. Catering them. To go all-in on my half-baked idea. Yes, I know I can't do teams but I teamed up with Kate, whose warmth and softness had, over the course of our friendship, rubbed away some of my sharper edges. At my wedding, she'd read a piece from *Appetite* by Nigel Slater, about pairings in food – items that may not ostensibly go together, but actually, are quite perfect. When I'd found it and taken it to Sam, suggesting it as a possible reading, his response was simple. 'Of course. Although I think we both know this is about you and Kate.'

Sometimes, Kate and I do dishes that are based on something external the couple both love – a place, or a particular cuisine, even a TV programme. Sometimes, it's just their favourite food: sharing bowls of crumble with big jugs of crème anglaise (of course), or joints of porchetta, burnished and crackling. We serve huge platters, to be passed down the table between groups of people who may never all be in the same room again, but are joined together by their love of the couple.

I've stood by a lake in Suffolk in the middle of summer, batting hundreds of tiny black flies off a pristine, primrose-yellow buttercream cake. I've crouched in a field in Edinburgh, in the pouring rain, trying to connect a fifty-foot hosepipe to plumb a kitchen. I've faced down failing generators, and no-show grocery orders, and once, trying to erect a wedding cake at the wrong venue.

And you know what? I cry every single time. At every wedding I attend, whether I am a guest or a caterer, I cry. I cannot help it. It is Pavlovian. The music swells, or the father of the bride gets to his feet to make his speech, and even if I don't know the couple from Adam and can't hear the words they're saying from the kitchen, I cry. But not because I can't cry for my mum. Not any more. I cry because I am so happy that these people, whoever they are, are doing the mad, hopeful thing, doing their best to put a bit more joy into this world. Which is all any of us can do, really.

*

I wanted my wedding cake to represent that together-ness that makes each wedding so individual and special to that couple. It was four tiers tall, golden brown at the bottom, lightening with each tier to ivory: the bottom tier was cardamom cake with coffee buttercream, the next sticky ginger with caramelized biscuit flavour icing, second from top a rosemary and honey cake with burnt buttercream, and the very top a fruit cake made to the traditional recipe from Sam's family, and covered in marzipan and fondant. I had made dozens of ginger-bread figures, decorated with white icing, which told our story: on the cake was Sam's much loved, sadly deceased golden retriever Waffle, back to back with my angry, fat cat, Gus, who had moved from London a couple of years previously to live with my dad (initially a temporary arrangement, but became long-term when grumpy Gus fell head over heels in love with Dad, following him everywhere. Once, I walked in on them dancing). There were the two colleges we'd attended at university, spitting distance from each other, where we'd spent three years contemporaneously, but failed to meet. There was the Victoria Wetherspoon's, where we finally did meet. There was the big barn we were getting married in, and the yurt that I'd decorated with origami birds, alongside a little boar, to represent Siena where we got engaged, and a bumble bee and a hive, as a nod to us taking the mishmashed surname 'Pollen', and there were reindeer and snow-covered pine trees, wishful thinking for our December wedding day. And at the top were a gingerbread bride and groom, iced to match my dress and Sam's suit. Perched on the edges of the tiers were sugar roses I'd made in the likeness of those in my bouquet, and real eucalyptus trailed up the cake. It was the best thing I'd ever made.

Gingerbread

Makes: 24 biscuits
Bakes: 9 minutes
Takes: 10 minutes, plus chilling

For the gingerbread
450g plain flour, plus extra for dusting
1 teaspoon salt
1 tablespoon ground ginger
2 teaspoons ground cinnamon
¼ teaspoon ground mixed spice
150g dark brown sugar
80g butter
1 egg
180g golden syrup
1 tablespoon treacle

For the icing
250g icing sugar
1 egg white

1. Whisk the flour, salt and spices together in a large mixing bowl.

2. In a separate bowl, sieve the dark brown sugar; this will stop you getting brown sticky spots in your finished biscuits. Cream the butter and sugar together until they are pale and smooth. Add the egg and mix it through the creamed butter and sugar.

3. Add the syrup and treacle and make sure they are evenly distributed through the mix, then stir in the dry ingredients. Wrap the dough in clingfilm and refrigerate for at least an hour.

4. Preheat the oven to 190°C fan/210°C/gas 6½. Remove from the fridge, remove the clingfilm,

and place on a surface lightly dusted with flour. Roll out to the thickness of a pound coin, and stamp out your preferred design with a cutter. Using a flat knife, transfer the biscuits to a lined baking tray.

5. Bake for 8–9 minutes, by which time the biscuits should be slightly coloured but not browned. They will still be soft when you take them out of the oven, so allow them to completely cool before trying to move them.

6. To make the icing, whisk the icing sugar and egg white together, starting slowly to prevent clouds of icing sugar billowing all over your kitchen. Whisk for 5 minutes, until the icing is a bright white paste. Dilute with water until it reaches the consistency of shampoo. You can colour the icing at this point; I use gel colourings, as they won't change the consistency of the icing; be aware if you use liquid colouring that it will loosen the mixture. Pop into a piping bag and squeeze on to your cooled biscuits, or spread using a teaspoon or palette knife.

Acknowledgements

When you write a book, there are, of course, a hundred people to thank. But when you write a book about a time in your life where you struggled, where you were supported and loved despite being a giant pain, it can feel like there are a thousand. There are so many people who showed me kindnesses and generosity and offered me practical help when I lost my mum; who didn't raise their eyebrows when I decided to leave the Bar; and who didn't laugh themselves stupid when I said I was going to write a book about it all. If I named them all, this book would double in length, but I am endlessly grateful to them. There are a number of people to whom I owe particular thanks.

My agent, Zoe Ross, who has coaxed, cajoled, and most importantly, championed this half baked idea from the start. I cannot thank you enough.

My editor, Juliet Annan. I can't believe my good luck in you taking on this book, and for believing in every aspect of it with such enthusiasm. Thank you for shaping this book into something I am so proud of; it has been a privilege to work with you.

Assallah, it has been such a joy to have you on my team! Thank you for your care and encouragement, for fielding all my stupid questions, and for making me laugh even when I was crippled by book nerves.

The meticulous, patient and kind Annie Lee, who licked this book into the form you now see, rather than the ungrammatical, imprecise amorphous blob that it was before she had it.

Olivia Mead, publicist extraordinaire, Natalie Wall, wonderful editorial manager, and the whole team at Penguin for their hard work, enthusiasm and kindness.

Kate, I cannot believe you are able to hear me mention this book without rolling your eyes: your patience, your kitchen companionship (your upper body strength!), but above all your friendship has been one of my greatest happinesses of the last three years.

My girls: Ruth, Steph, Charis and Suzy. Thank you for being my witnesses, for picking me up when I fall (figuratively and literally), for calling me out when I'm an idiot, for loving me even though I'm extremely annoying.

The Corpus lot: Ellie, Daisy, Zen, Ollie, Grace, Lizzy and George. Thank you for the Marmite on toast, the Corpus rosé, and for joining the union just to vote for me.

Genevieve, Graeme and Duncan. Thank you for being brilliant barristers so I can live vicariously through you. Thank you for all the noisy pubs. Genevieve and Duncan, I'm really sorry for lumbering you with Graeme all these years; what can I say? He's like a limpet. Duncan (and Suze!), thank you for trusting me enough to make my first ever wedding cake for you.

Everyone at 5 Paper Buildings, but especially Dale, Julian, Miranda, Deanna, Fooks, BDJ, Milo, Teresa, Charlene, Andrew, Carolina and Josh. It was a privilege to be surrounded by some of the most skilled, passionate and talented members of the Bar. I will never forget your kindness both during the worst time of my life, and following my subsequent volte-face. Andrew, a special thank you to you for your hard work, care and reassurance: any errors are entirely mine.

Vicky, Rachael and Hannah: you were with me while so much of this was so new. I can't think of three people I'd rather be shut in a small room with for a whole year.

All my fellow students at Le Cordon Bleu, but particularly Keiron, Rose, Katie and Mimi, who bore the brunt of my grumpiness when I couldn't pipe meringue properly, and made me laugh every single day. Thank you to the teaching staff at Le Cordon Bleu – Chefs Julie, Graham, Nick, Nicolas, Matthew, Javier, Olivier, Dominique and Jérôme – for your encouragement and forbearance in the face of my lack of natural talent.

As I was embarking on this slightly wiggly journey into the world of food writing, some very kind people helped me. My editors at the *Spectator*, Lara Prendergast, Danielle Wall and Will Gore. Thank you for taking a chance on me, and for giving me the space and freedom to develop my writing style and write about everything from blancmange to Brexit. The judges and organizers of the YBF awards, who loved my mum's minestrone as much as I did. I have been lucky enough to call some of the finest food writers out there my friends. Deb Robertson (and her glorious kitchen), Thane Prince, Diana Henry and Sue Quinn, thank you for your advice, encouragement and friendship. Nicola Swift, thank you for inviting me over for beef all those years ago – and for all the naan breads.

To my difficult aunts, SGP, Ella, ASP, Emma, Sarah, Eley, Marika, Alice, Minx, Fez, Xtin. Thank you for everything.

To those who have supported me tirelessly. All of Mummy's friends who reached out to me while I was first grieving, and patiently answered queries while I was writing: thank you.

To my therapist, 'John', without whom there would not have been quite so happy an ending.

The Palins: Jennie, Maurice, Meurig, Jess, Angie, Charles, Sebastian and Matilda. Thank you for your love and good humour, for your fruit cakes and bread sauce.

My family: Mo and Kris, Gerry, Marcus, Hallam, Christine and Ian, thank you for your support and love over all the years, but especially the last six. Daddy and Gill, I don't even know where to begin with your love and generosity. Thank you for absolutely everything. Maddy, you are the funniest, cleverest, best person I know. You have no idea how proud Mummy would be of you.

To Ruby, my co-worker, my companion, my distraction. Thank you for your soft head, your excellent ears, and occasionally making me brave the outside world and take in fresh air, whether I wanted it or not.

And to Sammy, this book would not exist without you. You have given so much time, energy and spirit. Thank you for making me that Welsh rarebit, for making me want to cook, and for persuading me to write. Thank you for reading every damn word I write: any mistakes are yours, and I accept no responsibility for them.